TERRORISM AND COMMUNISM

This essential new series features classic texts by key figures that took center stage during a period of insurrection. Each book is introduced by a major contemporary radical writer who shows how these incendiary works still have the power to inspire, to provoke and maybe to ignite new revolutions . . .

TERRORISM AND COMMUNISM:

A REPLY TO KARL KAUTSKY

———————◆———————

LEON TROTSKY

FOREWORD BY SLAVOJ ŽIŽEK

PREFACE BY H.N. BRAILSFORD

VERSO

London • New York

First published as *Dictatorship vs Democracy* by the Workers Party of America 1920
This edition published by Verso 2007
© Verso 2007
Foreword © Slavoj Žižek 2007
All rights reserved

1 3 5 7 9 10 8 6 4 2

Verso
UK: 6 Meard Street, London W1F 0EG
USA: 180 Varick Street, New York, NY 10014-4606
www.versobooks.com

Verso is the imprint of New Left Books

ISBN-13: 978-1-84467-178-6

British Library Cataloguing in Publication Data
A catalogue record for this book is available from the British Library

Library of Congress Cataloging-in-Publication Data
A catalog record for this book is available from the Library of Congress

Typeset in Bembo by Hewer Text UK Ltd, Edinburgh
Printed in the USA by Courier Stoughton Inc.

CONTENTS

FOREWORD

Trotsky's *Terrorism and Communism*, or, Despair and Utopia in the Turbulent Year of 1920

By Slavoj Žižek

Karl Kraus, the Viennese cultural critic and chronicler (author, among other things, of the famous claim that psychoanalysis is itself the disease it tries to cure), knew of Trotsky from the latter's *séjour* in Vienna before the First World War. One of the legends about Kraus is that, in the early 1920s, when he was told that Trotsky saved the October Revolution by organizing the Red Army, he exclaimed: 'Who would have expected that of Herr Bronstein from Café Central!' This remark relies on the transubstantiation in the style of the famous anecdote on Zhuang-Tze and the butterfly: it was not Trotsky, the great revolutionary, who, during his exile in Vienna, spent time in Café Central; it was the gentle and loquacious Herr Bronstein from Café Central who later become the dreaded Trotsky, the scourge of the counter-revolutionaries.

There are other figures of 'Herr Bronstein' which enact a similar mystifying transubstantiation of Trotsky and thus stand in the way of properly understanding his importance. First, there is the gentrified image of Trotsky popularized today by the latter-day Trotskyists them-selves: Trotsky the anti-bureaucratic libertarian critic of the Stalinist Thermidor, partisan of workers' self-organization, supporter of psycho-analysis and modern art, friend of surrealists, etc. (and one should include in this 'etc.' the brief love affair with Frida Kahlo) . . . this is the domesticated figure that leads one not to be surprised that some of Bush's neocons are ex-Trotskyists (exemplary is here the fate of *Partisan Review*: it started in the 1930s as the voice of the Communist intellectuals and artists; then it became Trotskyist, then the organ of liberal Cold Warriors – now it supports Bush in the War on Terror). This Trotsky almost makes one sympathetic to Stalin's anti-Trotskyist wisdom.

Those critical of Trotsky invented another figure of 'Herr Bronstein': Trotsky as the 'wandering Jew' of the 'permanent revolution' who could not find peace in the routine post-revolutionary process of (re)constructing a new order. No wonder that, in the 1930s, even many conservatives looked favourably both upon the Stalinist cultural counter-revolution as well as upon the expulsion of Trotsky – both were read as an abandonment of the earlier Jewish-international revolutionary spirit and as the return to Russian roots. Even such a critic of Bolshevism as Nikolai Berdaiev expressed in the 1940s, just before his death, a certain sympathy for Stalin, and considered returning to the USSR. Along these lines, Trotsky appears like a kind of Russian Che Guevara in contrast to Fidel: Fidel, the actual leader, supreme authority of the state, versus Che, the eternal revolutionary rebel who could not resign himself to just running a state. Is this not something like a Soviet Union in which Trotsky would not have been rejected as the arch-traitor? Imagine if, in the middle of the 1920s, Trotsky had emigrated and renounced Soviet citizenship in order to instigate permanent revolution around the world, and then had died soon afterwards – after his death, Stalin would have dutifully elevated him into a cult . . .

All this makes *Terrorism and Communism*, Trotsky's reply to Karl Kautsky's vicious attacks on the Bolsheviks, so important: it belies both these figures. Kautsky, who is today deservedly forgotten, was in the 1920s the *éminence grise* of the German Social Democratic Party, by far the strongest Social Democratic party in the world, and the guardian of Marxist orthodoxy against both Bernsteinian revisionism and leftist extremism. *Terrorism and Communism* presents a Trotsky who knew how to be hard, to exercise terror, and a Trotsky fully ready to accept the task of reconstructing daily life.

There is nonetheless a third figure of 'Herr Bronstein', one which relies precisely on *Terrorism and Communism*: Trotsky the precursor of Stalin who, in 1920, already called for one-party rule, militar-ization of labour . . . No wonder *Terrorism and Communism* is disowned even by many a Trotskyist, from Isaac Deutscher to Ernest Mandel (who characterized it as Trotsky's 'worst book', his relapse into anti-democratic dictatorship). There are passages in *Terrorism and Communism* which effectively seem to point forwards to the Stalinist 1930s with their spirit of total industrial mobilization to drag Russia out of its backwardness. After Stalin's death, a well-read copy of *Terrorism and Communism* was found among his private papers, full of handwritten notes which signalled Stalin's enthusiastic approval – what more does one need as a proof?

This is why *Terrorism and Communism* is Trotsky's key book, his 'symptomal' text which should on no account be politely ignored but, on the contrary, focused on. We leave to the *canailles* of cynical wisdom the dubious pleasure of dwelling on the (from the hindsight of today's perspective) all too obvious illusions of the book, starting with Trotsky's reliance on the forthcoming West European revolution. One should not forget that this belief was shared by all Bolsheviks, Lenin included, who saw the survival of their power not as opening up the space for 'constructing socialism in one country', but as buying them a breathing space, surviving till relief arrived in the guise of the West European revolution that would release the pressure.[1] The crucial problem lies elsewhere: the battle for Trotsky should be won on the very 'Stalinist' terrain of terror and industrial mobilization: it is *here* that a minimal, but crucial, difference between Trotsky and Stalin has to be demonstrated.

WHY WAR COMMUNISM?

Let us begin with the historical moment when the book was written: 1920, the last stages of the civil war, when Russia had been 'looted, weakened, exhausted [and was] falling apart', to quote Trotsky's own straight and honest description. Disease, hunger and cold stalked the land; the lives of the workers had gotten worse, not better; the promises of the revolution were more distant than ever – here, again, is Trotsky's own candid admission from a speech given on the third anniversary of the October Revolution:

> We went into this struggle with magnificent ideals, with magnificent enthusiasm, and it seemed to many people that the promised land of communist fraternity, the flowering not only of material but spiritual life, was much closer than it has actually turned out to

be. . . . The promised land – the new kingdom of justice, freedom, contentment and cultural uplift – was so near it could be touched. . . . If back then, three years ago, we had been given the opportunity of looking ahead, we would not have believed our eyes. We would not have believed that three years after the proletarian revolution it would be so hard for us, so harsh to be living on this earth . . .[2]

Therein resides the greatness of the Bolsheviks: at this point of utter disappointment, when their position was 'in the highest degree tragic', they did not withdraw and concede defeat, but *persisted*. Was, however, the price they paid for this persistence, for their success in surviving, not too high? Here is the predominant story of the fateful year 1920 shared by fanatical anti-communist historians, new-generation 'revisionists' and even some erstwhile Trotskyists themselves (such as Deutscher): Russia was 'a theater of the absurd' in which the depressing reality was presented 'as if it were what it was supposed to be, as imagined by the Communist leaders'.[3] And what did the Communist leaders imagine reality to be? They basically *hallucinated*: their reaction to the utter social catastrophe was a weird millenarian euphoria, that is, it appeared to them that the catastrophe opened up a chance of a 'short-cut to Communism': 'In a veritable ideological delirium, the most colossal economic collapse of the century was transmogrified into really-existing Communism, the radiant future *hic et nunc*.'[4] For example, grain-requisitioning by force was 'regarded by the Party, from Lenin down, as not merely socialism, but even communism'.[5] The Bolsheviks were thus 'inclined to see the essential features of fully fledged communism embodied in the war economy of 1919–20'.[6] The next logical step from here is, of course, to identify the war economy with Stalin's concentration camps:

A decade later Stalin, who in 1920–1 had supported Lenin's 'liberal' policy, was to adopt Trotsky's ideas in all but name. Neither Stalin nor Trotsky, nor the adherents of either, then admitted the fact. . . . What was only one of many facets in Trotsky's experimental thinking was to become Stalin's alpha and omega.[7]

The path from Trotsky to Stalin is thus the path from accidental origin to its repetition which elevated it into necessity. It is as if the historical accident of the civil-war devastation touched upon something that was there in the Bolshevik 'unconscious' from the very beginning, serving as 'the day residue' which brought it to life: the 'bureaucratic fantasy of imposing communism by decree'. No wonder, then, that, even after the accidental pretext disappeared (the civil war was over), Bolsheviks could not resist the temptation to stick to the same formulae: political terror (ruthless suppression of all opposition), militarization of labour, total regulation of production by the centralized state planning. The conclusion was formulated succinctly by Orlando Figes: 'The perversion was implicit in the system from the start.'[8] Here are some of Trotsky's harshest formulations:

> The introduction of compulsory labour service is unthinkable without the application, to a greater or lesser degree, of the methods of militarization of labour. . . . If organized economic life is unthinkable without compulsory labour service, the latter is not to be realized without the abolition of the fiction of the freedom of labour, and without the substitution for it of the obligatory principle, which is supplemented by real compulsion. . . . For we can have no way to socialism except by the authoritative regulation of the economic forces and resources of the country, and the centralized distribution of labour-power in harmony with the general state plan. The labour state considers itself empowered to send every worker to the place where his work is necessary.

To add insult to injury, as it were, Trotsky even presages the infamous Stalinist thesis that, in the passage from capitalism to socialism, the state 'withers away' through the strengthening of its organs, specifically of its organs of coercion:

> under socialism there will be no compulsion . . . the principle of compulsion contradicts socialism . . . under socialism we shall be moved by the feeling of duty, the habit of working, the attractiveness of labour, etc., etc. This is unquestionable. Only this unquestionable truth must be a little extended. In point of fact, under socialism there will not exist the apparatus of compulsion itself, namely, the state: for it will have melted away entirely into a producing and consuming commune. Nonetheless, the road to socialism lies through a period of the highest possible intensification of the principle of the state. And you and I are just passing through that

period. Just as a lamp, before going out, shoots up in a brilliant flame, so the state, before disappearing, assumes the form of the dictatorship of the proletariat, i.e., the most ruthless form of state, which embraces the life of the citizens authoritatively in every direction.

Such an enactment of destructive fantasies could not but end in a vicious cycle of self-propelling violence: 'It was a sure sign of the Utopian character of war communism that it went on ignoring realities until it drove itself into an impasse and could maintain itself only by ever increasing doses of violence.'[9] It took the Bolsheviks a full year after the end of the civil war to come to their senses and adopt a pragmatic and efficient way to deal with the catastrophe – stepping back and introducing the NEP (the 'New Economic Policy' which respected the basic market relations, paying peasants a fair price for their products, and allowed private small industry and services). The economic situation improved very fast: in a couple of months, the hunger and chaos were over, stores were full of goods, the country returned to (a type of) normal functioning.[10]

However, a close reading of *Terrorism and Communism* quickly reveals what is wrong with this story of the alleged Bolshevik 'delirium': Trotsky repeatedly emphasizes that the militarization of labour was 'dictated by a situation of fear – a natural, saving fear when faced with the ruin of the country'. There is no hallucinated 'short-cut to communism' here, but only the full awareness that war communismn was 'the regime of a blockaded fortress with a disorganized economy and exhausted resources': 'compulsory labour used to keep the masses from dying of cold and hunger. Harsh times require harsh measures, and we Bolsheviks are not the ones to flinch when the fate of the revolution and the country hang in the balance.' In his superb analysis, Lars T. Lih furthermore demonstrates how, when, at this point of utter devastation, the Bolsheviks spoke about 'transition' and 'central plan', one should not confuse this with the later Soviet 'central plan' and 'transition to socialism': the transition is not the one from capitalism to socialism, but from utter war devastation to a minimal normal functioning of society; and, accordingly, the 'plan' is simply the plan of how to achieve this, how to get things moving again.[11] If a proof is needed, the reader should look at the four stages of the 'plan' Trotsky describes in the book – the first one tells us everything:

We have first of all to afford the working class the very possibility of living – though it be in the most difficult conditions – and thereby to preserve our industrial centres and save the towns. This is the point of departure. If we do not wish to melt the town into agriculture, and transform the whole country into a peasant state, we must support our transport, even at the minimum level, and secure bread for the towns, fuel and raw materials for industry, fodder for the cattle. Without this we shall not make one step forward. Consequently, the first part of the plan comprises the improvement of transport, or, in any case, the prevention of its further deterioration and the preparation of the most necessary supplies of food, raw materials and fuel. The whole of the next period will be in its entirety filled with the concentration and straining of labour-power to solve these root problems; and only in this way shall we lay the foundations for all that is to come.

Indeed, as Trotsky himself put it in clear and unambiguous terms: 'There was no socialism here and there could not have been.' War communism with its militarization of labour was a desperate short-term device to create as soon as possible conditions for its own abolition – which effectively did occur a year later with the introduction of the NEP. This is also why the standard critical reproach to Bolsheviks 'Why didn't you introduce the NEP immediately at the end of the civil war? Why wait a whole disastrous year?' misses the point: in order for the NEP to be applicable at all, society must minimally function – transport, industrial production (to give something to the peasants in exchange for food), stable money, etc; and these conditions were created by war communism. The passage from war communism to the NEP was thus not a shift from ideological terror blind to reality to commonsense pragmatism; they were both part of a consistent strategy to drag the country out of the morass – the moment war communism had done its job, it was abandoned.

However, in the eyes of the critics of Bolsheviks, the militarization of labour is only one aspect of a more fundamental problem, the one of 'democracy versus dictatorship'. Here, indeed, the contrast seems to be as clear as possible – on the one hand, there is Trotsky's open recognition that the dictatorship of the proletariat means the dictatorship of the party:

We have more than once been accused of having substituted for the dictatorship of the soviets the dictatorship of our party. Yet it can be said with complete justice that the dictatorship of the soviets became possible only by means of the dictatorship of the party. It is thanks to the clarity of its theoretical vision and its strong revolutionary organization that the party has afforded to the soviets the possibility of becoming transformed from shapeless parliaments of labour into the apparatus of the supremacy of labour. In this 'substitution' of the power of the party for the power of the working class there is nothing accidental, and in reality there is no substitution at all. The Communists express the fundamental interests of the working class.

On the other hand, there is Kautsky's defence of multiparty democracy with all its ingredients, inclusive of the freedom of the press; for him, the victory of socialism was effectively conceived as the parliamentary victory of the Social Democratic Party, and he even suggested that the appropriate political form of the passage from capitalism to socialism is the parliamentary coalition of progressive bourgeois and socialist parties. (One is tempted to bring this logic to its extreme and suggest that, for Kautsky, the only acceptable revolution would have been to have a referendum and get at least 51 per cent of voters to approve it . . .) No wonder that, in the early 1920s, in his opposition to the Bolshevik dictatorship, Kautsky prefigured Ernst Nolte in describing the Fascists as 'copycat terrorists', the Bolsheviks' 'fraternal adversaries', claiming that Bolshevism had served as a school of repressive techniques for Fascism: 'Fascism is nothing other than the counterpart of Bolshevism; Mussolini is simply aping Lenin.'[12]

Another aspect of this fundamental difference is the different appraisal of the role of the 'soviets' (councils) as the direct self-organization of the working class: for Kautsky, soviets were 'in relation to the party and professional organizations of more developed countries, not a higher form of organization, but first and foremost a substitute [*Notbehelf*], arising out of the absence of political organizations', while for Trotsky, they were superior not only to the parliamentary state apparatus, but ultimately to the party itself:

If the party and the trade unions were organizations of preparation for the revolution, the soviets are the weapon of the revolution itself. After its victory, the soviets become the organs of power. The role of the party and the unions, without decreasing, is nevertheless essentially altered.

This aspect provides the key to the true stakes of the debate: not simply democracy versus dictatorship, but the class 'dictatorship' which is inscribed into the very form of parliamentary dictatorship – this is the point made by Trotsky in his reply:

> The dictatorship is necessary because it is a case, not of partial changes, but of the very existence of the bourgeoisie. No agreement is possible on this ground. Only force can be the deciding factor. The dictatorship of the proletariat does not exclude, of course, either separate agreements, or considerable concessions, especially in connection with the lower middle class and the peasantry. But the proletariat can only conclude these agreements after having gained possession of the apparatus of power, and having guaranteed to itself the possibility of independently deciding on which points to yield and on which to stand firm, in the interests of the general socialist task.

The true question is thus not who directly holds power, a coalition of political agents or the 'dictatorship' of one sole agent, but how the very field in which the total political process takes place is structured: is it the process of parliamentary representation with parties 'reflecting' the voters' opinions, or a more direct self-organization of the working classes, which relies on a much more active role of the participants in the political process? Trotsky's basic reproach to parliamentary democracy is not that it gives too much power to uneducated masses, but, paradoxically, that *it passivizes the masses too much, leaving the initiative to the apparatus of state power (in contrast to the 'soviets' in which the working classes directly mobilize themselves and exert their power).*

A commonsense reproach arises here: why, then, call this 'dictatorship'? Why not 'true democracy' or even simply the 'power of the proletariat'? 'Dictatorship' does not mean here the opposite of democracy, but democracy's own underlying mode of functioning – from the very beginning, the thesis on 'dictatorship of the proletariat' involved the presupposition that it is the opposite of other form(s) of dictatorship, since the entire field of state power is that of dictatorship.

When Lenin and Trotsky designate liberal democracy as a form of bourgeois dictatorship, they did not rely on a simplistic notion of how democracy is really manipulated, a mere façade, on how some secret clique is really in power and controls things, so that, if threatened with losing power in democratic elections, this clique would show its true face and assume direct power. What they meant is that the very *form* of the bourgeois–democratic state embodies a 'bourgeois' logic.

In other words, one should use the term 'dictatorship' in the precise sense in which democracy also is a form of dictatorship, that is, as a purely *formal* determination. Many like to point out how self-questioning is constitutive of democracy, how democracy always allows, solicits us even, to question its own features. However, this self-referentiality has to stop at some point: even the most 'free' elections cannot put into question the legal procedures that legitimize and organize them, the state apparatuses that guarantee (by force, if necessary) the electoral process, etc. The state in its institutional aspect is a massive presence which cannot be accounted for in the terms of the representation of interests – the democratic illusion is that it can; Alain Badiou conceptualized this excess as the excess of the state's representation over what it represents. One can also put it in Benjaminian terms: while democracy can more or less eliminate constituted violence, it still has to rely continuously on constitutive violence.

This critique of parliamentary democracy may appear as something that belongs to another era, to the era of discredited illusions; does it, however, not deserve a fresh look from today's perspective, when the complaint about the indifference and passivity of the majority of voters, about the progressive loss of the power of the democratic process, is gaining ground even in Western democratic countries? Trotsky's insight into how parliamentary democracy is the means of passivizing the majority also sustains his critique of Kautsky's confidence that parliamentary elections function as the faithful 'mirror' of the opinions of the people: in periods of relative stability, one could consider that 'parliamentary elections reflected the balance of power with sufficient exactness. The imperialist war, which upset all bourgeois society, displayed the complete uselessness of the old criteria.' Therein resides Kautsky's mistake: he teaches the workers 'to believe its reflection in the crooked mirror of democracy which has been shattered by the jackboot of militarism into a thousand fragments'. In the social chaos of world war and crisis, the 'hypnotic suggestion of peaceful legality' broke its spell: in such unstable times, the very psychological stability of large crowds of people disintegrates, in reaction to large-scale traumatic events, the majority can swing in a matter of days from one to another extreme, oscillations are so strong and fast that the democratic 'reflection' loses its effectivity:

> A determined push from left or right is sufficient to move the proletariat, for a certain period, to one or the other side. We saw this in 1914, when, under the united pressure of imperialist governments and socialist patriotic parties, the working class was all at once thrown out of its equilibrium and hurled onto the path of imperialism.

In such dynamic times where the situation is 'open' and extremely unstable, the role of the Communists is not to passively 'reflect' the opinion of the majority, but to instigate the working classes to mobilize their forces and thus to *create* a new majority:

> If the parliamentary regime, even in the period of 'peaceful', stable development, was a rather crude method of discovering the opinion of the country, and in the epoch of revolutionary storm completely lost its capacity to follow the course of the struggle and the development of revolutionary consciousness, the Soviet regime, which is more closely, straightly, honestly bound up with the toiling majority of the people, does achieve meaning, *not in statically reflecting a majority, but in dynamically creating it.*

This last point relies on a crucial philosophical premise which renders deeply problematic the standard dialectical-materialist theory of knowledge as 'reflection' (propagated by Lenin himself in his *Materialism and Empiriocriticism*). What is, for Trotsky, wrong with Kautsky's worry that the Russian working class took power 'too early' is that this concern implies the positivist vision of history as an 'objective' process which predetermines the possible coordinates of political interventions; within this horizon, it is unimaginable that a radical political intervention would change these very 'objective' coordinates and thus, in a way, *create* the conditions for its own success:

The argument which is repeated again and again in criticisms of the Soviet system in Russia, and particularly in criticisms of revolutionary attempts to set up a similar structure in other countries, is the argument based on the balance of power. The Soviet regime in Russia is utopian – 'because it does not correspond to the balance of power'. Backward Russia cannot put objects before itself which would be appropriate to advanced Germany. And for the proletariat of Germany it would be madness to take political power into its own hands, as this 'at the present moment' would disturb the balance of power.

There is more than opportunism in this obsession with the 'balance of power' (the opportunism encapsulated by Trotsky in a wonderful observation from his earlier Viennese days: 'After a whispered conversation with the director of the police department, an Austrian Social Democratic politician in the good, and not so far off, old times always knew exactly whether the balance of power permitted a peaceful street demonstration in Vienna on May Day'). Trotsky is here faithful to Lenin who, in his writings of 1917, saved his utmost acerbic irony for those who engage in the endless search for some kind of 'guarantee' for the revolution; this guarantee assumes two main forms: either the reified notion of social necessity (one should not risk the revolution too early; one has to wait for the right moment, when the situation is 'mature' with regard to the laws of historical development: 'it is too early for the socialist revolution, the working class is not yet mature') or the normative ('democratic') legitimacy ('the majority of the population is not on our side, so the revolution would not really be democratic') – it is as if, before the revolutionary agent risks the seizure of state power, it should get permission from some figure of the big Other (organize a referendum which will ascertain that the majority supports the revolution). With Lenin, as with Lacan, the revolution *ne s'autorise que d'elle-même*: one should assume responsibility for the revolutionary *act* not covered by the big Other – the fear of taking power 'prematurely', the search for the guarantee, is the fear of the abyss of the act. Therein resides the ultimate dimension of what Lenin incessantly denounces as 'opportunism', and his wager is that 'opportunism' is a position which is in itself, inherently, false, masking the fear to accomplish the act with the protective screen of 'objective' facts, laws, or norms. Lenin's answer is not the reference to a different set of 'objective facts', but the repetition of the argument made a decade earlier by Rosa Luxemburg against Kautsky: those who wait for the objective conditions of the revolution to arrive will wait for ever – such a position of the objective observer (and not of an engaged agent) is itself the main obstacle to the revolution. Lenin's counterargument against the formal-democratic critics of the second step is that this 'pure democratic' option itself is utopian: in the concrete Russian circumstances, the bourgeois-democratic state has no chance of surviving – the only 'realistic' way to protect the true gains of the February revolution (freedom of organization and the press, for example) is to move forward to the socialist revolution, otherwise, the tsarist reaction would win.

FROM LENIN TO STALIN

The entire history of the Soviet Union can be comprehended as homologous with Freud's famous image of Rome, a city whose history is deposited in its present in the guise of the different layers of the archaeological remainders, each new level covering up the preceding one, like (another model) the seven layers of Troy, so that history, in its regression towards ever older epochs, proceeds like the archaeologist, discovering new layers by probing deeper and deeper into the ground. Was the (official ideological) history of the Soviet Union not the same accumulation of exclusions, of turning persons into non-persons, of the retroactive rewriting of history? Quite logically, 'de-Stalinization' was signalled by the opposite process of 'rehabilitation', of admitting 'errors' in the past policies of the party. The gradual 'rehabilitation' of the demonized ex-leaders of the Bolsheviks could thus serve as perhaps the most sensitive index of how far (and in what direction) the 'de-Stalinization' of the Soviet Union was going. The first to be rehabilitated were the senior military leaders shot in 1937 (Tukhachevsky and others); the last to be rehabilitated, already in the Gorbachev era, just before the collapse of the Communist regime, was Bukharin – this last rehabilitation, of course, was a clear sign of the turn towards capitalism: the Bukharin who was rehabilitated was the one who, in the 1920s, advocated the pact between workers and peasants (owners of their land), launching the famous slogan 'Enrich yourselves!' and opposed forced collectivization. Significantly, however, one figure was *never* rehabilitated, excluded by the Communists as well as by the anti-communist Russian nationalists: Trotsky, the 'wandering Jew' of the revolution, the true anti-Stalin, the archenemy, opposing 'permanent revolution' to the idea of 'building socialism in one country'.[13] Recall one of the most tragic documents of the Soviet history, Nikolai Bukharin's death-cell letter to Stalin from 10 December 1937; here is what Bukharin offers to Stalin in exchange for his life:

> If my life is to be spared, I would like to request (though I would first have to discuss it with my wife) the following: That I be exiled to America. I would wage a mortal war against Trotsky, I would win over large segments of the wavering intelligentsia. You could send an expert security officer with me and, as added insurance, you could detain my wife here for six months until I have proven that I am really punching Trotsky and company on the nose.[14]

One is tempted to risk here the parallel with Freud's distinction between primordial (founding) and secondary repression in the unconscious: Trotsky's exclusion amounted to something like the 'primordial repression' of the Soviet state, to something which cannot ever be readmitted through 'rehabilitation', since the entire order relied on this negative gesture of exclusion. Trotsky is the one for whom there is no place either in pre-1990 really-existing socialism or in post-1990 really-existing capitalism in which even the communist nostalgiacs do not know what to do with Trotsky's permanent revolution – perhaps, the signifier 'Trotsky' is the most appropriate designation of what is worth redeeming in the Leninist legacy. One should recall here 'Hölderlin's Hyperion', a weird, but crucial, short essay by Georg Lukács from 1935, in which Lukács praises Hegel's endorsement of the Napoleonic Thermidor against Hölderlin's intransigent fidelity to the heroic revolutionary utopia:

> Hegel comes to terms with the post-Thermidorian epoch and the close of the revolutionary period of bourgeois development, and he builds up his philosophy precisely on an understanding of this new turning-point in world history. Hölderlin makes no compromise with the post-Thermidorian reality; he remains faithful to the

old revolutionary ideal of renovating 'polis' democracy and is broken by a reality which has no place for his ideals, not even on the level of poetry and thought.[15]

Lukács is here referring to Marx's notion that the heroic period of the French Revolution was the necessary enthusiastic breakthrough followed by the unheroic phase of market relations: the true social function of the revolution was to establish the condition for the prosaic reign of bourgeois economy, and true heroism resides not in blindly clinging to the early revolutionary enthusiasm, but in recognizing 'the rose in the cross of the present', as Hegel liked to paraphrase Luther, that is, in abandoning the position of the Beautiful Soul and fully accepting the present as the only possible domain of actual freedom. It is thus this 'compromise' with social reality which enabled Hegel's crucial philosophical step forward, that of overcoming proto-fascist notion of 'organic' community in his *System der Sittlichkeit* manuscript and engaging in the dialectical analysis of the antagonisms of bourgeois civil society. (Therein resides the properly dialectical paradox of the proto-fascist endeavour to return to a premodern 'organic' community: far from being simply 'reactionary', fascist 'feudal Socialism' is a kind of compromise-solution, an ersatz attempt to build socialism within the constraints of capitalism itself.)

It is obvious that this analysis of Lukács is deeply allegorical: it was written a couple of months after Trotsky launched his thesis of Stalinism as the Thermidor of the October Revolution. Lukács's text has thus to be read as an answer to Trotsky: he accepts Trotsky's characterization of Stalin's regime as 'Thermidorian', giving it a positive twist – instead of bemoaning the loss of utopian energy, one should, in a heroically resigned way, accept its consequences as the only actual space of social progress ... For Marx, of course, the sobering 'day after' which follows the revolutionary intoxication signals the original limitation of the 'bourgeois' revolutionary project, the falsity of its promise of universal freedom: the 'truth' of universal human rights are the rights of commerce and private property. If we read Lukács's endorsement of the Stalinist Thermidor, it implies (arguably against his conscious intention) an utterly anti-Marxist pessimistic perspective: the proletarian revolution itself is also characterized by the gap between its illusory universal assertion of freedom and the ensuing awakening in the new relations of domination and exploitation, which means that the communist project of realizing 'actual freedom' necessarily failed – or does it?

Historians who try to demonstrate the continuity between Lenin's politics and Stalinism like to focus on the figure of Felix Dzerzhinsky, the founder of the Cheka (later GPU, NKVD, KGB . . .), the Bolshevik secret police: as a rule, he is portrayed as what Deleuze would have called the 'dark precursor' of Stalinism. In the texture of the pre-Stalinist development of the Soviet Union in the first ten years after the October Revolution, Dzerzhinsky has to be 'read in reverse', as a voyager who travelled back in time from the Stalinist future a decade ahead. Such a reading often acquires properly fantasmatic dimensions, as in those historians who emphasize Dzerzhinsky's cold blank gaze, allegedly a bodily expression of his ruthless mind, deprived of all human warmth and compassion. No wonder, then, that the West received with chilled surprised the news that the Putin government in Russia decided to return the Dzerzhinsky statue to the square in front of the infamous Lubyanka palace, the seat of the dreaded KGB . . . There are, however, some surprises in store for those who cling to this received image. Lesley Chamberlain's *The Philosophy Steamer*, a book about the expulsion from the Soviet Union in 1921 of the group of most exposed non-Marxist intellectuals, a work which insists precisely on the straight path (if not direct continuity) between Leninism and Stalinism, has as an appendix short biographical notes on all the persons involved – here is the entry on Dzerzhinsky:

FELIKS DZERZHINSKY (1877–1926) Polish-born head of the Cheka, later the GPU, oversaw the expulsions. Dzerzhinsky spent a quarter of his life – eleven years – in tsarist prisons and Siberian exile, including three years of hard labour. 'His identification with, and championship of, the underprivileged and the oppressed' (Leggett)[16] was unquestionable. Dzerzhinsky remains an enigmatic figure.[17]

There are many further details which throw an unexpected light on this emblematic figure; however, the point is not primarily to emphasize how much 'softer', 'more human', the early Bolsheviks were. One should in no way cover up the harshness of their rule – the point lies elsewhere: precisely when they resorted to terror (and they often did it openly, calling the beast by its name, 'Red Terror'), this terror was of a different type from Stalinist terror. Of course, many a historian, while ready to concede this point, would nonetheless insist that there was a deeper necessity which led from the first to the second mode of terror: is the shift of ruthless revolutionary purity into corrupted terror not a commonplace of the histories of revolutions? No doubt the early Bolsheviks would have been shocked at what the Soviet Union turned into in the 1930s (as many of them were, and were also ruthlessly exterminated in the great purges); however, their tragedy was that they were not able to perceive in the Stalinist terror the ultimate offspring of their own acts. What they needed was their own version of the old Oriental insight 'tatvam asi' ('thou art that') . . . This accepted wisdom – which, let me state it clearly, cannot be dismissed as cheap anti-communism: it has its own coherent logic, and it does acknowledge a tragic grandeur within the Bolshevik old guard – is what one should nonetheless render problematic. Here, the left should propose its own alternative to the now-fashionable rightist what-if histories: the answer to the eternal leftist query 'What would have happened if Lenin had survived ten years longer with his health intact, and succeeded in deposing Stalin?' is not as clear as it may appear (one could say, basically, *nothing* – that is to say, nothing really different: the same Stalinism, just deprived of its worst excesses), in spite of many good arguments in favour of some kind of continuity (did Rosa Luxemburg herself not already back in 1918 foretell the rise of bureaucratic Stalinism?).

Here we suggest that, although it is clear that Stalinism emerged from the initial conditions of the October Revolution and its immediate aftermath, one should not *a priori* discount the possibility that, had Lenin remained healthy for a couple of years and deposed Stalin, something entirely different would have emerged – not, of course, the utopia of 'democratic socialism', but nonetheless something substantially different from Stalinist 'socialism in one country', the result of a much more 'pragmatic' and improvised series of political and economic decisions, fully aware of its own limitations. Lenin's desperate last struggle against the reawakened Russian nationalism, his support of Georgian 'nationalists', his vision of a much more decentralized federation, and so forth, were not just tactical compromises: they implied a vision of state and society which was, in its entirety, incompatible with the Stalinist perspective. Here is how, two years before his death, when it became clear that there would be no immediate all-European revolution, and that the idea of building socialism in one country was nonsense, Lenin viewed the situation:

What if the complete hopelessness of the situation, by stimulating
the efforts of the workers and peasants tenfold, offered us the opportunity to create the fundamental requisites of civilization in a
different way from that of the West European countries?[18]

One should take note of how Lenin uses here a class-neutral term
'to create the fundamental requisites of civilization', plus of how he
uses the same language of despair as Trotsky. To put it once again
in Deleuzian terms, Lenin's moment is the 'dark precursor', the
vanishing mediator, the displaced object never at its own place, between
the two series, the initial 'orthodox' Marx's series of revolution in
the most developed countries, and the new 'orthodox' series of Stalinist
'socialism in one country' and then of the Maoist identification of
the Third World nations with the new world proletariat. The shift
from Lenin to Stalinism is here clear and easy to determine: Lenin
perceived the situation as desperate, unexpected, but as such one
which had to be creatively exploited for new political choices; with
the notion of 'socialism in one country', Stalin renormalized the
situation into a new narrative of linear development in 'stages'. That
is to say, while Lenin was fully aware that an 'anomaly' had happened
(revolution in a country which has no presuppositions for developing
a socialist society), he rejected the vulgar evolutionist conclusion that
revolution had taken place 'too early', so that one could only take a
step backwards to developing modern democratic capitalist society,
which would then slowly create conditions for a new socialist
revolution. What Lenin is proposing here is effectively an implicit
theory of 'alternate history': under the 'premature' domination of the
force of the future, the same 'necessary' historical process (of modern
civilization) can be (re)run in a different way.

It is with regard to political terror that one can locate the gap
which separates Lenin's era from Stalinism: in Lenin's times, terror
was openly admitted (Trotsky sometimes even boasted, in an almost
cocky way, about the non-democratic nature of the Bolshevik regime
and the terror it used), while in Stalin's times, the symbolic status of
the terror thoroughly changed – terror turned into the publicly non-
acknowledged obscene shadowy supplement of public official discourse.
It is significant that the climax of terror (1936–37) took place as the
new constitution was installed in 1936 – this constitution was supposed
to end the state of emergency and to mark the return of normality:

the suspension of the civil rights of whole strata of the population (kulaks, ex-capitalists) was rescinded, the right to vote was now universalized, and so on and so forth. The key idea of this constitution was that now, after the stabilization of the socialist order and the annihilation of the enemy classes, the Soviet Union was no longer a class society: the subject of the state was no longer the working classes (workers and peasants), but 'the People'. However, this does not mean that the Stalinist constitution was a simple hypocrisy concealing the social reality – the possibility of terror is inscribed into its very core: since the class war was now proclaimed as over and the Soviet Union was conceived of as the classless country of the People, those who still opposed (or were presumed to oppose) the regime were no longer mere class enemies in a conflict that tears apart the social body, but enemies of the People, insects, worthless scum to be excluded from humanity itself.

One can also formulate this difference in the terms of the status of the prohibition: in the early 'Red Terror', prohibition was openly admitted and announced, while under Stalinism, prohibition itself was prohibited – one had to pretend and act as if there was no terror, as if life had returned to normal. This difference, although it may look like hair-splitting, is crucial, for it changes everything: from the early Bolshevik 'dictatorship' which was open and transparent in its very exercise of violence (thereby also openly admitting its temporary character, its exceptional status), we pass to the Stalinist dictatorship which relied on its self-denial and thus on a basic mystification.

Therein resides the importance of Trotsky. Although Trotskyism often functions as a kind of politico-theoretical obstacle, preventing the radical self-critical analysis needed by the contemporary left, the figure of Trotsky nonetheless remains crucial in so far as it stands for an element which disturbs the alternative 'either (social) democratic socialism or Stalinist totalitarianism': what we find in Trotsky, in his writings and his revolutionary practice in the early years of the Soviet Union, is revolutionary terror, party rule, etc., but *in a different mode* from that of Stalinism. One should thus, on account of the very fidelity to Trotsky's real achievements, dispel the popular myths of a soft and democratic Trotsky. And, again, the conclusion 'even if Trotsky had won, the ultimate result would have been basically the same' (or, even more, the claim that Trotsky was at the origin of Stalinism, namely, that, from the late 1920s onwards, Stalin merely applied and developed measures first envisaged by Trotsky in the years of war communism) is erroneous: history is open, one cannot tell what would have happened if Trotsky had won. The problem lies elsewhere: in the fact that Trotsky's strategy and attitude in the mid-1920s made it *impossible for his orientation to win* in the struggle for state power.

In the diaries of Georgi Dimitrov[19] we get a unique glimpse into how Stalin was fully aware of what brought him to power, giving an unexpected twist to his well-known slogan 'people (cadres) are our greatest wealth'. When, at a dinner in November 1937, Dimitrov praises the 'great luck' of the international workers, in that they had such a genius as their leader, Stalin, Stalin answered: '. . . *I do not agree with him*. He even expressed himself in a non-Marxist way. . . . *Decisive* are the middle cadres'. He puts it in an even clearer way a paragraph earlier:

> Why did we win over Trotsky and others? It is well known that, after Lenin, Trotsky was the most popular in our land. . . . But we had the support of the middle cadres, and they explained our grasp of the situation to the masses . . . Trotsky did not pay any attention to these cadres.

Here, Stalin spelled out the secret of his rise to power: as a rather anonymous general secretary, he nominated tens of thousands of cadres who owed their rise to him . . . This is why Stalin did not yet want Lenin dead in early 1922, rejecting his demand to be given poison to end his life after the debilitating stroke: had Lenin died already in early 1922, the question of succession would not yet have been resolved in Stalin's favour, since Stalin as the general secretary did not yet sufficiently penetrate the party apparatus with his appointees – he needed another year or two, so that, when Lenin effectively died, he could count on the support of thousands of mid-level cadres nominated by him to triumph over the big names of the Bolshevik 'aristocracy'.

THE UTOPIAN FERVOUR OF 1920

What we have said so far is, however, only the first step – in order to adequately comprehend the turbulent year of 1920, we should proceed in two steps. First, at the level of a detailed historical analysis, one should refute the predominant narrative of dogmatic madness, of the utopian dream of the short-cut to communism, of turning the catastrophe into a blessing in disguise. It is, however, crucial to supplement this step with the full recognition of the utopian fervour that sustained the Bolsheviks: despair and true utopia go together, the only way to survive the catastrophic period of civil war, social disintegration, hunger and cold, is to mobilize 'crazy' utopian energies. Is this not one of the basic lessons of the much-maligned 'millenarian' movements, exemplary being the German peasants' revolt in the sixteenth century and its leader Thomas Münzer? The very catastrophe has to be read in the apocalyptic mode, as a sign that 'the end of time is nigh', that a new Beginning is around the corner. Such an authentically Paulinian apocalyptic atmosphere is clearly discernible in passages like the following:

> What the Third International demands of its supporters is a recognition, not in words but in deeds, that civilized humanity has entered a revolutionary epoch; that all the capitalist countries are speeding towards colossal disturbances and an open class war; and that the task of the revolutionary representatives of the proletariat is to prepare for that inevitable and approaching war the necessary spiritual armory and buttress of organization.

One should read such outbursts of the apocalyptic revolutionary fervour also against the background of its expressions in poetry – recall the most famous poem about the October Revolution, Alexander Blok's 'The Twelve' from 1918, about twelve Red Guards patrolling a desolated city at night. The apocalyptic atmosphere clearly echoes Blok's earlier symbolist link of catastrophe and utopia:

> To get the bourgeoisie
> We'll start a fire
> a worldwide fire, and drench it
> in blood –
> The good Lord bless us!
>
> You bourgeoisie, fly as a sparrow!
> I'll drink your blood,
> your warm blood, for love,
> for dark-eyed love.

The famous finale directly identifies the twelve Red Guards with the apostles led by Christ:

> On they march with sovereign tread . . .
> 'Who else goes there? Come out! I said
> come out!' It is the wind and the red
> flag plunging gaily at their head.
>
> Crack ~ crack ~ crack! But only the echo
> answers from among the eaves . . .
> The blizzard splits his seams, the snow
> laughs wildly up the whirlwind's sleeve . . .
>
> Crack ~ crack ~ crack!
> Crack ~ crack ~ crack!
> . . . So they march with sovereign tread . . .
> Behind them the hungry dog drags,
> and wrapped in wild snow at their head
> carrying a blood-red flag –
> soft-footed where the blizzard swirls,
> invulnerable where bullets slice –
> crowned with a crown of snowflake pearls,
> a flowery diadem of ice,
> ahead of them goes Jesus Christ.

In a wonderful essay on *Chevengur*, Platonov's great peasant utopia written in 1927 and 1928 (just prior to forced collectivization), Fredric Jameson describes the two moments of the revolutionary process. It begins with the gesture of radical negativity:

> this first moment of world-reduction, of the destruction of the idols and the sweeping away of an old world in violence and pain, is itself the precondition for the reconstruction of something else. A first moment of absolute immanence is necessary, the blank slate of absolute peasant immanence or ignorance, before new and undreamed-of sensations and feelings can come into being.[20]

Then follows the second stage, the invention of a new life – not only the construction of the new social reality in which our utopian dreams would be realized, but the (re)construction of these dreams themselves:

> a process that it would be too simple and misleading to call recon-
> struction or Utopian construction, since in effect it involves the
> very effort to find a way to begin imagining Utopia to begin with.
> Perhaps in a more Western kind of psychoanalytic language . . .
> we might think of the new onset of the Utopian process as a kind
> of desiring to desire, a learning to desire, the invention of the desire
> called Utopia in the first place, along with new rules for the
> fantasizing or daydreaming of such a thing – a set of narrative
> protocols with no precedent in our previous literary institutions.[21]

The reference to psychoanalysis is crucial and very precise: in a radical revolution, people not only realize their old (emancipatory, etc.) dreams; rather, they have to reinvent their very modes of dreaming. It is here that the link between the October Revolution and the artistic vanguard acquires all its weight: what they shared was the idea of building a new man, of literally reconstructing it – or, as Trotsky himself put it:

> What is man? He is by no means a finished or harmonious being.
> No, he is still a highly awkward creature. Man, as an animal, has
> not evolved by plan but spontaneously, and has accumulated many
> contradictions. The question of how to educate and regulate, of
> how to improve and complete the physical and spiritual construction
> of man, is a colossal problem which can only be understood on
> the basis of socialism. . . . To produce a new, 'improved version'
> of man – that is the future task of communism. And for that we
> first have to find out everything about man, his anatomy, his
> physiology and that part of his physiology which is called his
> psychology. Man must look at himself and see himself as a raw
> material, or at best as a semi-manufactured product, and say: 'At
> last, my dear *homo sapiens*, I will work on you.'[22]

It was against this threat of full modernization that Stalinist cultural politics reacted with its big shift of the early and mid-1930s from proletarian egalitarianism to the full assertion of the Russian inheritance. In the cultural sphere, figures such as Pushkin and Tchaikovsky were elevated far above modernism; traditional aesthetic norms of beauty were reasserted; homosexuality was outlawed, sexual promiscuity condemned, and marriage proclaimed the elementary cell of the new society. It was the end of the short marriage of convenience between Soviet power and artistic and scientific modernism: the new cultural politics not only demanded a return to artistic forms that would be attractive to large crowds, but also – cynical as it may sound – the return to elementary traditional forms of morality. In the Stalinist show trials, the victims were held responsible, accused of guilt, forced to confess . . . in short, obscene as it may sound, they were treated as autonomous ethical subjects, not as objects of bio-politics.

Should we then draw the conclusion that, with regret, one should endorse Stalinism as the defence against a much worse threat? What about applying here also Lacan's motto '*le père ou pire*', and risk *the choice of the worse*: what if the effective result of choosing to pursue to the end the bio-political dream would have been something unpredictable that would have shaken the very coordinates of this dream? The stakes were here extremely high – nobody was more aware of them than Trotsky himself, as is clear from his dream about dead Lenin from the night of 25 June 1935:

> Last night, or rather early this morning, I dreamed I had a conversation with Lenin. Judging by the surroundings, it was on a ship, on the third-class deck. Lenin was lying in a bunk; I was either standing or sitting near him, I am not sure which. He was questioning me anxiously about my illness. 'You seem to have accumulated nervous fatigue, you must rest . . .' I answered that I had always recovered from fatigue quickly, thanks to my native *Schwungkraft*, but that this time the trouble seemed to lie in some deeper processes . . . 'then you should seriously (he emphasized the word) consult the doctors (several names) . . .' I answered that I had already had many consultations and began to tell him about my trip to Berlin; but looking at Lenin I recalled that he was dead. I immediately tried to drive away this thought, so as to finish the conversation. When I had finished telling him about my therapeutic trip to Berlin in 1926, I wanted to add, 'This was after your death'; but I checked myself and said, 'After you fell ill . . .'[23]

In his interpretation of this dream, Lacan[24] focuses on the obvious link with Freud's dream in which his father appears to him, a father who does not know that he is dead. So what does it mean that Lenin does not know he is dead? There are two radically opposed ways to read Trotsky's dream. According to the first reading, the terrifyingly ridiculous figure of the undead Lenin

> doesn't know that the immense social experiment he single-handedly brought into being (and which we call Soviet communism) has come to an end. He remains full of energy, although dead, and the vituperation expended on him by the living – that he was the originator of the Stalinist terror, that he was an aggressive personality full of hatred, an authoritarian in love with power and totalitarianism, even (worst of all) the rediscoverer of the market in his NEP – none of those insults manage to confer a death, or even a second death, upon him. How is it, how can it be, that he still thinks he is alive? And what is our own position here – which would be that of Trotsky in the dream, no doubt – what is our own non-knowledge, what is the death from which Lenin shields us?[25]

The dead Lenin who does not know that he is dead thus stands for our own obstinate refusal to renounce the grandiose utopian projects and accept the limitations of our situation: there is no big Other, Lenin was mortal and made errors like all others, so it is time for us to let him die, to put to rest this obscene ghost which haunts our political imaginary, and to approach our problems in a non-ideological and pragmatic way. But there is another sense in which Lenin is still alive: he is alive in so far as he embodies what Badiou calls the 'eternal Idea' of universal emancipation, the immortal striving for justice that no insults and catastrophes manage to kill. One should recall here Hegel's sublime words on the French Revolution from his *Lectures on the Philosophy of World History*:

> It has been said that the French revolution resulted from philosophy, and it is not without reason that philosophy has been called *Weltweisheit* [world wisdom]; for it is not only truth in and for itself, as the pure essence of things, but also truth in its living form as exhibited in the affairs of the world. We should not, therefore, contradict the assertion that the revolution received its first impulse

from philosophy. . . . Never since the sun had stood in the firmament and the planets revolved around him had it been perceived that man's existence centres in his head, i.e. in thought, inspired by which he builds up the world of reality. . . . [N]ot until now had man advanced to the recognition of the principle that thought ought to govern spiritual reality. This was accordingly a glorious mental dawn. All thinking being shared in the jubilation of this epoch. Emotions of a lofty character stirred men's minds at that time; a spiritual enthusiasm thrilled through the world, as if the reconciliation between the divine and the secular was now first accomplished.[26]

This, of course, did not prevent Hegel from coldly analyzing the inner necessity of this explosion of abstract freedom turning into its opposite, self-destructive revolutionary terror; however, one should never forget that Hegel's critique is immanent, accepting the basic principle of the French Revolution (and its key supplement, the Haitian Revolution). And one should do exactly the same apropos the October Revolution (and, later, the Chinese Revolution): it was, as Badiou pointed out, the first case in the entire history of humanity of the successful revolt of the exploited poor – they were the zero-level members of the new society, they set the standards. Against all hierarchical orders, egalitarian universality directly came to power. The revolution stabilized itself in a new social order, a new world was created and miraculously survived, amid unthinkable economic and military pressure and isolation. This was effectively 'a glorious mental dawn. All thinking being shared in the jubilation of this epoch'.

This difference is the ultimate distinction between Stalin and Trotsky. In Stalin, 'Lenin lives for ever' as an obscene spirit which 'does not know it is dead', artificially kept alive as an instrument of power. In Trotsky, the dead Lenin continues to live like Joe Hill – he lives wherever there are people who still struggle for the same Idea.

SELECTED
FURTHER READING

OTHER RELEVANT TEXTS BY TROTSKY*

Social Democracy and the Wars of Intervention in Russia, 1918–1921. Between Red and White, London, New Park Publications, 1975.
My Life. An Attempt at an Autobiography, Harmondsworth, Penguin Books, 1975.
The History of the Russian Revolution, London, Pluto Press, 1977.
The Military Writings and Speeches of Leon Trotsky: How the Revolution Armed, London, New Park Publications, 1981.

RELEVANT TEXTS BY KAUTSKY

The Class Struggle (Erfurt Program), Chicago, Charles H. Kerr & Co., 1910.
The Dictatorship of the Proletariat, Manchester, National Labour Press, 1918.
Terrorism and Communism: A Contribution to the Natural History of Revolution, Manchester, National Labour Press, 1919.
Social Democracy versus Communism, New York, Rand School Press, 1946.

RESPONSES TO KAUTSKY BY OTHER BOLSHEVIK LEADERS

V.I. Lenin, 'The Proletarian Revolution and the Renegade Kautsky' (1918), in *Collected Works*, Vol. 28, Moscow, Progress Publishers, 1974.
Karl Radek, *Dictatorship and Terrorism,* Detroit MI, Marxist Educational Society, 1921.

* Many of these texts are available in digital format on the Marxist Internet Archive, www.marxists.org.

BACKGROUND READING

Isaac Deutscher, *The Prophet Armed: Trotsky, 1879–1921*, London and New York, Verso, 2003.

Lars T. Lih, 'Bolshevik *Razverstka* and War Communism,' *Slavic Review* 45, no. 4 (1986): 673–88.

_____. 'The Mystery of the *ABC*,' *Slavic Review* 56, no. 1 (1997): 50–72.

_____. '"Our Position is in the Highest Degree Tragic": Bolshevik "Euphoria" in 1920', in *History and Revolution: Refuting Revisionism*, edited by Mike Haynes and Jim Wolfreys, London and New York, Verso, 2007.

Silvana Malle, *The Economic Organization of War Communism 1918–1921*, Cambridge, Cambridge University Press, 1985.

Massimo Salvadori, *Karl Kautsky and the Socialist Revolution, 1880-1938*, London, New Left Books, 1979.

Victor Serge, *Year One of the Russian Revolution*, London, Bookmarks and Pluto Press, 1992.

GLOSSARY OF NAMES

Abramovich, Rafael (1881–1963): leading Bund and Menshevik figure. Opposed the entry of the Bund into the Communist Party and, in exile, became editor of Menshevik journal *Sotsialistichesky Vestnik*. Author of a number of works, including *The Soviet Revolution, 1917–1939* (1962).

Adler, Friedrich (1879–1960): eldest son of Victor Adler. Was leader of the Left of the Party and opposed the First World War. Sentenced to death, he was amnestied in 1917. Played an active role in the "Second-and-a-Half International" – hovering between the Second International and the new Communist International – founded in 1921 in Vienna, and then became secretary of the renamed Second International from 1924–39. Emigrated to the USA in 1940 and died in Zurich in 1960.

Adler, Max (1873–1937): With Otto Bauer and Rudolf Hilferding, one of the leading theorists of Austro-Marxism. A legal scholar, Adler was philosophically influenced by neo-Kantianism; on the Left of the Austrian Social Democratic Party, he argued for a combination of workers' councils and parliamentary democracy.

Adler, Victor (1852–1918): founding father and chairman (1889–1918) of the Austrian Social Democratic Party, deputy in Austrian Reichstag 1905–18; influential in the Second International. Associated with the Right of his party and supported entry into the First World War. Joined the government in October 1918 as Secretary of State for Foreign Affairs and died the following month.

Alekseev, Mikhail Vasil'evich (1857–1918): a leader of counter-revolutionary White forces in 1917–18.

Arakcheev, Count Aleksei Andreevich (1769–1834): Russian general who served under Tsars Paul I and Alexander I, during which period he served as the War Minister, the Head of the War Department of the State Council of Imperial Russia, and the head of the Imperial Chancellery. Notorious for his ruthless despotism in instituting military-agricultural colonies which caused great suffering to the soldiers. After the coronation of Nicholas I in 1825, he was dismissed and exiled to Novgorod.

Arnould, Arthur (1833–1895): novelist (under the pseudonym of A. Matthey) who participated in the Paris Commune. Author of two significant works on the Commune : *L'Etat et la Révolution* (1877) and the *Histoire populaire et parlementaire de la Commune de Paris* (1878).

Austerlitz, Friedrich (1862–1931): chief editor of the daily newspaper of the Austrian Social Democratic Party, *Arbeiter Zeitung*. Author of a number of extreme pro-war articles in 1914, then became a pacifist in 1916.

Bauer, Otto (1881–1938): leading Austrian Social Democrat and one of the main theorists of Austro-Marxism. Particularly well-known for his book on the national question, published in 1907 (*Die Sozialdemokratie und die Nationalitätenfrage*). Founder of *Der Kampf*, the theoretical journal of the Austrian Social Democrats in 1907 and between 1907 and 1914 was secretary of the deputies of the party. After Victor Adler's death in 1918, became leader of the Austrian Social Democratic Party. From November 1918 to July 1919, Bauer was appointed Minister of Foreign Affairs. Forced into exile in 1934, he organized resistance first from Brno, Czechoslovakia, and later from Paris, France. He continued his literary and theoretical work until his death in Paris.

Bernstein, Eduard (1850–1932): leading figure of German Social Democracy. Became the most renowned theorist of the 'revisionist' tendency, which argued for a brand of evolutionary socialism or reformism.

Bernsteinism – *see* Bernstein

Bethmann-Hollweg, Theobald von (1856–1921): Chancellor of the German Empire from 1909 to 1917.

Blanqui, Louis Auguste (1805–1881): French revolutionary activist and leader, particularly renowned for his notion of the role of active minorities in insurrections.

Blanquists – *see* Blanqui

Brest-Litovsk, Treaty of: peace negotiations between Russia and Germany began at Brest-Litovsk on 3 December 1917. Despite very unfavourable terms for the Bolsheviks, including large losses of territory, and strong opposition within the party and from the Left SRs, the treaty was signed on 3 March 1918.

Chaikovsky, Nikolai Vasil'evich (1851–1926): Russian revolutionary with roots in the Narodnik movement. Opposed Bolshevik seizure of power and headed the White government in Arkhangelsk during the Russian Civil War.

Chernov, Viktor Mikhailovich (1876–1952): founder and most prominent leader of the Social Revolutionary Party. After the February Revolution he served as Minister of Agriculture in the Kerensky government. After October 1917, became a member of an anti-Bolshevik government in Samara, before fleeing to Europe and then the United States.

Clemenceau, Georges (1841–1929): leading French statesman, prime minister in 1917 and chief inspirer of the Versailles Treaty.

Czernin, Ottokar Count (1872–1932): Minister of Foreign Affairs of the Austro-Hungarian Empire who represented Austria-Hungary at Brest-Litovsk.

Dan, Fedor Il'ich (1871–1947): one of the leading Mensheviks from 1903 onwards, aligned increasingly with the right wing of the movement. Supported Menshevik involvement in the Provisional Government and continuing the war against Germany and Austria. Opposed the October Revolution, expelled from USSR in 1922. Author of *The Origins of Bolshevism* (1943).

David, Eduard (1863–1930): one of the leading members of the revisionist wing in the German Social Democratic Party.

Denikin, Anton Ivanovich (1872–1947): prominent Tsarist general who became one of the leaders of the counter-revolution during the years of the Civil War. In the autumn of 1919, Denikin's troops led a march on Moscow, which reached Orel. After the defeat of the Whites, Denikin departed for Europe to write his memoirs.

Ebert, Friedrich (1871–1925): right-wing Social Democrat who became Chancellor of Germany in 1918 and the first president of the Weimar Republic in 1919. He played a major role in combating revolution.

Entente: Entente Powers or The Triple Entente, the main allies during the First World War were France, Russia, Britain, Italy and the United States against the Central Powers (Germany, Austria-Hungary).

Erfurt Programme: adopted by the German Social Democratic Party at Erfurt in 1891. Formulated under the political guidance of August Bebel and the ideological tutelage of Karl Kautsky, it superseded the earlier Gotha Programme. Kautsky also wrote the official SPD commentary on the programme, called *The Class Struggle*, which became the *locus classicus* for the orthodoxy of the 'Marxism of the Second International'.

Galliffet, Gaston (1830–1909): French marquis and general who distinguished himself by his savagery in the suppression of the Paris Commune of 1871. Thousands of Communards were shot and tortured to death on his orders. In 1899–1900 the Socialist Millerand served in the same cabinet with Gallifet.

Gambetta, Léon (1838–1882): leading French republican statesman who opposed both the Empire and the Commune. Was prime minister between 1881 and 1882.

Gambettists – *see* Gambetta

Giolitti, Giovanni (1842–1928): prime minister of Italy five times between 1892 and 1921.

Girondins: name given to the right or moderate wing of the Convention during the French Revolution (1792–3), as opposed to the Jacobins or Montagnards.

Haase, Hugo (1863–1919): German Social Democrat, deputy in the Reichstag in 1897. During First World War, he headed the 'moderate opposition' within the German party. On 1 March 1917, he became chairman of the Central Committee of the Independent Socialist Party of Germany. During the Spartacist uprising of January 1919, he tried to play the role of 'peacemaker'. In October of the same year, he was assassinated on the steps of the Reichstag.

Havas: French news agency.

Henderson, Arthur (1863–1935): one of the leaders of the British Labour Party and a prominent member of its right wing. Advocated war to the end during the First World War. In 1929, served as Minister of Foreign Affairs in the MacDonald government. Later became a disarmament advocate, and winner of the 1934 Nobel Peace Prize.

Hilferding, Rudolf (1877–1941): third leading figure of Austro-Marxism, particularly well-known for his book *Finance Capital*, published in 1910. Part of the moderate opposition to the First World War and after the Russian Revolution supported the idea of combining soviet and parliamentary democracy. When the Independent Social Democratic Party split at its Halle Congress in 1920, Hilferding stayed with the right wing. Served in the Streseman cabinet in 1923. After the rise of the Nazis, Hilferding fled, ending up in France where he was handed over by the Vichy authorities to the Occupation forces. He died in prison in 1941.

Hungarian Soviet Republic: formed on 21 March 1919 when the government of Count Károlyi was obliged to resign and hand over power to the Social Democratic Party. The latter proposed sharing power with the leaders of the Hungarian Communist Party. A Council of People's Commissars was formed, comprising both Communists (Bela Kun, Tibor Szamuely, Eugen Varga and others) and Social Democrats. The Entente replied to this revolution with blockade and war, attacking the Republic with the White troops of Romania and Czechoslovakia. After a four-month struggle the Romanian army took Budapest and proclaimed the dictatorship of Admiral Horthy, who instituted a reign of intense repression.

Independent Labour Party: founded in Britain in 1893 with Chairman James Keir Hardie, elected as Independent Labour MP for West Ham in the previous year's general election. Robert Smillie, Tom Mann, John Bruce Glasier, Henry Hyde Champion, Ben Tillett, Philip Snowden, and Edward Carpenter were also involved with the party. The ILP played a central role in the formation of the Labour Representation Committee in 1900 and when the Labour Party was formed in 1906 the ILP affiliated to it but remained to its left. Opposed the First World War on pacifist grounds. The ILP disaffiliated from the Second International in August 1920, but its right wing opposed affiliation to the Third International. The ILP was a key element of the 'centrist' Second-and-a-Half International between 1921 and 1923.

Independents (Independent Social Democratic Party of Germany, *Unabhängige Sozialdemokratische Partei Deutschlands*, or USPD): founded by German Social Democrats who had voted against the extension of war credits in December 1915 and were ultimately expelled in 1916. Officially founded in April 1917 at a congress in Gotha, the USPD grew rapidly in membership and influence after the 1918 revolution which toppled the Kaiser. The Independents tried to maintain a 'centrist' position balancing between the counterrevolutionary policies of the SPD and the strategy supported by the Spartacists/German Communist Party. This attempt finally failed at the Halle Congress of October 1920 where the party split on the question of affiliation to the Third International. A majority went on to fuse with the Communist Party, whilst a large minority continued under the banner of the USPD and played a major role in the 'Second-and-a-Half International' in 1921. Ultimately, however, most of this section re-merged with the SPD in 1924.

Jacobins: first representing a moderate tendency during the French Revolution, this society included a range of political figures in 1789: Mirabeau, La Fayette and Robespierre, amongst others. After a split away by the more moderate elements in 1791, the Club increasingly moved towards republican positions. The Girondins left it after the September Massacres of 1792 and thereafter it became a powerful centre for the Montagnards (see below). Closed after 9 Thermidor, it was reconstituted several times until its definitive dissolution in 1799.

Jaurès, Jean (1859–1914): one of the most prominent leaders of the pre-1914 Second International and of the French Socialists. Renowned as a great orator, founding the newspaper *l'Humanité* in 1904. Entered the labour movement from a Radical background in 1890. After the Dreyfus affair, Jaurès was instrumental in forming a political bloc between the Radicals and the Socialists to support Millerand when the latter entered the bourgeois government. By the mid-1890s, Jaurès began to play a major role in the Second International, supporting the reformist wing on almost all questions. As a sincere opponent of war, Jaurès conducted in the pre-1914 days a bitter campaign against the First World War which resulted in his assassination in July 1914.

Jaurèsism – see Jaurès

Joffe, Adolph Abramovich (1883–1927): Russian Communist revolutionary and Soviet diplomat. Associated with Trotsky in the 1920s and committed suicide in the face of the rise of Stalin.

Jourde, François (1843–1893) : one of the key figures of the Paris Commune, with particular responsibility for the Bank of France, which caused him to be criticized by some for his excessive prudence. After the fall of the Commune, deported to New Caledonia, from which he escaped in 1874. After a period in several cities in Europe, returned to France after the 1880 amnesty.

Kadets: abbreviation for Kadet Party, or Constitutional Democrats – the liberal party of the Russian bourgeoisie.

Kaledin, Aleksei Maksimovich (1861–1918): Russian Full General of Cavalry who led the Don Cossack White movement in the opening stages of the Russian Civil War.

Kautsky, Karl (1854–1938): born in the Austro-Hungarian Empire, Kautsky became the most important of the theoreticians of German Social Democracy (popularly referred to as the 'Pope of Marxism'). Founding editor of the party's theoretical journal *Die Neue Zeit* (1883–1917), Kautsky was a prolific author of books, pamphlets, programmatic documents, articles and reviews on a vast range of political, economic, philosophical, historical and sociological subjects. He was the co-author of the Erfurt Programme and edited Marx's *Theories of Surplus-Value* for publication. Originally associated with a left position in the SPD and the Second International (he famously opposed Bernstein's 'revisionism'), Kautsky increasingly became associated with a 'centrist' position in the eyes of his radical critics. During the First World War, Kautsky voted for war credits but drifted to a pacifist oppositional position and became a founder of the Independent Social Democratic Party until 1919, when he rejoined the SPD. He was hostile to the Bolshevik Revolution and developed his critique in a number of texts, including *Terrorism and Communism*, to which Trotsky responds here. In 1924, Kautsky moved back to Vienna until he was forced into exile in Amsterdam, where he died in 1938.

Kerensky, Alexandr (1881–1970): reformist prime minister in Russia after the February 1917 revolution, overthrown by the October insurrection.

Kolchak, Aleksandr Vasil'evich (1874–1920): Tsarist admiral who, after the Soviet power had been temporarily overthrown in Siberia, installed himself as a puppet ruler supported by the Allies. In November 1918 the Cossack *atamans* (chieftains) elected him supreme commander. When the counter-revolution suffered defeat he was left stranded by the Allies and was arrested during an uprising in Irkutsk province. Executed in February 1920 by the order of the Irkutsk Revolutionary Committee.

Kornilov, Lavr Georgievich (1870–1918): senior Russian general who led a *coup d'état* attempt against Kerensky's Provisional Government in July–August 1917. The coup was defeated by mass mobilization by Bolsheviks and workers, leading to a further stage in radicalization of the revolution.

Krasnov, Pyotr Nikolaevich (1869–1947): one of the leaders of the counterrevolutionary White armies during the Civil War.

Kühlmann, Richard von (1873–1948): Minister of Foreign Affairs of the German Imperial government who conducted the peace negotiations at Brest-Litovsk for Germany.

Labriola, Antonio (1843–1904): Italian Marxist philosopher best known for his work *Essays on the Materialist Conception of History*.

Lafargue, Paul (1842–1911): French socialist journalist, literary critic, political writer and activist best known for his opuscule *The Right to Be Lazy*. Married Karl Marx's daughter Laura, with whom he committed suicide as part of a pact in 1911.

Lassalle, Ferdinand (1825–1864): German jurist and the leading figure in the early German socialist movement.

Lavrov, Pyotr Lavrovich (1823–1900): Russian sociologist and philosopher who was one of the key spokespeople for Narodism (peasant-based socialism). Forced to flee Tsarism to Paris in 1870, he joined the First International and participated in the Paris Commune, about which he later wrote a book.

Liebknecht, Karl (1871–1919): leader of the German revolutionary labour movement, founder with Rosa Luxemburg of the German Communist Party. Long before the First World War, he earned revolutionary renown through his struggle against militarism. He was sentenced to 18 months in prison for writing his pamphlet, *Militarism and Anti-Militarism*. Liebknecht's name is a symbol of revolutionary internationalism and irreconcilable opposition to imperialist war due to his sole vote against war credits in the Reichstag in December 1914. As member of the revolutionary committee, he headed the uprising of the Berlin workers in January 1919. After this uprising was suppressed he was arrested by the Scheidemann government and on 15 January 1919 was assassinated, together with Luxemburg, by counterrevolutionaries.

Lissagaray, Prosper-Olivier (1838–1901): French socialist journalist particularly well-known for his classic historical account of the Commune, *History of the Paris Commune of 1871* (1876) which he based on interviews with exiled survivors and documentary sources.

Lloyd George, David (1863–1945): one of the authors of the Versailles Treaty, and Liberal Party prime minister, 1916–1922. Beginning his career as a liberal reformer, he came into prominence in 1908 as the sponsor of the 8-hour day for the miners, however he conducted the war ruthlessly, and campaigned against the Russian Revolution. After the victory of the Bolsheviks in the Civil War, he became an advocate of re-establishing economic ties with the Soviet Union.

Longuet, Jean (1876–1938): French lawyer and Socialist, and grandson of Karl Marx, who in the First World War held a pacifist position but invariably voted for war credits. Founder and editor of the newspaper *Le Populaire*. At the Strasbourg Congress in 1918, the majority of the French SP went over to Longuet's position. After the Tours Congress in 1920, where the Communists gained the majority, he split from the party, joined the Second-and-a-Half International and returned later to the Second International.

Loriot, Fernand (1870–1932): a veteran French Socialist. During the closing years of the war of 1914–18 he was the leader of the extreme left wing in the French Socialist Party, supporting the Zimmerwald Left. In 1920–21 Loriot took active part in the split of the Socialists and the formation of the French Communist Party, and became one of its leaders. Attended the Third Congress of the Communist International and was elected to the presidium. A few years later, he dropped out of the Communist movement and joined forces with the revolutionary syndicalist Pierre Monatte.

Ludendorff, Erich Friedrich Wilhelm (1865–1937): German Army officer, Quartermaster General during the First World War, victor of Liège, and, with Paul von Hindenburg, one of the victors of the battle of Tannenberg. After the war, he briefly supported Adolf Hitler and the Nazi Party.

Luxemburg, Rosa (1871–1919): of Polish nationality, Luxemburg was one of the greatest theoreticians of the left wing of German Social Democracy, and then of the Spartacists and the Communist Party, and author of a number of key books including *The Accumulation of Capital*. She also participated in the Polish and

Russian revolutionary movements, and from 1910 headed the revolutionary opposition within the German SPD. During the First World War, she was imprisoned for her opposition to the conflict. In 1918, together with Liebknecht, she founded the German Communist Party. She was murdered in 1919.

MacMahon, Patrice Maurice de (1808–1893): Duke of Magenta, Marshal of France, and head of the army of Versaillais who overran and repressed the Paris Commune. Served as first president of the Third Republic, from 1875 to 1879.

Martov, Iulii (Y.O. Zederbaum) (1873–1923): the ideological leader of Menshevism, began his career by working with Lenin in 1895 in the Petersburg League of Struggle for the Emancipation of the Working Class. Collaborated with Lenin in founding *Iskra* and the theoretical magazine *Zarya*. Lifelong break with Lenin began in 1903. During the period of the October Revolution, Martov occupied a left position in Menshevik ranks, remaining in the Second Congress of the Soviets after the departure of the Right SRs and the Mensheviks. Permitted to emigrate, he left for Berlin where he founded the central publication of the Mensheviks in emigration (*Sotsialistichesky Vestnik*).

Mensheviks: reformist wing of the Russian Social Democratic Workers' Party (RSDLP), from 1903 to 1912 when it and the Bolsheviks became separate parties. The Mensheviks opposed the October 1917 revolution and subsequently split between right and left wings.

Miliukov, Pavel (1859–1943): Russian historian, leader of the Russian liberal bourgeoisie and its party, the Kadets (Constitutional Democrats). After the February 1917 revolution, he held the post of Foreign Minister in the Provisional Government and tried to continue the foreign policy of Tsarism. After the October revolution, he emigrated to France, where he edited a Russian daily newspaper.

Millerand, Alexandre (1859–1943): French socialist who worked with Jaurès. Notoriously, in 1899 he joined the bourgeois government of Waldeck-Rousseau alongside the Marquis de Galliffet, thereby sparking an international controversy on the Left. Continuing his rightward drift, he became president of France from 1920 to 1924 and prime minister of France January–September 1920.

Mirbach, Count Wilhelm (1871–1918): German Ambassador to Soviet Russia after the conclusion of the Brest-Litovsk Treaty. The

Left Social Revolutionaries assassinated him in the summer of 1918 in order, they hoped, to re-ignite war with Germany.

Monatte, Pierre (1881–1960): one of the leaders of the French Communist Party, which he joined toward the end of 1922. Prior to the First World War, Monatte stood in the ranks of the French revolutionary syndicalists, who constituted during the war years the core of the labour movement's opposition to the pro-war Left. After the war ended, Monatte continued his revolutionary work but did not immediately join the Communist Party. Expelled from the Communist Party in late 1924, he founded the journal *La Révolution prolétarienne*.

Montagnards: name given to the deputies sitting on the higher benches (the 'Mountain') of the French Legislative Assembly and then of the Convention. Often used interchangeably with 'Jacobins'. They differed from the Girondins in resting their support on the popular movement, by showing their support for regulation of the economy and, finally, by an equalizing vision of social relations. Robespierre was one of their most eminent representatives.

Noske, Gustav (1868–1946): German trade-union functionary and member of the extreme right wing of the Social Democratic Party. During the postwar years became known as the executioner of the revolution, so ferocious was his repression. Served as Defence Minister between 1919 and 1920.

Piłsudski, Józef Klemens (1867–1935): early in his career was persecuted by the Tsarist government as an activist and revolutionary leader in the Polish Socialist Party (PPS). After the First World War, when Poland won independence, became head of the government through a *coup d'état*. Later became dictator (1926–1935) of the Second Polish Republic, as well as head of its armed forces.

Plekhanov, Georgi Valentinovich (1856–1918): Russian revolutionary and leading Marxist theoretician. One of the founders of the Social Democratic movement in Russia, Plekhanov was allied to the Menshevik wing and opposed the October Revolution.

Poincaré, Raymond (1860–1934): French conservative statesman who served as prime minister of France on five separate occasions and as president of France from 1913 to 1920.

Pood: Russian unit of mass equivalent to 16.38kg (36.11lbs).

Potresov, Alexandr Nikolaevich (1869–1934): prominent right wing Menshevik.

Proudhon, Pierre-Joseph (1809–1865): French mutualist political philosopher of the socialist tradition, considered to be among the leading early anarchist thinkers. Proudhon is most famous for his assertion that 'Property is theft!', in *What Is Property? Or, an Inquiry into the Principle of Right and Government*, his first major work, published in 1840.

Proudhonism: see Proudhon.

Rada: assembly of representatives of various public organizations in Ukraine, formed after the February Revolution and claimed to be the spokesman for the Ukrainian nation. After October 1917, the Rada supported the White counter-revolution. After its overthrow by the Bolsheviks in 1918, the Rada favoured the German occupation, which, when established, dissolved the Rada government and made Hetman Skoropadsky the sole ruler of the country.

Radoslavov, Vasil (1854–1929): leading Bulgarian liberal politician who twice served as prime minister. He was premier of the country throughout most of the First World War.

Renaudel, Pierre (1871–1935): leader of the extreme right and pro-war wing of the French Socialist Party.

Renner, Karl (1870–1950): leading figure of the moderate wing of the Austrian Social Democrats and author of a major work on the sociology of the law. Supported the war of 1914–18. After the Hapsburg dynasty was overthrown, he became chancellor in the coalition government. When the revolutionary wave subsided, Renner, together with his colleagues, was ejected from the government. He became president of the Second Republic in 1945.

Revisionism: right wing current of thought in German Social Democracy which argued for a revision of theoretical orthodoxy in the direction of a more gradualist and pacific vision.

Rigault, Raoul (1846–1871): French Blanquist and militant atheist who served many prison sentences for political offences. During the Paris Commune, became head of the security and police apparatus and was responsible for the arrest of hostages and requisitioning in the churches. Died fighting in the Latin Quarter against the Versaillais.

Rodzianko, Mikhail Vladimirovich (1859–1924): one of the founders and leaders of the Russian Octobrist party. Deputy of the Third Russian State Duma, and elected chairman after the resignation of Aleksandr Guchkov in 1911. He then continued as chairman of the Fourth State Duma until its dissolution in February

1917. One of the key politicians during the Russian February Revolution. Presided over the Provisional Committee of the State Duma, and, among other things, led abdication talks with Tsar Nicholas II. Emigrated to Yugoslavia in 1920 where he died.

Rosmer, Alfred (1877–1964): French revolutionary who participated with Pierre Monatte in the syndicalist movement. Broke in 1919–20 with syndicalism and in 1920 attended the Second Congress of the Communist International, serving as a member of its presidium. He actively defended the line of the Communist International within the French Communist Party and was one of the leaders of its left wing. Joined the Left Opposition in the early days of its existence, but subsequently distanced himself from it while maintaining contact with Trotsky. Author of *Le Mouvement ouvrier pendant la guerre* (1936) and the memoir *Lenin's Moscow* (1953).

Savinkov, Boris Viktorovich (1879–1925): Russian writer and revolutionary terrorist. As one of the leaders of the Fighting Organization of the Socialist-Revolutionary Party, he was responsible for the most spectacular assassinations of imperial officials in 1904 and 1905. Later, he became assistant war minister in the Provisional Government. Savinkov emigrated in 1920, but in 1924 he attempted to return to Russia, was arrested and either was killed in prison or committed suicide.

Sazhen: Russian unit of measure equivalent to 2.13m (7ft).

Scheidemann, Philipp (1865–1939): right wing German Social Democrat politician, who proclaimed the Republic on 9 November 1918, and who became the first Chancellor of the Weimar Republic. After the defeat of the Spartacists in 1919, he became the head of a coalition government but resigned in protest at the Treaty of Versailles.

Second International: founded in 1889 as the international organization of socialist and labour parties, with a permanent bureau based in Brussels. In 1914, almost all the sections of the International supported their respective governments rather than opposing the war. Was reorganized in 1920 in clear opposition to the Communist International and in 1923 merged with the 'Two-and-a-Half' International.

Seitz, Karl (1869–1950): moderate Austrian Social Democrat who became first federal president of Austria in 1918 until 1920, and chairman of the party. Elected mayor of Vienna in 1923.

Skoropadsky, Pavlo (1873–1945): Ukrainian aristocrat and general in the Russian Imperial army. Became the conservative leader in Ukraine's unsuccessful struggle for independence following the Russian Revolution of 1917. Declared *hetman* (leader) of the government of a 'Ukrainian State' (*Ukrayinska Derzhava*) in April 1918 after a *coup d'état*. His highly reactionary government, and his period in power, are both referred to as 'the Hetmanate', which lasted until December 1918.

Social Revolutionaries (SRs): Russian peasant socialist party. Split in 1917, the Left SRs participated for a period in the Soviet government, the right SRs opposed the revolution.

Sombart, Werner (1863–1941): leading German economist and sociologist, initially associated with the Left, but moved rightwards. Most famous for his work *Modern Capitalism* (1916).

Thiers, Louis Adolphe (1797–1877): French politician and historian. Thiers was a prime minister under King Louis-Philippe of France. Following the overthrow of the Second Empire he again came to prominence as the French leader who suppressed the Paris Commune of 1871.

Tsereteli, Irakli (1881–1959): one of the most prominent right wing Mensheviks from Georgia, deputy to the Second Duma. After the February Revolution he was one of the leaders of the so-called 'revolutionary defensists' and entered as Minister of Posts and Telegraph into the coalition government. After the October Revolution, Lenin ordered Tsereteli's arrest, so he remained in Georgia where he obtained a seat in the Parliament of the Democratic Republic of Georgia (1918–21). After occupation of Georgia by the Red Army, he fled to France and then to the United States.

Tsyperovich, Grigorii Vladimirovich (1872–1932): leading Russian trade-union leader. Born the son of a poor tailor, he joined the Social Democratic movement as a youth and spent long periods in jail and exile, including ten years in Srednekolymsk. Released in 1905, he rejoined the revolutionary movement in southern Russia (Odessa). Later he graduated from the economics faculty of St Petersburg University, and then spent more than two years abroad. Upon his return to Russia, he became active in the trade-union movement, and wrote especially on economic questions in the trade-union press. After October he became a member of the Central Council of Trade Unions (VTsSPS), then worked in the Petrograd Council of Trade Unions. From July to October 1919 he headed the Council. He joined the Bolshevik party in that year.

Tugan-Baranovsky, Mikhaylo Ivanovych (1865–1919): major economist in Russia, of Ukrainian origin. Was one of the founders of the National Academy of Science of Ukraine, as well as Minister of Finance of the Ukrainian People's Republic.

Turati, Filippo (1857–1932): Italian lawyer and one of the founders of the Italian Socialist Party. Leader of the reformist wing, he voted against war credits in the First World War, but supported President Wilson's programme. At the conclusion of the war, remained an opponent of the Russian Revolution and of the Communist International. After the split of the Italian party in 1922, he headed the Reformist party.

Uritsky, Moisei Solomonovich (1873–1918): Bolshevik leader of Ukrainian origin, who served as head of the Petrograd Cheka. Assassinated in August 1918, an event which, together with the assassination attempt on Lenin, is often posited as the beginning of the Red Terror.

Vandervelde, Emile (1866–1938): lawyer and professor, right wing leader of the Belgian Socialist Party and former leader of the Second International. Was among the first Socialists to enter the war cabinet, becoming premier. As Belgium's representative, he signed the Versailles Treaty. Participated in various coalition governments in the 1920s.

Vermorel, August Jean-Marie (1841–1871): French socialist journalist who played an active part in the Commune and was wounded on the barricades. Taken to Versailles, where he died.

Versaillais: term for the counterrevolutionary forces that rallied to Versailles during the Commune and who inflicted terrible repression on it when the latter fell.

Verst: Russian unit of length, equivalent to 500 *sazhen*, or 1.07km (3,500ft).

Vollmar, Georg Heinrich von (1850–1922): leading figure of the right wing of German Social Democracy. Elected to the Reichstag in 1881, serving until 1887, then from 1890 to 1918.

Wolff: German news agency.

Yudenich, Nikolai Nikolaevich (1862–1933): general of the Russian Imperial Army during the First World War and later a leader of the counter-revolution in north-western Russia during the Russian Civil War.

Zinoviev, Grigory Yevseevich (1883–1936): Bolshevik leader, head of Petrograd government and president of the Communist International.

CHRONOLOGY

1917

February   Workers strike and soldiers mutiny in Petrograd. Petrograd Soviet is created

March   Abdication of Nicholas II and establishment of the Provisional Government under Lvov. Spread of soviets. Peasants unrest against landlords. Mensheviks and Social Revolutionaries give Provisional Government their conditional support

April   Lenin returns from Switzerland and publishes his *April Theses*. Miliukov's note to Allies provokes street demonstration in Petrograd. Miliukov and Guchkov resign from cabinet

May   Lvov forms coalition ministry involving Mensheviks and Social Revolutionaries

June   First All-Russia Congress of Soviets of Workers' and Soldiers' Deputies. Russian military offensive on Eastern front. Proposal to grant regional autonomy to Ukraine

July   Resignation of Kadet ministers. Armed demonstration of workers and sailors in Petrograd. Lenin flees. Kerensky becomes premier

August   State Conference in Moscow. Germans take Riga. Kornilov mutiny is suppressed

September   Bolsheviks take over the Petrograd Soviet. Democratic Conference in Petrograd

October   Bolshevik Central Committee, cajoled by Lenin, decides to seize power. Second Congress of Soviets; overthrow of the Provisional Government and the establishment of

Sovnarkom. Issuance of revolutionary decrees: on Peace, on Land, on the Press. Arrests of Kadets and others

November Left Social Revolutionaries definitively form own party. Constituent Assembly elections. Ceasefire on Eastern front

December Extraordinary Commission (Cheka) is formed. Left Social Revolutionaries join Sovnarkom. Banks are nationalized. Soviet forces invade Ukraine and Ukrainian Soviet government is announced

1918

January Opening and dispersal of the Constituent Assembly. Sovnarkom decides to form Red Army. Bolsheviks dispute the proposal for a separate peace with Central Powers

February Basic Law on the Land is introduced

March Bolsheviks rename themselves as the Russian Communist Party (Bolsheviks). Treaty of Brest-Litovsk: Russia withdraws from the First World War and renounces claims over the territory of Ukraine, Belorussia, Lithuania, Latvia and Estonia. Bolsheviks defeated in several Russian town soviets

April Germans establish puppet regime of Skoropadsky in Ukraine

May Czechoslovak Legion revolts

June Social Revolutionary government is formed in Samara. Massive campaign of industrial nationalization. Decree on the committees of the village poor

July Suppression of the Party of Left Social Revolutionaries. Romanov family shot in the Urals

August Assassination attempt on Lenin

September Red Terror is formally proclaimed. Red Army recaptures Kazan

November End of First World War. Russian Soviet republic declares the treaty of Brest-Litovsk null and void. Kolchak is proclaimed Supreme Ruler in Omsk. Estonian Soviet republic is announced

December Committees of the village poor are abolished. Kolchak takes Perm in Urals. Latvian and Lithuanian Soviet republics are announced. Petlyura takes over Ukrainian government

1919

January   System of Politburo and Orgburo is introduced to Bolshevik Party Central Committee. Red Army takes eastern Ukraine. Belorussian Soviet republic is established

February   Delivery quota system of grain requisitioning is formalized. Red Army takes Kiev

March   First Congress of Communist International. Eighth Congress of Russian Communist Party. Short-lived Soviet republics are created in Hungary and Munich. Ukrainian Soviet republic is restored

April   Kolchak's advance is halted

May   Beginning of Denikin's offensive

August   Red Army evacuates Ukraine

October   Yudenich advances towards Petrograd. Denikin is defeated. Then Yudenich is defeated

December   Red Army recaptures Kiev

1920

January   Allies end blockade of Soviet Russia. Labour armies are introduced

February   Kolchak is executed. Estonian state independence is recognized by the Russian Soviet republic

April   Intensification of military hostility with Poland. Azerbaijani Soviet republic is formed

May   Pilsudski captures Kiev, but is forced to retreat in July

July   Lithuanian state independence is recognized by the Russian Soviet republic

August   Latvian state independence is recognized by the Russian Soviet republic. Poles defeat Red Army at battle of the Vistula

December   Armenian Soviet republic is established

1921

February   Politburo agrees to introduce New Economic Policy. Georgian Soviet republic is formed

March   Kronstadt naval garrison mutinies. Tenth Party Congress confirms New Economic Policy and bans Workers' Opposition and other factions in the party

NOTE ON THE TEXT

This edition of Trotsky's text (also available on the Marxist Internet Archive www.marxists.org) was published by the Workers Party of America (as the Communist Party of the United States was then called) in 1920 under the title *Dictatorship vs Democracy*. Subsequent editions have been published under the titles *Terrorism or Communism* or *Terrorism and Communism*. This version has been corrected for consistency in spelling and transliteration. References in parentheses in the text are Trotsky's, and all notes are by the editor.

LEON TROTSKY

TERRORISM AND
COMMUNISM: A REPLY
TO KARL KAUTSKY

PREFACE

By H.N. Brailsford

It has been said of the Bolsheviks that they are more interesting than Bolshevism. To those who hold to the economic interpretation of history that may seem a heresy. Nonetheless, I believe that the personality not merely of the leaders but also of their party goes far to explain the making and survival of the Russian Revolution. To us in the West they seem a wholly foreign type. With socialist leaders and organizations we and our fathers have been familiar for three-quarters of a century. There has been no lack of talent and even of genius among them. The movement has produced its great theorist in Marx, its orator in Jaurès, its powerful tacticians like Bebel, and it has influenced literature in Morris, Anatole France and Shaw. It bred, however, no considerable man of action, and it was left for the Russians to do what generations of Western socialists had spent their lives in discussing. There was in this Russian achievement an almost barbaric simplicity and directness. Here were men who really believed the formulae of our theorists and the resolutions of our congresses. What had become for us a sterilized and almost respectable orthodoxy rang to their ears as a trumpet call to action. The older generation has found it difficult to pardon their sincerity. The rest of us want to understand the miracle.

The real audacity of the Bolsheviks lay in this, that they made a proletarian revolution precisely in that country which, of all portions of the civilized world, seemed the least prepared for it by its economic development. For an agrarian revolt, for the subdivision of the soil, even for the overthrow of the old governing class, Russia was certainly ready. But any spontaneous revolution, with its foundations laid in the masses of the peasantry, would have been individualistic and not communistic. The daring of the Bolsheviks lay in their belief that the minute minority of the urban working class could, by its concentration, its greater intelligence and its relative capacity for organization, dominate the inert peasant mass, and give to their outbreak of land hunger the character and form of a constructive proletarian revolution. The bitter struggle among Russian parties which lasted from March 1917, down to the defeat of Wrangel in November 1920, was really an internecine competition among them for the leadership of the peasants. Which of these several groups could enlist their confidence, to the extent of inducing them not merely to fight, but to accept the discipline, military and civilian, necessary for victory? At the start the Bolsheviks had everything against them. They are nearly all townsmen. They talked in terms of a foreign and very German doctrine. Few of them, save Lenin, grasped the problems of rural life at all. The landed class should at least have known the peasant better. Their chief rivals were the Social Revolutionaries; a party which from its first beginnings had made a cult of the Russian peasant, studied him, idealized him and courted him, which even seemed in 1917 to have won him. Many circumstances explain the success of the Bolsheviks, who proved once again in history the capacity of the town, even when its population is relatively minute, for swift and concentrated action. They also had the luck of dealing with opponents who committed the supreme mistake of invoking foreign aid. But none of these advantages would have availed without an immense superiority of character. The Slav temperament, dreamy, emotional, undisciplined, showed itself at its worst in the incorrigible self-indulgence of the more aristocratic 'Whites', while the 'intellectuals' of the moderate socialist and liberal groups have been ruined for action by their exclusively literary and aesthetic education. The Bolsheviks may be a less cultivated group, but, in their underground life of conspiracy, they had learned sobriety, discipline, obedience and mutual confidence. Their rigid dogmatic Marxist faith gives to them the power of action which belongs only to those who believe without criticism or question. Their ability to lead depends much less than most Englishmen suppose on their ruthlessness and their readiness to practise the arts of intimidation and suppression. Their chief asset is their self-confidence. In every emergency they are always sure that they have the only workable plan. They stand before the rest of Russia as one man. They never doubt or despair and, even when they compromise, they do it with an air of truculence. Their survival amid invasion, famine, blockade and economic collapse has been from first to last a triumph of the unflinching will and the fanatical faith. They have spurred a lazy and demoralized people to notable feats of arms and to still more astonishing feats of endurance. To hypnotize a nation in this fashion is, perhaps, the most remarkable feat of the human will in modern times.

This book is, so far, by far the most typical expression of the Bolshevik temperament which the revolution has produced. Characteristically it is a polemic, and not a constructive essay. Its self-confidence, its dash, even its insolence, are a true expression of the movement. Its author bears a world-famous name. Everyone can visualize the powerful head, the singularly handsome features, the athletic figure of the man. He makes in private talk an impression of decision and definiteness. He is not rapid or expansive in speech, for everything that he says is calculated and clear-cut. One has the sense that one is in the presence of abounding yet disciplined vitality. The background is an office which by its military order and punctuality rebukes the habitual slovenliness of Russia. On the platform his manner was much quieter than I expected. He spoke rather slowly, in a pleasant tenor voice, walking to and fro across the stage and choosing his words, obviously anxious to express his thoughts forcibly but also exactly. A flash of wit and a striking phrase came frequently, but the manner was emphatically not that of a demagogue. The man, indeed, is a natural aristocrat, and his tendency, which Lenin, the aristocrat by birth, corrects, is towards military discipline and authoritative regimentation.

There is nothing surprising today in the note of authority which one hears in Trotsky's voice and detects in his writing, for he is the chief of a considerable army, which owes everything to his talent for organization. It was at Brest-Litovsk that he displayed the audacity which is genius. Up to that moment there was little in his career to distinguish him from his comrades of the revolutionary underworld – a university course cut short by prison, an apprenticeship to agitation in Russia, some years of exile spent in Vienna, Paris and New York, the distinction which he shares with Tchitcherin of 'sitting' in a British prison, a ready wit, a gift of trenchant speech, but as yet neither the solid achievement nor the legend which gives confidence. Yet this obscure agitator, handicapped in such a task by his Jewish birth, faced the diplomatist and soldiers of the central empires, flushed as they were with victory and the insolence of their kind, forced them into public debate, staggered them by talking of first principles as though the defeat and impotence of Russia counted for nothing, and actually used the negotiations to shout across their heads his summons to their own subjects to revolt. He showed in this astonishing performance the grace and audacity of a 'matador'. This unique bit of drama revealed the persistent belief of the Bolsheviks in the power of the defiant challenge, the magnetic effect of sheer will. Since this episode his services to the revolution have been more solid but not less brilliant. He had no military knowledge or experience, yet he took in hand the almost desperate task of creating an army. He has often been compared to Carnot. But, save that both had lost officers, there was little in common between the French and the Russian armies in the early stages of the two revolutions. The French army had not been demoralized by defeat, or wearied by long inaction, or sapped by destructive propaganda. Trotsky had to create his Red Army from the foundations. He imposed firm discipline, and yet contrived to preserve the plan of the revolutionary spirit. Hampered by the inconceivable difficulties that arose from ruined railways and decayed industries, he nonetheless contrived to make a military machine which overthrew the armies of Kolchak, Denikin and Wrangel, with the flower of the old professional officers at their head. As a feat of organization under inordinate difficulties, his work ranks as the most remarkable performance of the revolution.

It is not the business of a preface to anticipate the argument of a book, still less to obtrude personal opinions. Kautsky's laboured essay, to which this book is the brilliant reply, has been translated into English, and is widely known. The case against the possibility of political democracy in a capitalist society could hardly be better put than in these pages, and the polemic against purely evolutionary methods is formidable. The English reader of today is aware, however, that the Russian Revolution has not stood still since Trotsky wrote. We have to realize that, even in the view of the Bolsheviks themselves, the evolution towards communism is in Russia only in its early stages. The recent compromises imply, at the best, a very long period of transition, through controlled capitalist production, to socialism. Experience has proved that catastrophic revolution and the seizure of political power do not in themselves avail to make a socialist society. The economic development in that direction has actually been retarded, and Russia, under the stress of civil war, has retrograded into a primitive village system of production and exchange. To every reader's mind the question will be present whether the peculiar temperament of the Bolsheviks has led them to overestimate the importance of political power, to underestimate the inert resistance of the majority, and to risk too much for the illusion of dictating. To that question history has not yet given the decisive answer. The daemonic will that made the revolution and defended it by achieving the impossible may yet vindicate itself against the dull trend of impersonal forces.

INTRODUCTION

The origin of this book was the learned brochure by Kautsky with the same name. My work was begun at the most intense period of the struggle with Denikin and Yudenich, and more than once was interrupted by events at the front. In the most difficult days, when the first chapters were being written, all the attention of Soviet Russia was concentrated on purely military problems. We were obliged to defend first of all the very possibility of socialist economic reconstruction. We could busy ourselves little with industry, further than was necessary to maintain the front. We were obliged to expose Kautsky's economic slanders mainly by analogy with his political slanders. The monstrous assertions of Kautsky — to the effect that the Russian workers were incapable of labour discipline and economic self-control — could, at the beginning of this work, nearly a year ago, be combated chiefly by pointing to the high state of discipline and heroism in battle of the Russian workers at the front created by the civil war. That experience was more than enough to explode these bourgeois slanders. But now a few months have gone by, and we can turn to facts and conclusions drawn directly from the economic life of Soviet Russia.

As soon as the military pressure relaxed after the defeat of Kolchak and Yudenich and the infliction of decisive blows on Denikin, after the conclusion of peace with Estonia and the beginning of negotiations with Lithuania and Poland, the whole country turned its mind to things economic. And this one fact, of a swift and concentrated transference of attention and energy from one set of problems to another — very different, but requiring not less sacrifice — is incontrovertible evidence of the mighty vigour of the Soviet order. In spite of political tortures, physical sufferings and horrors, the labouring masses are infinitely distant from political decomposition, from moral collapse, or from apathy. Thanks to a regime which, though it has inflicted great hardships upon them, has given their life a purpose and a high goal, they preserve an extraordinary moral stubbornness and ability unexampled in history, and concentrate their attention and will on collective problems. Today, in all branches of industry, there is going on an energetic struggle for the establishment of strict labour discipline, and for the increase of the productivity of labour. The party organizations, the trade unions, the factory and workshop administrative committees, rival one another in this respect, with the undivided support of the public opinion of the working class as a whole. Factory after factory willingly, by resolution at its general meeting, increases its working day. Petrograd and Moscow set the example, and the provinces emulate Petrograd. Communist Saturdays and Sundays – that is to say, voluntary and unpaid work during hours appointed for rest – spread ever wider and wider, drawing into their reach many, many hundreds of thousands of working men and women. The industry and productivity of labour at the Communist Saturdays and Sundays, according to the report of experts and the evidence of figures, is of a remarkably high standard.

Voluntary mobilizations for labour problems in the party and in the Young Communist League are carried out with just as much enthusiasm as hitherto for military tasks. Voluntarism supplements and gives life to universal labour service. The committees for universal labour service recently set up have spread all over the country. The attraction of the population to work on a mass scale (clearing snow from the roads, repairing railway lines, cutting timber, chopping and bringing up of wood to the towns, the simplest building operations, the cutting of slate and of peat) becomes more and more widespread and organized every day. The ever-increasing employment of military formations on the labour front would be quite impossible in the absence of elevated enthusiasm for labour.

True, we live in the midst of a very difficult period of economic depression – exhausted, poverty-stricken and hungry. But this is no argument against the Soviet regime. All periods of transition have been characterized by just such tragic features. Every class society (serf, feudal, capitalist), having exhausted its vitality, does not simply leave the arena, but is violently swept off by an intense struggle, which immediately brings to its participants even greater privations and sufferings than those against which they rose.

The transition from feudal economy to bourgeois society – a step of gigantic importance from the point of view of progress – gave us a terrifying list of martyrs. However the masses of serfs suffered under feudalism, however difficult it has been, and is, for the proletariat to live under capitalism, never have the sufferings of the workers reached such a pitch as at the epochs when the old feudal order was being violently shattered, and was yielding place to the new. The French Revolution of the eighteenth century, which attained its titanic dimensions under the pressure of the masses exhausted with suffering, itself deepened and rendered more acute their misfortunes for a prolonged period and to an extraordinary extent. Can it be otherwise?

Palace revolutions, which end merely by personal reshufflings at the top, can take place in a short space of time, having practically no effect on the economic life of the country. Quite another matter are revolutions which drag into their whirlpool millions of workers. Whatever be the form of society, it rests on the foundation of labour. Dragging the mass of the people away from labour, drawing them for a prolonged period into the struggle, thereby destroying their connection with production, the revolution in all these ways strikes deadly blows at economic life, and inevitably lowers the standard which it found at its birth. The more perfect the revolution, the greater are the masses it draws in; and the longer it is prolonged, the greater is the destruction it achieves in the apparatus of production, and the more terrible inroads does it make upon public resources. From this there follows merely the conclusion which did not require proof – that a civil war is harmful to economic life. But to lay this at the door of the Soviet economic system is like accusing a new-born human being of the birth-pangs of the mother who brought him into the world. The problem is to make a civil war a short one; and this is attained only by resoluteness in action. But it is just against revolutionary resoluteness that Kautsky's whole brochure is directed.

Since the time that the brochure under examination appeared, not only in Russia, but throughout the world – and first of all in Europe – the greatest events have taken place, or processes of great importance have developed, undermining the last buttresses of Kautskianism.

In Germany, the civil war has been adopting an ever fiercer character. The external strength in organization of the old party and trade union democracy of the working class has not only not created conditions for a more peaceful and 'humane' transition to socialism – as follows from the present theory of Kautsky – but, on the contrary, has served as one of the principal reasons for the long-drawn-out character of the struggle, and its constantly growing ferocity. The more German social democracy became a conservative, retarding force, the more energy, lives and blood have had to be spent by the German proletariat, devoted to it, in a series of systematic attacks on the foundation of bourgeois society, in order, in the process of the struggle itself, to create an actually revolutionary organization, capable of guiding the proletariat to final victory. The conspiracy of the German generals, their fleeting seizure of power, and the bloody events which followed, have again shown what a worthless and wretched masquerade is so-called democracy, during the collapse of imperialism and a civil war. This democracy that has outlived itself has not decided one question, has not reconciled one contradiction, has not healed one wound, has not warded off risings either of the right or of the left; it is helpless, worthless, fraudulent, and serves only to confuse the backward sections of the people, especially the lower middle classes.

The hope expressed by Kautsky, in the conclusion of his book, that the Western countries, the 'old democracies' of France and England – crowned as they are with victory – will afford us a picture of a healthy, normal, peaceful, truly Kautskian development of socialism, is one of the most puerile illusions possible. The so-called Republican democracy of victorious France, at the present moment, is nothing but the most reactionary, grasping government that has ever existed in the world. Its internal policy is built upon fear, greed and violence, in just as great a measure as its external policy. On the other hand, the French proletariat, misled more than any other class has ever been misled, is more and more entering on the path of direct action. The repressions which the government of the Republic has hurled upon the General Confederation of Labour show that even syndicalist Kautskianism – i.e., hypocritical compromise – has no legal place within the framework of bourgeois democracy. The revolutionizing of the masses, the growing ferocity of the propertied classes and the disintegration of intermediate groups – three parallel processes which determine the character and herald the coming of a cruel civil war – have been going on before our eyes in full blast during the last few months in France.

In Great Britain, events, different in form, are moving along the selfsame fundamental road. In that country, the ruling class of which is oppressing and plundering the whole world more than ever before, the formulae of democracy have lost their meaning even as weapons of parliamentary swindling. The specialist best qualified in this sphere, Lloyd George, appeals now not to democracy, but to a union of conservative and liberal property holders against the working class. In his arguments there remains not a trace of the vague democracy of the 'Marxist' Kautsky. Lloyd George stands on the ground of class realities, and for this very reason speaks in the language of civil war. The British working class, with that ponderous learning by experience which is its distinguishing feature, is approaching that stage of its struggle before which the most heroic pages of Chartism will fade, just as the Paris Commune will grow pale before the coming victorious revolt of the French proletariat.

Precisely because historical events have, with stern energy, been developing in these last months their revolutionary logic, the author of this present work asks himself: Does it still require to be published? Is it still necessary to confute Kautsky theoretically? Is there still theoretical necessity to justify revolutionary terrorism?

Unfortunately, yes. Ideology, by its very essence, plays in the socialist movement an enormous part. Even for practical England the period has arrived when the working class must exhibit an ever increasing demand for a theoretical statement of its experiences and its problems. On the other hand, even proletarian psychology includes in itself a terrible inertia of conservatism – all the more that, in the present case, there is a question of nothing less than the traditional ideology of the parties of the Second International which first roused the proletariat, and recently were so powerful. After the collapse of official social patriotism (Scheidemann, Victor Adler, Renaudel, Vandervelde, Henderson, Plekhanov, etc.), international Kautskianism (the staff of the German Independents, Friedrich Adler, Longuet, a considerable section of the Italians, the British Independent Labour Party, the Martov group, etc.) has become the chief political factor on which the unstable equilibrium of capitalist society depends. It may be said that the will of the working masses of the whole of the civilized world, directly influenced by the course of events, is at the present moment incomparably more revolutionary than their consciousness, which is still dominated by the prejudices of parliamentarism and compromise. The struggle for the dictatorship of the working class means, at the present moment, an embittered struggle with Kautskianism within the working class. The lies and prejudices of the policy of compromise, still poisoning the atmosphere even in parties tending towards the Third International, must be thrown aside. This book must serve the ends of an irreconcilable struggle against the cowardice, half-measures and hypocrisy of Kautskianism in all countries.

P.S.: Today (May 1920) the clouds have again gathered over Soviet Russia. Bourgeois Poland, by its attack on the Ukraine, has opened the new offensive of world imperialism against the Soviet Republic.[1] The gigantic perils again growing up before the revolution, and the great sacrifices again imposed on the labouring masses by the war, are once again pushing Russian Kautskianism onto the path of open opposition to the Soviet government, in reality, onto the path of assistance to the world murderers of Soviet Russia. It is the fate of Kautskianism to try to help the proletarian revolution when it is in satisfactory circumstances, and to raise all kinds of obstacles in its way when it is particularly in need of help. Kautsky has more than once foretold our destruction, which must serve as the best proof of his, Kautsky's, theoretical rectitude. In his fall, this 'successor of Marx' has reached a stage at which his sole serious political programme consists in speculations on the collapse of the proletarian dictatorship.

He will be once again mistaken. The destruction of bourgeois Poland by the Red Army, guided by Communist working men, will appear as a new manifestation of the power of the proletarian dictatorship, and will thereby inflict a crushing blow on bourgeois scepticism (Kautskianism) in the working-class movement. In spite of mad confusion of external forms, watchwords and appearances, history has extremely simplified the fundamental meaning of its own process, reducing it to a struggle of imperialism against communism. Pilsudski is fighting, not only for the lands of the Polish magnates in the Ukraine and in White Russia, not only for capitalist property and for the Catholic Church, but also for parliamentary democracy and for evolutionary socialism, for the Second International, and for the right of Kautsky to remain a critical hanger-on of the bourgeoisie. We are fighting for the Communist International, and for the international proletarian revolution. The stakes are great on either side. The struggle will be obstinate and painful. We hope for the victory, for we have every historical right to it.

Moscow, 29 May 1920

I

THE BALANCE OF POWER

The argument which is repeated again and again in criticisms of the Soviet system in Russia, and particularly in criticisms of revolutionary attempts to set up a similar structure in other countries, is the argument based on the balance of power. The Soviet regime in Russia is utopian – 'because it does not correspond to the balance of power'. Backward Russia cannot put objectives before itself which would be appropriate to advanced Germany. And for the proletariat of Germany it would be madness to take political power into its own hands, as this 'at the present moment' would disturb the balance of power. The League of Nations is imperfect, but still corresponds to the balance of power. The struggle for the overthrow of imperialist supremacy is utopian – the balance of power only requires a revision of the Treaty of Versailles. When Longuet hobbled after Wilson this took place, not because of the political decomposition of Longuet, but in honour of the law of the balance of power. The Austrian president, Seitz, and the chancellor, Renner, must, in the opinion of Friedrich Adler, exercise their bourgeois impotence at the central posts of the bourgeois republic, for otherwise the balance of power would be infringed. Two years before the world war, Karl Renner, then not a chancellor, but a 'Marxist' advocate of opportunism, explained to me that the regime of 3 June – that is, the union of landlords and capitalists crowned by the monarchy – must inevitably maintain itself in Russia during a whole historical period, as it answered to the balance of power.

What is this balance of power, after all – that sacramental formula which is to define, direct and explain the whole course of history, wholesale and retail? Why exactly is it that the formula of the balance of power, in the mouth of Kautsky and his present school, inevitably appears as a justification of indecision, stagnation, cowardice and treachery?

By the balance of power they understand everything you please: the level of production attained, the degree of differentiation of classes, the number of organized workers, the total funds at the disposal of the trade unions, sometimes the results of the last parliamentary elections, frequently the degree of readiness for compromise on the part of the ministry, or the degree of effrontery of the financial oligarchy. Most frequently, it means that summary political impression which exists in the mind of a half-blind pedant, or a so-called realist politician, who, though he has absorbed the phraseology of Marxism, in reality is guided by the most shallow manoeuvres, bourgeois prejudices and parliamentary 'tactics'. After a whispered conversation with the director of the police department, an Austrian Social Democratic politician in the good, and not so far off, old times always knew exactly whether the balance of power permitted a peaceful street demonstration in Vienna on May Day. In the case of the Eberts, Scheidemanns and Davids, the balance of power was, not so very long ago, calculated exactly by the number of fingers which were extended to them at their meeting in the Reichstag with Bethmann-Hollweg, or with Ludendorff himself.

According to Friedrich Adler, the establishment of a Soviet dictatorship in Austria would be a fatal infraction of the balance of power; the Entente would condemn Austria to starvation. In proof of this, Friedrich Adler, at the July congress of soviets, pointed to Hungary, where at that time the Hungarian Renners had not yet, with the help of the Hungarian Adlers, overthrown the dictatorship of the soviets.[2]

At the first glance, it might really seem that Friedrich Adler was right in the case of Hungary. The proletarian dictatorship was overthrown there soon afterwards, and its place was filled by the ministry of the reactionary Friedrich. But it is quite justifiable to ask: Did the latter correspond to the balance of power? At all events, Friedrich and his hussar might not even temporarily have seized power had it not been for the Romanian army.[3] Hence, it is clear that, when discussing the fate of the Soviet government in Hungary, it is necessary to take account of the 'balance of power', at all events in two countries – in Hungary itself, and in its neighbour Romania. But it is not difficult to grasp that we cannot stop at this. If the dictatorship of the soviets had been set up in Austria before the maturing of the Hungarian crisis, the overthrow of the Soviet regime in Budapest would have been an infinitely more difficult task. Consequently, we have to include Austria also, together with the treacherous policy of Friedrich Adler, in that balance of power which determined the temporary fall of the Soviet government in Hungary.

Friedrich Adler himself, however, seeks the key to the balance of power, not in Russia and Hungary, but in the West, in the countries of Clemenceau and Lloyd George. They have in their hands bread and coal – and really bread and coal, especially in our time, are just as prominent factors in the mechanism of the balance of power as cannon in the constitution of Lassalle. Brought down from the heights, Adler's idea consists, consequently, in this: that the Austrian proletariat must not seize power until such time as it is permitted to do so by Clemenceau (or Millerand, i.e., a Clemenceau of the second order).

However, even here it is permissible to ask: does the policy of Clemenceau himself really correspond to the balance of power? At first glance it may appear that it corresponds well enough, and, if it cannot be proved, it is, at least, guaranteed by Clemenceau's gendarmes, who break up working-class meetings, and arrest and shoot Communists. But here we cannot but remember that the terrorist measures of the Soviet government – that is, the same searches, arrests and executions, only directed against the counter-revolutionaries – are considered by some people as a proof that the Soviet government does not correspond to the balance of power. In vain would we, however, begin to seek in our time, anywhere in the world, a regime which, to preserve itself, did not have recourse to measures of stern mass repression. This means that hostile class forces, having broken through the framework of every kind of law – including that of 'democracy' – are striving to find their new balance by means of a merciless struggle.

When the Soviet system was being instituted in Russia, not only the capitalist politicians, but also the socialist opportunists of all countries proclaimed it an insolent challenge to the balance of forces. On this score, there was no quarrel between Kautsky, the Austrian Count Czernin and the Bulgarian premier, Radoslavov. Since that time, the Austro-Hungarian and German monarchies have collapsed, and the most powerful militarism in the world has fallen into dust. The Soviet regime has held out. The victorious countries of the Entente have mobilized and hurled against it all they could. The Soviet government has stood firm. Had Kautsky, Friedrich Adler and Otto Bauer been told that the system of the dictatorship of the proletariat would hold out in Russia – first against the attack of German militarism, and then in a ceaseless war with the militarism of the Entente countries – the sages of the Second International would have considered such a prophecy a laughable misunderstanding of the 'balance of power'.

The balance of political power at any given moment is determined under the influence of fundamental and secondary factors of differing degrees of effectiveness, and only in its most fundamental quality is it determined by the stage of the development of production. The social structure of a people lags extraordinarily behind the development of its productive forces. The lower middle classes, and particularly the peasantry, retain their existence long after their economic methods have been made obsolete, and have been condemned, by the technical development of the productive powers of society. The consciousness of the masses, in its turn, lags extraordinarily behind the development of their social relations, the consciousness of the old socialist parties trails a whole epoch behind the state of mind of the masses, and the consciousness of the old parliamentary and trade union leaders, more reactionary than the consciousness of their party, represents a petrified mass which history has been unable hitherto either to digest or reject. In the parliamentary epoch, during the period of stability of social relations, the psychological factor – without great error – was the foundation upon which all current calculations were based. It was considered that parliamentary elections reflected the balance of power with sufficient exactness. The imperialist war, which upset all bourgeois society, displayed the complete uselessness of the old criteria. The latter completely ignored those profound historical factors which had gradually been accumulating in the preceeding period, and have now, all at once, appeared on the surface, and have begun to determine the course of history.

The political worshippers of routine, incapable of surveying the historical process in its complexity, in its internal clashes and contradictions, imagined to themselves that history was preparing the way for the socialist order simultaneously and systematically on all sides, so that concentration of production and the development of a communist morality in the producer and the consumer mature simultaneously with the electric plough and a parliamentary majority. Hence the purely mechanical attitude towards parliamentarism, which, in the eyes of the majority of the statesmen of the Second International, indicated the degree to which society was prepared for socialism as accurately as the manometer indicates the pressure of steam. Yet there is nothing more senseless than this mechanized representation of the development of social relations.

If, beginning with the productive bases of society, we ascend the stages of the superstructure – classes, the state, laws, parties, and so on – it may be established that the weight of each additional part of the superstructure is not simply to be added to, but in many cases to be multiplied by, the weight of all the preceding stages. As a result, the political consciousness of groups which long imagined themselves to be among the most advanced, displays itself, at a moment of change, as a colossal obstacle in the path of historical development. Today it is quite beyond doubt that the parties of the Second International, standing at the head of the proletariat, which dared not, could not, and would not take power into their hands at the most critical moment of human history, and which led the proletariat along the road of mutual destruction in the interests of imperialism, proved a decisive factor of the counter-revolution.

The great forces of production – that shock-factor in historical development – were choked in those obsolete institutions of the super-structure (private property and the national state) in which they found themselves locked by all preceding development. Engendered by capitalism, the forces of production were knocking at all the walls of the bourgeois national state, demanding their emancipation by means of the socialist organization of economic life on a world scale. The stagnation of social groupings, the stagnation of political forces, which proved themselves incapable of destroying the old class groupings, the stagnation, stupidity and treachery of the directing socialist parties, which had assumed to themselves in reality the defence of bourgeois society – all these factors led to an elemental revolt of the forces of production, in the shape of the imperialist war. Human technical skill, the most revolutionary factor in history, arose with the might accumulated during scores of years against the disgusting conservatism and criminal stupidity of the Scheidemanns, Kautskys, Renaudels, Vanderveldes and Longuets, and, by means of its howitzers, machine guns, dreadnoughts and aeroplanes, it began a furious pogrom of human culture.

In this way the cause of the misfortunes at present experienced by humanity is precisely that the development of the technical command of men over nature has long ago grown ripe for the socialization of economic life. The proletariat has occupied a place in production which completely guarantees its dictatorship, while the most intelligent forces in history – the parties and their leaders – have been discovered to be still wholly under the yoke of the old prejudices, and only fostered a lack of faith among the masses in their own power. In quite recent years Kautsky used to understand this. 'The proletariat at the present time has grown so strong', wrote Kautsky in his pamphlet *The Path to Power*, 'that it can calmly await the coming war. There can be no more talk of a premature revolution, now that the proletariat has drawn from the present structure of the state such strength as could be drawn therefrom, and now that its reconstruction has become a condition of the proletariat's further progress.' From the moment that the development of productive forces, outgrowing the framework of the bourgeois national state, drew mankind into an epoch of crises and convulsions, the consciousness of the masses was shaken by dread shocks out of the comparative equilibrium of the preceding epoch. The routine and stagnation of its mode of living, the hypnotic suggestion of peaceful legality, had already ceased to dominate the proletariat. But it had not yet stepped, consciously and courageously, onto the path of open revolutionary struggle. It wavered, passing through the last moment of unstable equilibrium. At such a moment of psychological change, the part played by the summit – the state, on the one hand, and the revolutionary party on the other – acquires a colossal importance. A determined push from left or right is sufficient to move the proletariat, for a certain period, to one or the other side. We saw this in 1914, when, under the united pressure of imperialist governments and socialist patriotic parties, the working class was all at once thrown out of its equilibrium and hurled onto the path of imperialism. We have since seen how the experience of the war, the contrasts between its results and its first objects, is shaking the masses in a revolutionary sense, making them more and more capable of an open revolt against capitalism. In such conditions, the presence of a revolutionary party, which renders to itself a clear account of the motive forces of the present epoch, and understands the exceptional role amongst them of a revolutionary class; which knows its inexhaustible, but unrevealed, powers; which believes in that class and believes in itself; which knows the power of revolutionary method in an epoch of instability of all social relations; which is ready to employ that method and carry it through to the end – the presence of such a party represents a factor of incalculable historical importance.

And on the other hand, the socialist party, enjoying traditional influence, which does not render itself an account of what is going on around it, which does not understand the revolutionary situation, and, therefore, finds no key to it, which does not believe in either the proletariat or itself – such a party in our time is the most mischievous stumbling block in history, and a source of confusion and inevitable chaos.

Such is now the role of Kautsky and his sympathizers. They teach the proletariat not to believe in itself, but to believe its reflection in the crooked mirror of democracy which has been shattered by the jackboot of militarism into a thousand fragments. The decisive factor in the revolutionary policy of the working class must be, in their view, not the international situation, not the actual collapse of capitalism, not that social collapse which is generated thereby, not that concrete necessity of the supremacy of the working class for which the cry arises from the smoking ruins of capitalist civilization – not all this must determine the policy of the revolutionary party of the proletariat – but that counting of votes which is carried out by the capitalist tellers of parliamentarism. Only a few years ago, we repeat, Kautsky seemed to understand the real inner meaning of the problem of revolution. 'Yes, the proletariat represents the sole revolutionary class of the nation,' wrote Kautsky in his pamphlet *The Path to Power*. It follows that every collapse of the capitalist order, whether it be of a moral, financial, or military character, implies the bankruptcy of all the bourgeois parties responsible for it, and signifies that the sole way out of the blind alley is the establishment of the power of the proletariat. And today the party of prostration and cowardice, the party of Kautsky, says to the working class:

The question is not whether you today are the sole creative force in history; whether you are capable of throwing aside that ruling band of robbers into which the propertied classes have developed; the question is not whether anyone else can accomplish this task on your behalf; the question is not whether history allows you any postponement (for the present condition of bloody chaos threatens to bury you yourself, in the near future, under the last ruins of capitalism).

The problem is for the ruling imperialist bandits to succeed – yesterday or today – to deceive, violate and swindle public opinion, by collecting 51 per cent of the votes against your 49. Perish the world, but long live the parliamentary majority!

2

THE DICTATORSHIP OF THE PROLETARIAT

Marx and Engels hammered out the idea of the dictatorship of the proletariat, which Engels stubbornly defended in 1891, shortly before his death – the idea that the political autocracy of the proletariat is the 'sole form in which it can realize its control of the state.

That is what Kautsky wrote about ten years ago. The sole form of power for the proletariat he considered to be not a socialist majority in a democratic parliament, but the political autocracy of the proletariat, its dictatorship. And it is quite clear that, if our problem is the abolition of private property in the means of production, the only road to its solution lies through the concentration of state power in its entirety in the hands of the proletariat, and the setting-up for the transitional period of an exceptional regime – a regime in which the ruling class is guided, not by general principles calculated for a prolonged period, but by considerations of revolutionary policy.

The dictatorship is necessary because it is a case, not of partial changes, but of the very existence of the bourgeoisie. No agreement is possible on this ground. Only force can be the deciding factor. The dictatorship of the proletariat does not exclude, of course, either separate agreements, or considerable concessions, especially in connection with the lower middle class and the peasantry. But the proletariat can only conclude these agreements after having gained possession of the apparatus of power, and having guaranteed to itself the possibility of independently deciding on which points to yield and on which to stand firm, in the interests of the general socialist task.

Kautsky now repudiates the dictatorship of the proletariat at the very outset, as the 'tyranny of the minority over the majority'. That is, he discerns in the revolutionary regime of the proletariat those very features by which the honest socialists of all countries invariably describe the dictatorship of the exploiters, albeit masked by the forms of democracy.

Abandoning the idea of a revolutionary dictatorship, Kautsky transforms the question of the conquest of power by the proletariat into a question of the conquest of a majority of votes by the Social Democratic Party in one of the electoral campaigns of the future. Universal suffrage, according to the legal fiction of parliamentarism, expresses the will of the citizens of all classes in the nation, and, consequently, gives a possibility of attracting a majority to the side of socialism. While the theoretical possibility has not been realized, the socialist minority must submit to the bourgeois majority. This fetishism of the parliamentary majority represents a brutal repudiation, not only of the dictatorship of the proletariat, but of Marxism and of the revolution altogether. If, in principle, we are to subordinate socialist policy to the parliamentary mystery of majority and minority, it follows that, in countries where formal democracy prevails, there is no place at all for the revolutionary struggle. If the majority elected on the basis of universal suffrage in Switzerland pass draconian legislation against strikers, or if the executive elected by the will of a formal majority in North America shoots workers, have the Swiss and American workers the 'right' of protest by organizing a general strike? Obviously, no. The political strike is a form of extra-parliamentary pressure on the 'national will', as it has expressed itself through universal suffrage. True, Kautsky himself, apparently, is ashamed to go as far as the logic of his new position demands. Bound by some sort of remnant of the past, he is obliged to acknowledge the possibility of correcting universal suffrage by action. Parliamentary elections, at all events in principle, never took the place, in the eyes of the Social Democrats, of the real class struggle, of its conflicts, repulses, attacks, revolts; they were considered merely as a contributory fact in this struggle, playing a greater part at one period, a smaller at another, and no part at all in the period of dictatorship.

In 1891, that is, not long before his death, Engels, as we just heard, obstinately defended the dictatorship of the proletariat as the only possible form of its control of the state. Kautsky himself more than once repeated this definition. Hence, by the way, we can see what an unworthy forgery is Kautsky's present attempt to throw back the dictatorship of the proletariat at us as a purely Russian invention.

Who aims at the end cannot reject the means. The struggle must be carried on with such intensity as actually to guarantee the supremacy of the proletariat. If the socialist revolution requires a dictatorship – 'the sole form in which the proletariat can achieve control of the state' – it follows that the dictatorship must be guaranteed at all cost.

To write a pamphlet about dictatorship one needs an inkpot and a pile of paper, and possibly, in addition, a certain number of ideas in one's head. But in order to establish and consolidate the dictatorship, one has to prevent the bourgeoisie from undermining the state power of the proletariat. Kautsky apparently thinks that this can be achieved by tearful pamphlets. But his own experience ought to have shown him that it is not sufficient to have lost all influence with the proletariat, to acquire influence with the bourgeoisie.

It is only possible to safeguard the supremacy of the working class by forcing the bourgeoisie accustomed to rule to realize that it is too dangerous an undertaking for it to revolt against the dictatorship of the proletariat, to undermine it by conspiracies, sabotage, insurrections, or the calling-in of foreign troops. The bourgeoisie, hurled from power, must be forced to obey. In what way? The priests used to terrify the people with future penalties. We have no such resources at our disposal. But even the priests' hell never stood alone, but was always bracketed with the material fire of the Holy Inquisition, and with the scorpions of the democratic state. Is it possible that Kautsky is leaning to the idea that the bourgeoisie can be held down with the help of the categorical imperative, which in his last writings plays the part of the Holy Ghost? We, on our part, can only promise him our material assistance if he decides to equip a Kantian–humanitarian mission to the realms of Denikin and Kolchak. At all events, there he would have the possibility of convincing himself that the counter-revolutionaries are not naturally devoid of character, and that, thanks to their six years' existence in the fire and smoke of war, their character has managed to become thoroughly hardened. Every White Guard has long ago acquired the simple truth that it is easier to hang a Communist to the branch of a tree than to convert him with a book of Kautsky's. These gentlemen have no superstitious fear, either of the principles of democracy or of the flames of hell – the more so because the priests of the church and of official learning act in collusion with them, and pour their combined thunders exclusively on the heads of the Bolsheviks. The Russian White Guards resemble the German and all other White Guards in this respect – that they cannot be convinced or shamed, but only terrorized or crushed.

The man who repudiates terrorism in principle – i.e., repudiates measures of suppression and intimidation towards determined and armed counter-revolution – must reject all idea of the political supremacy of the working class and its revolutionary dictatorship. The man who repudiates the dictatorship of the proletariat repudiates the socialist revolution, and digs the grave of socialism.

At the present time, Kautsky has no theory of the social revolution. Every time he tries to generalize his slanders against the revolution and the dictatorship of the proletariat, he produces merely a *réchauffé* of the prejudices of Jaurèsism and Bernsteinism.

'The revolution of 1789', writes Kautsky, 'itself put an end to the most important causes which gave it its harsh and violent character, and prepared the way for milder forms of the future revolution' (p. 140).[4] Let us admit this, though to do so we have to forget the June days of 1848 and the horrors of the suppression of the Commune.[5] Let us admit that the great revolution of the eighteenth century, which by measures of merciless terror destroyed the rule of absolutism, of feudalism and of clericalism, really prepared the way for more peaceful and milder solutions of social problems. But, even if we admit this purely liberal standpoint, even here our accuser will prove to be completely in the wrong; for the Russian Revolution, which culminated in the dictatorship of the proletariat, began with just that work which was done in France at the end of the eighteenth century. Our forefathers, in centuries gone by, did not take the trouble to prepare the democratic way – by means of revolutionary terrorism – for milder manners in our revolution. The ethical mandarin, Kautsky, ought to take these circumstances into account, and accuse our forefathers, not us. Kautsky, however, seems to make a little concession in this direction. 'True,' he says, 'no man of insight could doubt that a military monarchy like the German, the Austrian, or the Russian could be overthrown only by violent methods. But in this connection there was always less thought' (amongst whom?) 'of the bloody use of arms, and more of the working-class weapon peculiar to the proletariat – the mass strike. And that a considerable portion of the proletariat, after seizing power, would again – as at the end of the eighteenth century – give vent to its rage and revenge in bloodshed could not be expected. This would have meant a complete negation of all progress' (p. 147). As we see, the war and a series of revolutions were required to enable us to get a proper view of what was going on in reality in the heads of some of our most learned theoreticians. It turns out that Kautsky did not think that a Romanov or a Hohenzollern could be put away by means of conversations; but at the same time he seriously imagined that a military monarchy could be overthrown by a general strike – i.e., by a peaceful demonstration of folded arms. In spite of the Russian Revolution, and the world discussion of this question, Kautsky, it turns out, retains the anarchoreformist view of the general strike. We might point out to him that, in the pages of its own journal, the *Neue Zeit*, it was explained twelve years ago that the general strike is only a mobilization of the proletariat and its setting-up against its enemy, the state; but that the strike in itself cannot produce the solution of the problem, because it exhausts the forces of the proletariat sooner than those of its enemies, and this, sooner or later, forces the workers to return to the factories. The general strike acquires a decisive importance only as a preliminary to a conflict between the proletariat and the armed forces of the opposition – i.e., to the open revolutionary rising of the workers. Only by breaking the will of the armies thrown against it can the revolutionary class solve the problem of power – the root problem of every revolution. The general strike produces the mobilization of both sides, and gives the first serious estimate of the powers of resistance of the counter-revolution. But only in the further stages of the struggle, after the transition to the path of armed insurrection, can that bloody price be fixed which the revolutionary class has to pay for power. But that it will have to pay with blood, that, in the struggle for the conquest of power and for its consolidation, the proletariat will have not only to be killed, but also to kill – of this no serious revolutionary ever had any doubt. To announce that the existence of a determined life-and-death struggle between the proletariat and the bourgeoisie 'is a complete negation of all progress', means simply that the heads of some of our most revered theoreticians take the form of a *camera obscura*, in which objects are represented upside down.

But, even when applied to more advanced and cultured countries with established democratic traditions, there is absolutely no proof of the justice of Kautsky's historical argument. As a matter of fact, the argument itself is not new. Once upon a time the revisionists gave it a character more based on principle. They strove to prove that the growth of proletarian organizations under democratic conditions guaranteed the gradual and imperceptible – reformist and evolutionary – transition to socialist society – without general strikes and risings, without the dictatorship of the proletariat.

Kautsky, at that culminating period of his activity, showed that, in spite of the forms of democracy, the class contradictions of capitalist society grew deeper, and that this process must inevitably lead to a revolution and the conquest of power by the proletariat.

No one, of course, attempted to reckon up beforehand the number of victims that will be called for by the revolutionary insurrection of the proletariat, and by the regime of its dictatorship. But it was clear to all that the number of victims will vary with the strength of resistance of the propertied classes. If Kautsky desires to say in his book that a democratic upbringing has not weakened the class egoism of the bourgeoisie, this can be admitted without further parley.

If he wishes to add that the imperialist war, which broke out and continued for four years, in spite of democracy, brought about a degradation of morals and accustomed men to violent methods and action, and completely stripped the bourgeoisie of the last vestige of awkwardness in ordering the destruction of masses of humanity – here also he will be right.

All this is true on the face of it. But one has to struggle in real conditions. The contending forces are not proletarian and bourgeois manikins produced in the retort of Wagner-Kautsky, but a real proletariat against a real bourgeoisie, as they have emerged from the last imperialist slaughter.

In this fact of merciless civil war that is spreading over the whole world, Kautsky sees only the result of a fatal lapse from the 'experienced tactics' of the Second International.

'In reality, since the time', he writes, 'that Marxism has dominated the socialist movement, the latter, up to the world war, was, in spite of its great activities, preserved from great defeats. And the idea of insuring victory by means of terrorist domination had completely disappeared from its ranks.

'Much was contributed in this connection by the fact that, at the time when Marxism was the dominating socialist teaching, democracy threw out firm roots in Western Europe, and began there to change from an end of the struggle to a trustworthy basis of political life' (p. 145).

In this 'formula of progress' there is not one atom of Marxism. The real process of the struggle of classes and their material conflicts has been lost in Marxist propaganda, which, thanks to the conditions of democracy, guarantees, forsooth, a painless transition to a new and 'wiser' order. This is the most vulgar liberalism, a belated piece of rationalism in the spirit of the eighteenth century – with the difference that the ideas of Condorcet are replaced by a vulgarization of the *Communist Manifesto*. All history resolves itself into an endless sheet of printed paper, and the centre of this 'humane' process proves to be the well-worn writing table of Kautsky.

We are given as an example the working-class movement in the period of the Second International, which, going forward under the banner of Marxism, never sustained great defeats whenever it deliberately challenged them. But did not the whole working-class movement, the proletariat of the whole world, and with it the whole of human culture, sustain an incalculable defeat in August 1914, when history cast up the accounts of all the forces and possibilities of the socialist parties, amongst whom, we are told, the guiding role belonged to Marxism, 'on the firm footing of democracy'? Those parties proved bankrupt. Those features of their previous work which Kautsky now wishes to render permanent – self-adaptation, repudiation of 'illegal' activity, repudiation of the open fight, hopes placed in democracy as the road to a painless revolution – all these fell into dust. In their fear of defeat, holding back the masses from open conflict, dissolving the general-strike discussions, the parties of the Second International were preparing their own terrifying defeat; for they were not able to move one finger to avert the greatest catastrophe in world history, the four years' imperialist slaughter, which foreshadowed the violent character of the civil war. Truly, one has to put a wadded nightcap not only over one's eyes, but over one's nose and ears, to be able today, after the inglorious collapse of the Second International, after the disgraceful bankruptcy of its leading party – the German Social Democracy – after the bloody lunacy of the world slaughter and the gigantic sweep of the civil war, to set up in contrast to us, the profundity, the loyalty, the peacefulness and the sobriety of the Second International, the heritage of which we are still liquidating!

3

DEMOCRACY

EITHER DEMOCRACY, OR CIVIL WAR

Kautsky has a clear and solitary path to salvation: democracy. All that is necessary is that every one should acknowledge it and bind himself to support it. The right-wing socialists must renounce the sanguinary slaughter with which they have been carrying out the will of the bourgeoisie. The bourgeoisie itself must abandon the idea of using its Noskes and Lieutenant Vogels to defend its privileges to the last breath. Finally, the proletariat must once and for all reject the idea of over-throwing the bourgeoisie by means other than those laid down in the constitution. If the conditions enumerated are observed, the social revolution will painlessly melt into democracy. In order to succeed it is sufficient, as we see, for our stormy history to draw a nightcap over its head, and take a pinch of wisdom out of Kautsky's snuffbox.

'There exist only two possibilties,' says our sage, 'either democracy, or civil war' (p. 220). Yet, in Germany, where the formal elements of 'democracy' are present before our eyes, the civil war does not cease for a moment. 'Unquestionably,' agrees Kautsky, 'under the present National Assembly Germany cannot arrive at a healthy condi-tion. But that process of recovery will not be assisted, but hindered, if we transform the struggle against the present Assembly into a struggle against the democratic franchise' (p. 230). As if the question in Germany really did reduce itself to one of electoral forms and not to one of the real possession of power!

The present National Assembly, as Kautsky admits, cannot 'bring the country to a healthy condition'. Therefore let us begin the game again at the beginning. But will the partners agree? It is doubtful. If the rubber is not favourable to us, obviously it is so to them. The National Assembly which 'is incapable of bringing the country to a healthy condition', is quite capable, through the mediocre dictatorship of Noske, of preparing the way for the dictatorship of Ludendorff. So it was with the Constituent Assembly which prepared the way for Kolchak. The historical mission of Kautsky consists precisely in having waited for the revolution to write his (ninth) book, which should explain the collapse of the revolution by all the previous course of history, from the ape to Noske, and from Noske to Ludendorff. The problem before the revolutionary party is a difficult one: its problem is to foresee the peril in good time, and to forestall it by action. And for this there is no other way at present than to tear the power out of the hands of its real possessors, the agrarian and capitalist magnates, who are only temporarily hiding behind Messrs Ebert and Noske. Thus, from the present National Assembly, the path divides into two: either the dictatorship of the imperialist clique, or the dictatorship of the proletariat. On neither side does the path lead to 'democracy'. Kautsky does not see this. He explains at great length that democracy is of great importance for its political development and its education in organization of the masses, and that through it the proletariat can come to complete emancipation. One might imagine that, since the day on which the Erfurt Programme was written, nothing worthy of notice had ever happened in the world!

Yet meanwhile, for decades, the proletariat of France, Germany and the other most important countries has been struggling and developing, making the widest possible use of the institutions of democracy, and building up on that basis powerful political organizations. This path of the education of the proletariat through democracy to socialism proved, however, to be interrupted by an event of no inconsiderable importance – the world imperialist war. The class state at the moment when, thanks to its machinations, the war broke out succeeded in enlisting the assistance of the guiding organizations of Social Democracy to deceive the proletariat and draw it into the whirlpool. So that, taken as they stand, the methods of democracy, in spite of the incontestable benefits which they afford at a certain period, displayed an extremely limited power of action; with the result that two generations of the proletariat, educated under conditions of democracy, by no means guaranteed the necessary political preparation for judging accurately an event like the world imperialist war. That experience gives us no reasons for affirming that, had the war broken out ten or fifteen years later, the proletariat would have been more prepared for it. The bourgeois democratic state not only creates more favourable conditions for the political education of the workers, as compared with absolutism, but also sets a limit to that development in the shape of bourgeois legality, which skilfully accumulates and builds on the upper strata of the proletariat's opportunist habits and law-abiding prejudices. The school of democracy proved quite insufficient to rouse the German proletariat to revolution when the catastrophe of the war was at hand. The barbarous school of the war, social-imperialist ambitions, colossal military victories and unparalleled defeats were required. After these events, which made a certain amount of difference in the universe, and even in the Erfurt Programme, to come out with commonplaces as to the meaning of democratic parliamentarism for the education of the proletariat signifies a fall into political childhood. This is just the misfortune which has overtaken Kautsky.

'Profound disbelief in the political struggle of the proletariat,' he writes, 'and in its participation in politics, was the characteristic of Proudhonism. Today there arises a similar (!) view, and it is recommended to us as the new gospel of socialist thought, as the result of an experience which Marx did not, and could not, know. In reality, it is only a variation of an idea which half a century ago Marx was fighting, and which he in the end defeated' (p. 79).

Bolshevism proves to be warmed-up Proudhonism! From a purely theoretical point of view, this is one of the most brazen remarks in the pamphlet.

The Proudhonists repudiated democracy for the same reason that they repudiated the political struggle generally. They stood for the economic organization of the workers without the interference of the state, without revolutionary outbreaks – for self-help of the workers on the basis of production for profit. As far as they were driven by the course of events onto the path of the political struggle, they, as lower-middle-class theoreticians, preferred democracy, not only to plutocracy, but to revolutionary dictatorship. What thoughts have they in common with us? While we repudiate democracy in the name of the concentrated power of the proletariat, the Proudhonists, on the other hand, were prepared to make their peace with democracy, diluted by a federal basis, in order to avoid the revolutionary monopoly of power by the proletariat. With more foundation Kautsky might have compared us with the opponents of the Proudhonists, the Blanquists, who understood the meaning of a revolutionary government, but did not superstitiously make the question of seizing it depend on the formal signs of democracy. But in order to put the comparison of the Communists with the Blanquists on a reasonable footing, it would have to be added that, in the Workers' and Soldiers' Councils, we had at our disposal such an organization for revolution as the Blanquists could not even dream of; in our party we had, and have, an invaluable organization of political leadership with a perfected programme of the social revolution. Finally, we had, and have, a powerful apparatus of economic transformation in our trade unions, which stand as a whole under the banner of communism and support the Soviet government. Under such conditions, to talk of the renaissance of Proudhonist prejudices in the shape of Bolshevism can only take place when one has lost all traces of theoretical honesty and historical understanding.

THE IMPERIALIST TRANSFORMATION OF DEMOCRACY

It is not for nothing that the word 'democracy' has a double meaning in the political vocabulary. On the one hand, it means a state system founded on universal suffrage and the other attributes of formal 'popular government'. On the other hand, by the word 'democracy' is understood the mass of the people itself, in so far as it leads a political existence. In the second sense, as in the first, the meaning of democracy rises above class distinctions. This peculiarity of terminology has its profound political significance. Democracy as a political system is the more perfect and unshakeable the greater is the part played in the life of the country by the intermediate and less differentiated mass of the population – the lower middle class of the town and the country. Democracy achieved its highest expression in the nineteenth century in Switzerland and the United States of America. On the other side of the ocean the democratic organization of power in a federal republic was based on the agrarian democracy of the farmers. In the small Helvetian Republic, the lower middle classes of the towns and the rich peasantry constituted the basis of the conservative democracy of the united cantons.

Born of the struggle of the Third Estate against the powers of feudalism, the democratic state very soon becomes the weapon of defence against the class antagonisms generated within bourgeois society. Bourgeois society succeeds in this the more, the wider beneath it is the layer of the lower middle class, the greater is the importance of the latter in the economic life of the country, and the less advanced, consequently, is the development of class antagonism. However, the intermediate classes become ever more and more helplessly behind historical development, and, thereby, become ever more and more incapable of speaking in the name of the nation. True, the lower-middle-class doctrinaires (Bernstein and company) used to demonstrate with satisfaction that the disappearance of the middle classes was not taking place with that swiftness that was expected by the Marxian school. And, in reality, one might agree that, numerically, the middle-class elements in the town, and especially in the country, still maintain an extremely prominent position. But the chief meaning of evolution has shown itself in the decline in importance on the part of the middle classes from the point of view of production: the amount of values which this class brings to the general income of the nation has fallen incomparably more rapidly than the numerical strength of the middle classes. Correspondingly falls their social, political and cultural importance. Historical development has been relying more and more, not on these conservative elements inherited from the past, but on the polar classes of society – i.e., the capitalist bourgeoisie and the proletariat.

The more the middle classes lost their social importance, the less they proved capable of playing the part of an authoritative arbitral judge in the historical conflict between capital and labour. Yet the very considerable numerical proportion of the town middle classes, and still more of the peasantry, continues to find direct expression in the electoral statistics of parliamentarism. The formal equality of all citizens as electors thereby only gives more open indication of the incapacity of democratic parliamentarism to settle the root questions of historical evolution. An 'equal' vote for the proletariat, the peasant and the manager of a trust formally placed the peasant in the position of a mediator between the two antagonists; but, in reality, the peasantry, socially and culturally backward and politically helpless, has in all countries always provided support for the most reactionary, filibustering and mercenary parties which, in the long run, always supported capital against labour.

Absolutely contrary to all the prophecies of Bernstein, Sombart, Tugan-Baranovsky and others, the continued existence of the middle classes has not softened, but has rendered to the last degree acute, the revolutionary crisis of bourgeois society. If the proletarianization of the lower middle classes and the peasantry had been proceeding in a chemically purified form, the peaceful conquest of power by the proletariat through the democratic parliamentary apparatus would have been much more probable than we can imagine at present. Just the fact that was seized upon by the partisans of the lower middle class – its longevity – has proved fatal even for the external forms of political democracy, now that capitalism has undermined its essential foundations. Occupying in parliamentary politics a place which it has lost in production, the middle class has finally compromised parliamentarism and has transformed it into an institution of confused chatter and legislative obstruction. From this fact alone, there grew up before the proletariat the problem of seizing the apparatus of state power as such, independently of the middle class, and even against it – not against its interests, but against its stupidity and its policy, impossible to follow in its helpless contortions.

'Imperialism', wrote Marx of the Empire of Napoleon III, 'is the most prostituted, and, at the same time, perfected form of the state which the bourgeoisie, having attained its fullest development, transforms into a weapon for the enslavement of labour by capital.' This definition has a wider significance than for the French Empire alone, and includes the latest form of imperialism, born of the world conflict between the national capitalisms of the great powers. In the economic sphere, imperialism presupposed the final collapse of the rule of the middle class; in the political sphere, it signified the complete destruction of democracy by means of an internal molecular transformation, and a universal subordination of all democracy's resources to its own ends. Seizing upon all countries, independently of their previous political history, imperialism showed that all political prejudices were foreign to it, and that it was equally ready and capable of making use, after their transformation and subjection, of the monarchy of Nicholas Romanov or Wilhelm Hohenzollern, of the presidential autocracy of the United States of America, and of the helplessness of a few hundred bogus legislators in the French parliament. The last great slaughter – the bloody font in which the bourgeois world attempted to be rebaptized – presented to us a picture, unparalleled in history, of the mobilization of all state forms, systems of government, political tendencies, religions and schools of philosophy, in the service of imperialism. Even many of those pedants who slept through the preparatory period of imperialist development during the last decades, and continued to maintain a traditional attitude towards ideas of democracy and universal suffrage, began to feel during the war that their accustomed ideas had become fraught with some new meaning. Absolutism, parliamentary monarchy, democracy – in the presence of imperialism (and, consequently, in the presence of the revolution rising to take its place), all the state forms of bourgeois supremacy, from Russian tsarism to North American quasi-democratic federalism, have been given equal rights, bound up in such combinations as to supplement one another in an indivisible whole. Imperialism succeeded by means of all the resources it had at its disposal, including parliamentarism, irrespective of the electoral arithmetic of voting, to subordinate for its own purposes at the critical moment the lower middle classes of the towns and country and even the upper layers of the proletariat. The national idea, under the watchword of which the Third Estate rose to power, found in the imperialist war its rebirth in the watchword of national defence. With unexpected clearness, national ideology flamed up for the last time at the expense of class ideology. The collapse of imperialist illusions, not only amongst the vanquished, but   after a certain delay amongst the victorious also, finally laid low what was once national democracy, and, with it, its main weapon, the democratic parliament. The flabbiness, rottenness and helplessness of the middle classes and their parties everywhere became evident with terrifying clearness. In all countries the question of the control of the state assumed first-class importance as a question of an open measuring of forces between the capitalist clique, openly or secretly supreme and disposing of hundreds of thousands of mobilized and hardened officers, devoid of all scruple, and the revolting, revolutionary proletariat; while the intermediate classes were living in a state of terror, confusion and prostration. Under such conditions, what pitiful nonsense are speeches about the peaceful conquest of power by the proletariat by means of democratic parliamentarism!

The scheme of the political situation on a world scale is quite clear. The bourgeoisie, which has brought the nations, exhausted and bleeding to death, to the brink of destruction – particularly the victorious bourgeoisie – has displayed its complete inability to bring them out of their terrible situation, and, thereby, its incompatibility with the future development of humanity. All the intermediate political groups, including here first and foremost the social patriotic parties, are rotting alive. The proletariat they have deceived is turning against them more and more every day, and is becoming strengthened in its revolutionary convictions as the only power that can save the people from savagery and destruction. However, history has not at all secured, just at this moment, a formal parliamentary majority on the side of the party of the social revolution. In other words, history has not transformed the nation into a debating society solemnly voting the transition to the social revolution by a majority of votes. On the contrary, the violent revolution has become a necessity precisely because the imminent requirements of history are helpless to find a road through the apparatus of parliamentary democracy. The capitalist bourgeois calculates:

While I have in my hands lands, factories, workshops, banks; while I possess newspapers, universities, schools; while – and this most important of all – I retain control of the army: the apparatus of democracy, however, you reconstruct it, will remain obedient to my will. I subordinate to my interests spiritually the stupid, conservative, characterless lower middle class, just as it is subjected to me materially. I oppress, and will oppress, its imagination by the gigantic scale of my buildings, my transactions, my plans and my crimes. For moments when it is dissatisfied and murmurs, I have created scores of safety valves and lightning conductors. At the right moment I will bring into existence opposition parties, which will disappear tomorrow, but which today accomplish their mission by affording the possibility of the lower middle class expressing their indignation without hurt therefrom for capitalism. I shall hold the masses of the people, under cover of compulsory general education, on the verge of complete ignorance, giving them no opportunity of rising above the level which my experts in spiritual slavery consider safe. I will corrupt, deceive and terrorize the more privileged or the more backward of the proletariat itself. By means of these measures I shall not allow the vanguard of the working class to gain the ear of the majority of the working class, while the necessary weapons of mastery and terrorism remain in my hands.

To this the revolutionary proletarian replies:

Consequently, the first condition of salvation is to tear the weapons of domination out of the hands of the bourgeoisie. It is hopeless to think of a peaceful arrival to power while the bourgeoisie retains in its hands all the apparatus of power. Three times over hopeless is the idea of coming to power by the path which the bourgeoisie itself indicates and, at the same time, barricades – the path of parliamentary democracy. There is only one way: to seize power, taking away from the bourgeoisie the material apparatus of government. Independently of the superficial balance of forces in parliament, I shall take over for social administration the chief forces and resources of production. I shall free the mind of the lower middle class from their capitalist hypnosis. I shall show them in practice what is the meaning of socialist production. Then even the most backward, the most ignorant, or most terrorized sections of the nation will support me, and willingly and intelligently will join in the work of social construction.

When the Russian Soviet government dissolved the Constituent Assembly, that fact seemed to the leading Social Democrats of Western Europe, if not the beginning of the end of the world, at all events a rude and arbitrary break with all the previous developments of socialism. In reality, it was only the inevitable outcome of the new position resulting from imperialism and the war. If Russian communism was the first to enter the path of casting up theoretical and practical accounts, this was due to the same historical reasons which forced the Russian proletariat to be the first to enter the path of the struggle for power.

All that has happened since then in Europe bears witness to the fact that we drew the right conclusion. To imagine that democracy can be restored in its general purity means that one is living in a pitiful, reactionary utopia.

THE METAPHYSICS OF DEMOCRACY

Feeling the historical ground shaking under his feet on the question of democracy, Kautsky crosses to the ground of metaphysics. Instead of inquiring into what is, he deliberates about what ought to be.

The principles of democracy – the sovereignty of the people, universal and equal suffrage, personal liberties – appear, as presented to him, in a halo of moral duty. They are turned from their historical meaning and presented as unalterable and sacred things-in-themselves.

This metaphysical fall from grace is not accidental. It is instructive that the late Plekhanov, a merciless enemy of Kantianism at the best period of his activity, attempted at the end of his life, when the wave of patriotism had washed over him, to clutch at the straw of the categorical imperative.

That real democracy with which the German people is now making practical acquaintance Kautsky confronts with a kind of ideal democracy, as he would confront a common phenomenon with the thing-in-itself. Kautsky indicates with certitude not one country in which democracy is really capable of guaranteeing a painless transition to socialism. But he does know, and firmly, that such democracy ought to exist. The present German National Assembly, that organ of helplessness, reactionary malice and degraded solicitations, is confronted by Kautsky with a different, real, true National Assembly, which possesses all virtues – excepting the small virtue of reality.

The doctrine of formal democracy is not scientific socialism, but the theory of so-called natural law. The essence of the latter consists in the recognition of eternal and unchanging standards of law, which among different peoples and at different periods find a different, more or less limited and distorted expression. The natural law of modern history – i.e., as it emerged from the Middle Ages – included first of all a protest against class privileges, the abuse of despotic legislation, and the other 'artificial' products of feudal positive law. The theoreticians of the, as yet, weak Third Estate expressed its class interests in a few ideal standards, which later on developed into the teaching of democracy, acquiring at the same time an individualist character. The individual is absolute; all persons have the right of expressing their thoughts in speech and print; every man must enjoy equal electoral rights. As a battle cry against feudalism, the demand for democracy had a progressive character. As time went on, however, the metaphysics of natural law (the theory of formal democracy) began to show its reactionary side – the establishment of an ideal standard to control the real demands of the labouring masses and the revolutionary parties.

If we look back to the historical sequence of world concepts, the theory of natural law will prove to be a paraphrase of Christian spiritualism freed from its crude mysticism. The gospels proclaimed to the slave that he had just the same soul as the slave-owner, and in this way established the equality of all men before the heavenly tribunal. In reality, the slave remained a slave, and obedience became for him a religious duty. In the teaching of Christianity, the slave found an expression for his own ignorant protest against his degraded condition. Side by side with the protest was also the consolation. Christianity told him: 'You have an immortal soul, although you resemble a packhorse.' Here sounded the note of indignation. But the same Christianity said: 'Although you are like a packhorse, yet your immortal soul has in store for it an eternal reward.' Here is the voice of consolation. These two notes were found in historical Christianity in different proportions at different periods and amongst different classes. But as a whole, Christianity, like all other religions, became a method of deadening the consciousness of the oppressed masses.

Natural law, which developed into the theory of democracy, said to the worker: 'All men are equal before the law, independently of their origin, their property, and their position; every man has an equal right in determining the fate of the people.' This ideal criterion revolutionized the consciousness of the masses in so far as it was a condemnation of absolutism, aristocratic privileges and the property qualification. But the longer it went on, the more it sent the consciousness to sleep, legalizing poverty, slavery and degradation: for how could one revolt against slavery when every man has an equal right in determining the fate of the nation?

Rothschild, who has coined the blood and tears of the world into the gold napoleons of his income, has one vote at the parliamentary elections. The ignorant tiller of the soil who cannot sign his name, sleeps all his life without taking his clothes off, and wanders through society like an underground mole, plays his part, however, as a trustee of the nation's sovereignty, and is equal to Rothschild in the courts and at the elections. In the real conditions of life, in the economic process, in social relations, in their way of life, people became more and more unequal; dazzling luxury was accumulated at one pole, poverty and hopelessness at the other. But in the sphere of the legal edifice of the state, these glaring contradictions disappeared, and there penetrated thither only unsubstantial legal shadows. The landlord, the labourer, the capitalist, the proletarian, the minister, the bootblack – all are equal as 'citizens' and as 'legislators'. The mystic equality of Christianity has taken one step down from the heavens in the shape of the 'natural', 'legal' equality of democracy. But it has not yet reached earth, where lie the economic foundations of society. For the ignorant day-labourer, who all his life remains a beast of burden in the service of the bourgeoisie, the ideal right to influence the fate of the nations by means of the parliamentary elections remained little more real than the palace which he was promised in the kingdom of heaven.

In the practical interests of the development of the working class, the socialist party took its stand at a certain period on the path of parliamentarism. But this did not mean in the slightest that it accepted in principle the metaphysical theory of democracy, based on extra-historical, super-class rights. The proletarian doctrines examined democracy as the instrument of bourgeois society entirely adapted to the problems and requirements of the ruling classes; but as bourgeois society lived by the labour of the proletariat and could not deny it the legalization of a certain part of its class struggle without destroying itself, this gave the socialist party the possibility of utilizing, at a certain period, and within certain limits, the mechanism of democracy, without taking an oath to do so as an unshakeable principle.

The root problem of the party, at all periods of its struggle, was to create the conditions for real, economic, living equality for mankind as members of a united human commonwealth. It was just for this reason that the theoreticians of the proletariat had to expose the meta-physics of democracy as a philosophic mask for political mystification.

The democratic party at the period of its revolutionary enthusiasm, when exposing the enslaving and stupefying lie of church dogma, preached to the masses: 'You are lulled to sleep by promises of eternal bliss at the end of your life, while here you have no rights and you are bound with the chains of tyranny.' The socialist party, a few decades later, said to the same masses with no less right: 'You are lulled to sleep with the fiction of civic equality and political rights, but you are deprived of the possibility of realizing those rights. Conditional and shadowy legal equality has been transformed into the convicts' chain with which each of you is fastened to the chariot of capitalism.'

In the name of its fundamental task, the socialist party mobilized the masses on the parliamentary ground as well as on others; but nowhere and at no time did any party bind itself to bring the masses to socialism only through the gates of democracy. In adapting ourselves to the parliamentary regime, we stopped at a theoretical exposure of democracy, because we were still too weak to overcome it in practice. But the path of socialist ideas which is visible through all deviations, and even betrayals, foreshadows no other outcome but this: to throw democracy aside and replace it by the mechanism of the proletariat, at the moment when the latter is strong enough to carry out such a task.

We shall bring one piece of evidence, albeit a sufficiently striking one. 'Parliamentarism', wrote Paul Lafargue in the Russian review *Sozialdemokrat*, in 1888, 'is a system of government in which the people acquires the illusion that it is controlling the forces of the country itself, when, in reality, the actual power is concentrated in the hands of the bourgeoisie – and not even of the whole bourgeoisie, but only of certain sections of that class. In the first period of its supremacy the bourgeoisie does not understand, or, more correctly, does not feel, the necessity for making the people believe in the illusion of self-government. Hence it was that all the parliamentary countries of Europe began with a limited franchise. Everywhere the right of influencing the policy of the country by means of the election of deputies belonged at first only to more or less large property-holders, and was only gradually extended to less substantial citizens, until finally in some countries it became from a privilege the universal right of all and sundry.

'In bourgeois society, the more considerable becomes the amount of social wealth, the smaller becomes the number of individuals by whom it is appropriated. The same takes place with power: in proportion as the mass of citizens who possess political rights increases, and the number of elected rulers increases, the actual power is concentrated and becomes the monopoly of a smaller and smaller group of individuals.' Such is the secret of the majority.

For the Marxist Lafargue, parliamentarism remains as long as the supremacy of the bourgeoisie remains. 'On the day', writes Lafargue, 'when the proletariat of Europe and America seizes the state, it will have to organize a revolutionary government, and govern society as a dictatorship, until the bourgeoisie has disappeared as a class.'

Kautsky in his time knew this Marxist estimate of parliamentarism, and more than once repeated it himself, although with no such Gallic sharpness and lucidity. The theoretical apostasy of Kautsky lies just in this point: having recognized the principle of democracy as absolute and eternal, he has stepped back from materialist dialectics to natural law. That which was exposed by Marxism as the passing mechanism of the bourgeoisie, and was subjected only to temporary utilization with the object of preparing the proletarian revolution, has been newly sanctified by Kautsky as the supreme principle standing above classes, and unconditionally subordinating to itself the methods of the proletarian struggle. The counter-revolutionary degeneration of parliamentarism finds its most perfect expression in the deification of democracy by the decaying theoreticians of the Second International.

THE CONSTITUENT ASSEMBLY

Speaking generally, the attainment of a majority in a democratic parliament by the party of the proletariat is not an absolute impossibility. But such a fact, even if it were realized, would not introduce any new principle into the course of events. The intermediate elements of the intelligentsia, under the influence of the parliamentary victory of the proletariat, might possibly display less resistance to the new regime. But the fundamental resistance of the bourgeoisie would be decided by such facts as the attitude of the army, the degree to which the workers were armed, the situation in the neighbouring states: and the civil war would develop under the pressure of these most real circumstances, and not by the mobile arithmetic of parliamentarism.

Our party has never refused to lead the way for proletarian dictatorship through the gates of democracy, having clearly summed up in its mind certain agitational and political advantages of such a 'legalized' transition to the new regime. Hence our attempt to call the Constituent Assembly. The Russian peasant, only just awakened by the revolution to political life, found himself face to face with half a dozen parties, each of which apparently had made up its mind to confuse his mind. The Constituent Assembly placed itself across the path of the revolutionary movement, and was swept aside.

The opportunist majority in the Constituent Assembly represented only the political reflection of the mental confusion and indecision which reigned amidst the middle classes in the town and country and amidst the more backward elements of the proletariat. If we take the viewpoint of isolated historical possibilities, one might say that it would have been more painless if the Constituent Assembly had worked for a year or two, had finally discredited the Socialist Revolutionaries and the Mensheviks by their connection with the Kadets, and had thereby led to the formal majority of the Bolsheviks, showing the masses that in reality only two forces existed: the revolutionary proletariat, led by the Communists, and the counter-revolutionary democracy, headed by the generals and the admirals. But the point is that the pulse of the internal relations of the revolution was beating not at all in time with the pulse of the development of its external relations. If our party had thrown all responsibility onto the objective formula of 'the course of events' the development of military operations might have forestalled us. German imperialism might have seized Petrograd, the evacuation of which the Kerensky government had already begun. The fall of Petrograd would at that time have meant a death blow to the proletariat, for all the best forces of the revolution were concentrated there, in the Baltic fleet and in the Red capital.

Our party may be accused, therefore, not of going against the course of historical development, but of having taken at a stride several political steps. It stepped over the heads of the Mensheviks and the Social Revolutionaries, in order not to allow German imperialism to step across the head of the Russian proletariat and conclude peace with the Entente on the back of the revolution before it was able to spread its wings over the whole world.

From the above it will not be difficult to deduce the answers to the two questions with which Kautsky pestered us. First, why did we summon the Constituent Assembly when we had in view the dictatorship of the proletariat? Second, if the first Constituent Assembly which we summoned proved backward and not in harmony with the interests of the revolution, why did we reject the idea of a new assembly? The thought at the back of Kautsky's mind is that we repudiated democracy, not on the ground of principle, but only because it proved against us. In order to seize this insinuation by its long ears, let us establish the facts.

The watchword 'All power to the soviets' was put forward by our party at the very beginning of the revolution – i.e., long before not merely the decree as to the dissolution of the Constituent Assembly but the decree as to its convocation. True, we did not set up the soviets in opposition to the future Constituent Assembly, the summoning of which was constantly postponed by the government of Kerensky, and consequently became more and more problematical. But in any case, we did not consider the Constituent Assembly, after the manner of the democrats, as the future master of the Russian land, who would come and settle everything. We explained to the masses that the soviets, the revolutionary organizations of the labouring masses themselves, can and must become the true masters. If we did not formally repudiate the Constituent Assembly beforehand, it was only because it stood in contrast, not to the power of the soviets, but to the power of Kerensky himself, who, in his turn, was only a screen for the bourgeoisie. At the same time we did decide beforehand that, if in the Constituent Assembly the majority proved in our favour, that body must dissolve itself and hand over the power to the soviets – as later the Petrograd town council did, elected as it was on the basis of the most democratic electoral franchise. In my book on the October Revolution, I tried to explain the reasons which made the Constituent Assembly the out-of-date reflection of an epoch through which the revolution had already passed. As we saw the organization of revolutionary power only in the soviets, and at the moment of the summoning of the Constituent Assembly the soviets were already the de facto power, the question was inevitably decided for us in the sense of the violent dissolution of the Constituent Assembly, since it would not dissolve itself in favour of the government of the soviets.

'But why', asks Kautsky, 'did you not summon a new Constituent Assembly?'

Because we saw no need for it. If the first Constituent Assembly could still play a fleeting progressive part, conferring a sanction upon the Soviet regime in its first days, convincing for the middle-class elements, now, after two years of victorious proletarian dictatorship and the complete collapse of all democratic attempts in Siberia, on the shores of the White Sea, in the Ukraine and in the Caucasus, the power of the soviets truly does not need the blessing of the faded authority of the Constituent Assembly. 'Are we not right in that case to conclude', asks Kautsky in the tone of Lloyd George, 'that the Soviet government rules by the will of the minority, since it avoids testing its supremacy by universal suffrage?' Here is a blow that misses its mark.

If the parliamentary regime, even in the period of 'peaceful', stable development, was a rather crude method of discovering the opinion of the country, and in the epoch of revolutionary storm completely lost its capacity to follow the course of the struggle and the development of revolutionary consciousness, the Soviet regime, which is more closely, straightly, honestly bound up with the toiling majority of the people, does achieve meaning, not in statically reflecting a majority, but in dynamically creating it. Having taken its stand on the path of revolutionary dictatorship, the working class of Russia has thereby declared that it builds its policy in the period of transition, not on the shadowy art of rivalry with chameleon-hued parties in the chase for peasant votes, but on the actual attraction of the peasant masses, side by side with the proletariat, into the work of ruling the country in the real interests of the labouring masses. Such democracy goes a little deeper down than parliamentarism.

Today, when the main problem – the question of life and death – of the revolution consists in the military repulse of the various attacks of the White Guard bands, does Kautsky imagine that any form of parliamentary 'majority' is capable of guaranteeing a more energetic, devoted, and successful organization of revolutionary defence? The conditions of the struggle are so defined, in a revolutionary country throttled by the criminal ring of the blockade, that all the middle-class groups are confronted only with the alternative of Denikin or the Soviet government. What further proof is needed when even parties, which stand for compromise in principle, like the Mensheviks and the Social Revolutionaries, have split along that very line?

When suggesting to us the election of a Constituent Assembly, does Kautsky propose the stopping of the civil war for the purpose of the elections? By whose decision? If he intends for this purpose to bring into motion the authority of the Second International, we hasten to inform him that that institution enjoys in Denikin's camp only a little more authority than it does in ours. But to the extent that the civil war between the workers' and peasants' army and the imperialist bands is still going on, the elections must of necessity be limited to Soviet territory. Does Kautsky desire to insist that we should allow the parties which support Denikin to come out into the open? Empty and contemptible chatter! There is not one government, at any time and under any conditions, which would allow its enemies to mobilize hostile forces in the rear of its armies.

A not unimportant place in the discussion of the question is occupied by the fact that the flower of the labouring population is at present on active service. The foremost workers and the most class-conscious peasants, who take the first place at all elections, as in all important political activities, directing the public opinion of the workers, are at present fighting and dying as commanders, commissars, or rank and file in the Red Army. If the most 'democratic' governments in the bourgeois states, whose regime is founded on parliamentarism, consider it impossible to carry on elections to parliament in wartime, it is all the more senseless to demand such elections during the war of the Soviet Republic, the regime of which is not for one moment founded on parliamentarism. It is quite sufficient that the revolutionary government of Russia, in the most difficult months and times, never stood in the way of periodic re-elections of its own elective institutions – the local and central soviets.

Finally, as a last argument – the last and the least – we have to present to the notice of Kautsky that even the Russian Kautskians, the Mensheviks like Martov and Dan, do not consider it possible to put forward at the present moment a demand for a Constituent Assembly, postponing it to better times in the future. Will there be any need of it then? Of this one may be permitted to doubt. When the civil war is over, the dictatorship of the working class will disclose all its creative energy, and will, in practice, show the most backward masses what it can give them. By means of a systematically applied universal labour service, and a centralized organization of distribution, the whole population of the country will be drawn into the general soviet system of economic arrangement and self-government. The soviets themselves, at present the organs of government, will gradually melt into purely economic organizations. Under such conditions it is doubtful whether anyone will think of erecting, over the real fabric of socialist society, an archaic crown in the shape of the Constituent Assembly, which would only have to register the fact that everything necessary has already been 'constituted' before it and without it.[1]

4

TERRORISM

The chief theme of Kautsky's brochure is terrorism. The view that terrorism is of the essence of revolution Kautsky proclaims to be a widespread delusion. It is untrue that he who desires revolution must put up with terrorism. As far as he, Kautsky, is concerned, he is, generally speaking, for revolution, but decidedly against terrorism. From there, however, complications begin.

'The revolution brings us', Kautsky complains, 'a bloody terrorism carried out by socialist governments. The Bolsheviks in Russia first stepped onto this path, and were, consequently, sternly condemned by all socialists who had not adopted the Bolshevik point of view, including the socialists of the German majority. But as soon as the latter found themselves threatened in their supremacy, they had recourse to the methods of the same terrorist regime which they attacked in the East' (p. 9). It would seem that from this follows the conclusion that terrorism is much more profoundly bound up with the nature of revolution than certain sages think. But Kautsky reaches an absolutely opposite conclusion. The gigantic development of White and Red terrorism in all the last revolutions – the Russian, the German, the Austrian and the Hungarian – is evidence to him that these revolutions turned aside from their true path and turned out to be not the revolution they ought to have been according to the theoretical visions of Kautsky. Without going into the question of whether terrorism 'as such' is 'immanent' to the revolution 'as such', let us consider a few of the revolutions as they pass before us in the living history of mankind.

Let us first regard the religious Reformation, which proved the watershed between the Middle Ages and modern history: The deeper were the interests of the masses that it involved, the wider was its sweep, the more fiercely did the civil war develop under the religious banner, and the more merciless did the terror become on the other side.

In the seventeenth century England carried out two revolutions. The first, which brought forth great social upheavals and wars, brought amongst other things the execution of King Charles I, while the second ended happily with the accession of a new dynasty. The British bourgeoisie and its historians maintain quite different attitudes to these two revolutions: the first is for them a rising of the mob – the 'Great Rebellion'; the second has been handed down under the title of the 'Glorious Revolution'. The reason for this difference in estimates was explained by the French historian Augustin Thierry. In the first English revolution, in the 'Great Rebellion', the active force was the people; while in the second it was almost 'silent'. Hence it follows that, in surroundings of class slavery, it is difficult to teach the oppressed masses good manners. When provoked to fury they use clubs, stones, fire and the rope. The court historians of the exploiters are offended at this. But the great event in modern 'bourgeois' history is, nonetheless, not the 'Glorious Revolution', but the 'Great Rebellion'.

The greatest event in modern history after the Reformation and the 'Great Rebellion', and far surpassing its two predecessors in significance, was the great French Revolution of the eighteenth century. To this classical revolution there was a corresponding classical terrorism. Kautsky is ready to forgive the terrorism of the Jacobins, acknowledging that they had no other way of saving the republic. But by this justification after the event no one is either helped or hindered. The Kautskys of the end of the eighteenth century (the leaders of the French Girondins) saw in the Jacobins the personification of evil. Here is a comparison, sufficiently instructive in its banality, between the Jacobins and the Girondins from the pen of one of the bourgeois French historians: 'Both one side and the other desired the republic.' But the Girondins 'desired a free, legal and merciful republic. The Montagnards desired a despotic and terrorist republic. Both stood for the supreme power of the people; but the Girondins justly understood all by the people, while the Montagnards considered only the working class to be the people. That was why only to such persons, in the opinion of the Montagnards, did the supremacy belong.' The antithesis between the noble champions of the Constituent Assembly and the bloodthirsty agents of the revolutionary dictatorship is here outlined fairly clearly, although in the political terms of the epoch.

The iron dictatorship of the Jacobins was evoked by the monstrously difficult position of revolutionary France. Here is what the bourgeois historian says of this period: 'Foreign troops had entered French territory from four sides. In the north, the British and the Austrians, in Alsace, the Prussians, in Dauphine and up to Lyon, the Piedmontese, in Roussillon the Spaniards. And this at a time when civil war was raging at four different points: in Normandy, in the Vendée, at Lyon, and at Toulon' (p. 176). To this we must add internal enemies in the form of numerous secret supporters of the old regime, ready by all methods to assist the enemy.

The severity of the proletarian dictatorship in Russia, let us point out here, was conditioned by no less difficult circumstances. There was one continuous front, on the north and south, in the east and west. Besides the Russian White Guard armies of Kolchak, Denikin and others, there are attacking Soviet Russia, simultaneously or in turn: Germans, Austrians, Czechoslovaks, Serbs, Poles, Ukrainians, Romanians, French, British, Americans, Japanese, Finns, Estonians, Lithuanians . . . In a country throttled by a blockade and strangled by hunger, there are conspiracies, risings, terrorist acts and destruction of roads and bridges.

'The government which had taken on itself the struggle with countless external and internal enemies had neither money, nor sufficient troops, nor anything except boundless energy, enthusiastic support on the part of the revolutionary elements of the country, and the gigantic courage to take all measures necessary for the safety of the country, however arbitrary and severe they were.' In such words did once upon a time Plekhanov describe the government of the . . . Jacobins (*Sozialdemokrat*, a quarterly review of literature and politics. Book I, February 1890, London. The article on 'The Centenary of the Great Revolution,' pp. 6–7).

Let us now turn to the revolution which took place in the second half of the nineteenth century, in the country of 'democracy' – in the United States of America. Although the question was not the abolition of property altogether, but only of the abolition of property in Negroes, nevertheless, the institutions of democracy proved absolutely powerless to decide the argument in a peaceful way. The Southern states, defeated at the presidential elections in 1860, decided by all possible means to regain the influence they had hitherto exerted in the question of slave-owning; and uttering, as was right, the proper-sounding words about freedom and independence, rose in a slave-owners' insurrection. Hence inevitably followed all the later consequences of civil war. At the very beginning of the struggle, the military government in Baltimore imprisoned in Fort MacHenry a few citizens, sympathizers with the slave-holding South, in spite of *habeas corpus*. The question of the lawfulness or the unlawfulness of such action became the object of fierce disputes between so-called 'high authorities'. The judge of the Supreme Court decided that the president had neither the right to arrest the operation of *habeas corpus* nor to give plenipotentiary powers to that end to the military authorities. 'Such, in all probability, is the correct constitutional solution of the question', says one of the first historians of the American Civil War. 'But the state of affairs was to such a degree critical, and the necessity of taking decisive measures against the population of Baltimore so great, that not only the government but the people of the United States also supported the most energetic measures.' (*The History of the American War*, by Fletcher, Lieut. Colonel in the Scots Guards, St Petersburg 1867, p. 95.)

Some goods that the rebellious South required were secretly supplied by the merchants of the North. Naturally, the Northerners had no other course but to introduce methods of repression. On 6 August 1861, the President confirmed a resolution of Congress as to 'the confiscation of property used for insurrectionary purposes'. The people, in the shape of the most democratic elements, were in favour of extreme measures. The Republican Party had a decided majority in the North, and persons suspected of secessionism, i.e., of sympathizing with the rebellious Southern states, were subjected to violence. In some Northern towns, and even in the states of New England, famous for their order, the people frequently burst into the offices of newspapers which supported the revolting slave-owners and smashed their printing presses. It occasionally happened that reactionary publishers were smeared with tar, decorated with feathers, and carried in such array through the public squares until they swore an oath of loyalty to the Union. The personality of a planter smeared in tar bore little resemblance to the 'end-in-itself'; so that the categorical imperative of Kautsky suffered in the civil war of the states a considerable blow. But this is not all. 'The government, on its part', the historian tells us, 'adopted repressive measures of various kinds against publications holding views opposed to its own: and in a short time the hitherto free American press was reduced to a condition scarcely superior to that prevailing in the autocratic European states'. The same fate overtook the freedom of speech. 'In this way,' Lieut. Colonel Fletcher continues, 'the American people at this time denied itself the greater part of its freedom. It should be observed', he moralizes, 'that the majority of the people was to such an extent occupied with the war, and to such a degree imbued with the readiness for any kind of sacrifice to attain its end, that it not only did not regret its vanished liberties, but scarcely even noticed their disappearance.' (Fletcher's *History of the American War*, pp. 162, 164.)

Infinitely more ruthlessly did the bloodthirsty slave-owners of the South employ their uncontrollable hordes. 'Wherever there was a majority in favor of slavery,' writes the Count of Paris, 'public opinion behaved despotically to the minority. All who expressed pity for the national banner . . . were forced to be silent. But soon this itself became insufficient; as in all revolutions, the indifferent were forced to express their loyalty to the new order of things. . . . Those who did not agree to this were given up as a sacrifice to the hatred and violence of the mass of the people. . . . In each centre of growing civilization (South-Western states) vigilance committees were formed, composed of all those who had been distinguished by their extreme views in the electoral struggle. . . . A tavern was the usual place of their sessions, and a noisy orgy was mingled with a contemptible parody of public forms of justice. A few madmen sitting around a desk on which gin and whisky flowed judged their present and absent fellow-citizens. The accused, even before having been questioned, could see the rope being prepared. He who did not appear at the court learned his sentence when falling under the bullets of the executioner concealed in the forest . . .' This picture is extremely reminiscent of the scenes which day by day took place in the camps of Denikin, Kolchak, Yudenich and the other heroes of Anglo-Franco-American 'democracy'.

We shall see later how the question of terrorism stood in regard to the Paris Commune of 1871. In any case, the attempts of Kautsky to contrast the Commune with us are false at their very root, and only bring the author to a juggling with words of the most petty character.

The institution of hostages apparently must be recognized as 'immanent' in the terrorism of the civil war. Kautsky is against terrorism and against the institution of hostages, but in favour of the Paris Commune. (NB: the Commune existed fifty years ago.) Yet the Commune took hostages. A difficulty arises. But what does the art of exegesis exist for?

The decree of the Commune concerning hostages and their execution in reply to the atrocities of the *Versaillais* arose, according to the profound explanation of Kautsky, 'from a striving to preserve human life, not to destroy it'. A marvellous discovery! It only requires to be developed. It could, and must, be explained that in the civil war we destroyed White Guards in order that they should not destroy the workers. Consequently, our problem is not the destruction of human life, but its preservation. But as we have to struggle for the preservation of human life with arms in our hands, it leads to the destruction of human life – a puzzle the dialectical secret of which was explained by old Hegel, without reckoning other still more ancient sages.

The Commune could maintain itself and consolidate its position only by a determined struggle with the *Versaillais*. The latter, on the other hand, had a large number of agents in Paris. Fighting with the agents of Thiers, the Commune could not abstain from destroying the *Versaillais* at the front and in the rear. If its rule had crossed the bounds of Paris, in the provinces it would have found – during the process of the civil war with the army of the National Assembly – still more determined foes in the midst of the peaceful population. The Commune when fighting the royalists could not allow freedom of speech to royalist agents in the rear.

Kautsky, in spite of all the developments in the world today, completely fails to realize what war is in general, and the civil war in particular. He does not understand that every, or nearly every, sympathizer with Thiers in Paris was not merely an 'opponent' of the Communards in ideas, but an agent and spy of Thiers, a ferocious enemy ready to shoot one in the back. The enemy must be made harmless, and in wartime this means that he must be destroyed.

The problem of revolution, as of war, consists in breaking the will of the foe, forcing him to capitulate and to accept the conditions of the conqueror. The will, of course, is a fact of the physical world, but in contradistinction to a meeting, a dispute, or a congress, the revolution carries out its object by means of the employment of material resources – though to a lesser degree than war. The bourgeoisie itself conquered power by means of revolts, and consolidated it by the civil war. In the peaceful period, it retains power by means of a system of repression. As long as class society, founded on the most deep-rooted antagonisms, continues to exist, repression remains a necessary means of breaking the will of the opposing side.

Even if, in one country or another, the dictatorship of the proletariat grew up within the external framework of democracy, this would by no means avert the civil war. The question as to who is to rule the country, i.e., of the life or death of the bourgeoisie, will be decided on either side, not by references to the paragraphs of the constitution, but by the employment of all forms of violence. However deeply Kautsky goes into the question of the food of the anthropopithecus (see pp. 122 *et seq.* of his brochure) and other immediate and remote conditions which determine the cause of human cruelty, he will find in history no other way of breaking the class will of the enemy except the systematic and energetic use of violence.

The degree of ferocity of the struggle depends on a series of internal and international circumstances. The more ferocious and dangerous is the resistance of the class enemy who have been overthrown, the more inevitably does the system of repression take the form of a system of terror.

But here Kautsky unexpectedly takes up a new position in his struggle with Soviet terrorism. He simply waves aside all reference to the ferocity of the counter-revolutionary opposition of the Russian bourgeoisie.

'Such ferocity', he says, 'could not be noticed in November 1917, in Petrograd and Moscow, and still less more recently in Budapest' (p. 149). With such a happy formulation of the question, revolutionary terrorism merely proves to be a product of the bloodthirstiness of the Bolsheviks, who simultaneously abandoned the traditions of the vegetarian anthropopithecus and the moral lessons of Kautsky.

The first conquest of power by the soviets at the beginning of November 1917 (New Style) was actually accomplished with insignificant sacrifices. The Russian bourgeoisie found itself to such a degree estranged from the masses of the people, so internally helpless, so compromised by the course and the result of the war, so demoralized by the regime of Kerensky, that it scarcely dared show any resistance. In Petrograd the power of Kerensky was overthrown almost without a fight. In Moscow its resistance was dragged out, mainly owing to the indecisive character of our own actions. In the majority of the provincial towns, power was transferred to the soviet on the mere receipt of a telegram from Petrograd or Moscow. If the matter had ended there, there would have been no word of the Red Terror. But in November 1917, there was already evidence of the beginning of the resistance of the propertied classes. True, there was required the intervention of the imperialist governments of the West in order to give the Russian counter-revolution faith in itself, and to add ever-increasing power to its resistance. This can be shown from facts, both important and insignificant, day by day during the whole epoch of the Soviet revolution.

Kerensky's 'staff' felt no support forthcoming from the mass of the soldiery, and was inclined to recognize the Soviet government, which had begun negotiations for an armistice with the Germans. But there followed the protest of the military missions of the Entente, followed by open threats. The staff was frightened; incited by 'Allied' officers, it entered the path of opposition. This led to armed conflict and to the murder of the chief of the field-staff, General Dukhonin, by a group of revolutionary sailors.

In Petrograd, the official agents of the Entente, especially the French Military Mission, hand in hand with the SRs and the Mensheviks, openly organized the opposition, mobilizing, arming, inciting against us the Kadets, and the bourgeois youth generally, from the second day of the Soviet revolution. The rising of the Junkers on 10 November brought about a hundred times more victims than the revolution of 7 November. The campaign of the adventurers Kerensky and Krasnov against Petrograd, organized at the same time by the Entente, naturally introduced into the struggle the first elements of savagery. Nevertheless, General Krasnov was set free on his word of honour. The Yaroslav rising (in the summer of 1918) which involved so many victims, was organized by Savinkov on the instructions of the French embassy, and with its resources. Archangel was captured according to the plans of British naval agents, with the help of British warships and aeroplanes. The beginning of the empire of Kolchak, the nominee of the American Stock Exchange, was brought about by the foreign Czechoslovak Corps maintained by the resources of the French government. Kaledin and Krasnov (liberated by us), the first leaders of the counter-revolution on the Don, could enjoy partial success only thanks to the open military and financial aid of Germany. In the Ukraine Soviet power was overthrown in the beginning of 1918 by German militarism. The Volunteer Army of Denikin was created with the financial and technical help of Great Britain and France. Only in the hope of British intervention and of British military support was Yudenich's army created. The politicians, the diplomats and the journalists of the Entente have for the last two years been debating with complete frankness the question of whether the financing of the civil war in Russia is a sufficiently profitable enterprise. In such circumstances, one needs truly a brazen forehead to seek the reason for the sanguinary character of the civil war in Russia in the malevolence of the Bolsheviks, and not in the international situation.

The Russian proletariat was the first to enter the path of the social revolution, and the Russian bourgeoisie, politically helpless, was emboldened to struggle against its political and economic expropriation only because it saw its elder sister in all countries still in power, and still maintaining economic, political and, to a certain extent, military supremacy.

If our November revolution had taken place a few months, or even a few weeks, after the establishment of the rule of the proletariat in Germany, France and England, there can be no doubt that our revolution would have been the most 'peaceful', the most 'bloodless' of all possible revolutions on this sinful earth. But this historical sequence — the most 'natural' at the first glance and, in any case, the most beneficial for the Russian working class — found itself infringed — not through our fault, but through the will of events. Instead of being the last, the Russian proletariat proved to be the first. It was just this circumstance, after the first period of confusion, which imparted desperation to the character of the resistance of the classes which had ruled in Russia previously, and forced the Russian proletariat, in a moment of the greatest peril, foreign attacks and internal plots and insurrections, to have recourse to severe measures of State terror. No one will now say that those measures proved futile. But, perhaps, we are expected to consider them 'intolerable'?

The working class, which seized power in battle, had as its object and its duty to establish that power unshakeably, to guarantee its own supremacy beyond question, to destroy its enemies' hankering for a new revolution, and thereby to make sure of carrying out socialist reforms. Otherwise there would be no point in seizing power.

The revolution 'logically' does not demand terrorism.

Just as 'logically' it does not demand an armed insurrection. What a profound commonplace! But the revolution does require of the revolutionary class that it should attain its end by all methods at its disposal – if necessary, by an armed rising: if required, by terrorism. A revolutionary class which has conquered power with arms in its hands is bound to, and will, suppress, rifle in hand, all attempts to tear the power out of its hands. Where it has against it a hostile army, it will oppose to it its own army. Where it is confronted with armed conspiracy, attempt at murder, or rising, it will hurl at the heads of its enemies an unsparing penalty. Perhaps Kautsky has invented other methods? Or does he reduce the whole question to the degree of repression, and recommend in all circumstances imprisonment instead of execution?

The question of the form of repression, or of its degree, of course, is not one of 'principle'. It is a question of expediency. In a revolutionary period, the party which has been thrown from power, which does not reconcile itself with the stability of the ruling class, and which proves this by its desperate struggle against the latter, cannot be terrorized by the threat of imprisonment, as it does not believe in its duration. It is just this simple but decisive fact that explains the widespread recourse to shooting in a civil war.

Or, perhaps, Kautsky wishes to say that execution is not expedient, that 'classes cannot be cowed'. This is untrue. Terror is helpless – and then only 'in the long run' – if it is employed by reaction against a historically rising class. But terror can be very efficient against a reactionary class which does not want to leave the scene of operations. Intimidation is a powerful weapon of policy, both internationally and internally. War, like revolution, is founded upon intimidation. A victorious war, generally speaking, destroys only an insignificant part of the conquered army, intimidating the remainder and breaking their will. The revolution works in the same way: it kills individuals, and intimidates thousands. In this sense, the Red Terror is not distinguishable from the armed insurrection, the direct continuation of which it represents. The state terror of a revolutionary class can be condemned 'morally' only by a man who, as a principle, rejects (in words) every form of violence whatsoever – consequently, every war and every rising. For this, one has to be merely and simply a hypocritical Quaker.

'But in that case, in what do your tactics differ from the tactics of tsarism?' we are asked by the high priests of liberalism and Kautskianism.

You do not understand this, holy men? We shall explain to you. The terror of tsarism was directed against the proletariat. The gendarmerie of tsarism throttled the workers who were fighting for the socialist order. Our Extraordinary Commissions shoot landlords, capitalists and generals who are striving to restore the capitalist order. Do you grasp this . . . distinction? Yes? For us Communists it is quite sufficient.

'FREEDOM OF THE PRESS'

One point particularly worries Kautsky, the author of a great many books and articles – the freedom of the press. Is it permissible to suppress newspapers?

During war all institutions and organs of the state and of public opinion become, directly or indirectly, weapons of warfare. This is particularly true of the press. No government carrying on a serious war will allow publications to exist on its territory which, openly or indirectly, support the enemy. Still more so in a civil war. The nature of the latter is such that each of the struggling sides has in the rear of its armies considerable circles of the population on the side of the enemy. In war, where both success and failure are repaid by death, hostile agents who penetrate into the rear are subject to execution. This is inhumane, but no one ever considered war a school of humanity – still less civil war. Can it be seriously demanded that, during a civil war with the White Guards of Denikin, the publications of parties supporting Denikin should come out unhindered in Moscow and Petrograd? To propose this in the name of the 'freedom of the press' is just the same as, in the name of open dealing, to demand the publication of military secrets. 'A besieged city', wrote a Communard, Arthur Arnould of Paris, 'cannot permit within its midst that hopes for its fall should openly be expressed, that the fighters defending it should be incited to treason, that the movements of its troops should be communicated to the enemy. Such was the position of Paris under the Commune.' Such is the position of the Soviet Republic during the two years of its existence.

Let us, however, listen to what Kautsky has to say in this connection. 'The justification of this system [i.e., repressions in connection with the press] is reduced to the naive idea that an absolute truth [!] exists, and that only the Communists possess it [!]. Similarly,' continues Kautsky, 'it reduces itself to another point of view, that all writers are by nature liars [!] and that only Communists are fanatics for truth [!]. In reality, liars and fanatics for what they consider truth are to be found in all camps' (p. 176). And so on, and so on, and so on.

In this way, in Kautsky's eyes, the revolution, in its most acute phase, when it is a question of the life and death of classes, continues as hitherto to be a literary discussion with the object of establishing. . . the truth. What profundity! . . . Our 'truth', of course, is not absolute. But as in its name we are, at the present moment, shedding our blood, we have neither cause nor possibility to carry on a literary discussion as to the relativity of truth with those who 'criticize' us with the help of all forms of arms. Similarly, our problem is not to punish liars and to encourage just men amongst journalists of all shades of opinion, but to throttle the class lie of the bourgeoisie and to achieve the class truth of the proletariat, irrespective of the fact that in both camps there are fanatics and liars.

'The Soviet government', Kautsky thunders, 'has destroyed the sole remedy that might militate against corruption: the freedom of the press. Control by means of unlimited freedom of the press alone could have restrained those bandits and adventurers who will inevitably cling like leeches to every unlimited, uncontrolled power' (p. 188). And so on.

The press as a trusty weapon of the struggle with corruption! This liberal recipe sounds particularly pitiful when one remembers the two countries with the greatest 'freedom' of the press – North America and France – which, at the same time, are countries of the most highly developed stage of capitalist corruption.

Feeding on the old scandal of the political anterooms of the Russian revolution, Kautsky imagines that without Kadet and Menshevik freedom the Soviet apparatus is honeycombed with 'bandits' and 'adventurers'. Such was the voice of the Mensheviks a year or eighteen months ago. Now even they will not dare to repeat this. With the help of Soviet control and party selection, the Soviet government, in the intense atmosphere of the struggle, has dealt with the bandits and adventurers who appeared on the surface at the moment of the revolution incomparably better than any government whatsoever, at any time whatsoever.

We are fighting. We are fighting a life-and-death struggle. The press is a weapon not of an abstract society, but of two irreconcilable, armed and contending sides. We are destroying the press of the counter-revolution, just as we destroyed its fortified positions, its stores, its communication, and its intelligence system. Are we depriving ourselves of Kadet and Menshevik criticisms of the corruption of the working class? In return we are victoriously destroying the very foundations of capitalist corruption.

But Kautsky goes further to develop his theme. He complains that we suppress the newspapers of the SRs and the Mensheviks, and even – such things have been known – arrest their leaders. Are we not dealing here with 'shades of opinion' in the proletarian or the socialist movement? The scholastic pedant does not see facts beyond his accustomed words. The Mensheviks and SRs for him are simply tendencies in socialism, whereas, in the course of the revolution, they have been transformed into an organization which works in active cooperation with the counter-revolution and carries on against us an open war. The army of Kolchak was organized by Social Revolutionaries (how that name rings false and hollow today!), and was supported by Mensheviks. Both carried on – and carry on – against us, for a year and a half, a war on the northern front. The Mensheviks who rule the Caucasus, formerly the allies of Hohenzollern, and today the allies of Lloyd George, arrested and shot Bolsheviks hand in hand with German and British officers. The Mensheviks and SRs of the Kuban Rada organized the army of Denikin. The Estonian Mensheviks who participate in their government were directly concerned in the last advance of Yudenich against Petrograd. Such are these 'tendencies' in the socialist movement. Kautsky considers that one can be in a state of open and civil war with the Mensheviks and SRs, who, with the help of the troops they themselves have organized for Yudenich, Kolchak and Denikin, are fighting for their 'shade of opinions' in socialism, and at the same time to allow those innocent 'shades of opinion' freedom of the press in our rear. If the dispute with the SRs and the Mensheviks could be settled by means of persuasion and voting – that is, if there were not behind their backs the Russian and foreign imperialists – there would be no civil war.

Kautsky, of course, is ready to 'condemn' – an extra drop of ink

– the blockade, and the Entente support of Denikin, and the White Terror. But in his high impartiality he cannot refuse the latter certain extenuating circumstances. The White Terror, you see, does not infringe their own principles, while the Bolsheviks, making use of the Red Terror, betray the principle of 'the sacredness of human life which they themselves proclaimed' (p. 210).

What is the meaning of the principle of the sacredness of human life in practice, and in what does it differ from the commandment 'Thou shalt not kill'? Kautsky does not explain. When a murderer raises his knife over a child, may one kill the murderer to save the child? Will not thereby the principle of the 'sacredness of human life' be infringed? May one kill the murderer to save oneself? Is an insurrection of oppressed slaves against their masters permissible? Is it permissible to purchase one's freedom at the cost of the life of one's jailers? If human life in general is sacred and inviolable, we must deny ourselves not only the use of terror, not only war, but also revolution itself. Kautsky simply does not realize the counter-revolutionary meaning of the 'principle' which he attempts to force upon us. Elsewhere we shall see that Kautsky accuses us of concluding the Treaty of Brest-Litovsk: in his opinion we ought to have continued war. But what then becomes of the sacredness of human life? Does life cease to be sacred when it is a question of people talking another language, or does Kautsky consider that mass murders organized on principles of strategy and tactics are not murders at all? Truly it is difficult to put forward in our age a principle more hypocritical and more stupid. As long as human labour-power, and, consequently, life itself, remain articles of sale and purchase, of exploitation and robbery, the principle of the 'sacredness of human life' remains a shameful lie, uttered with the object of keeping the oppressed slaves in their chains.

We used to fight against the death penalty introduced by Kerensky, because that penalty was inflicted by the courts martial of the old army on soldiers who refused to continue the imperialist war. We tore this weapon out of the hands of the old courts martial, destroyed the courts martial themselves, and demobilized the old army which had brought them forth. Destroying in the Red Army, and generally throughout the country, counter-revolutionary conspirators who strive by means of insurrections, murders and disorganization to restore the old regime, we are acting in accordance with the iron laws of a war in which we desire to guarantee our victory.

If it is a question of seeking formal contradictions, then obviously we must do so on the side of the White Terror, which is the weapon of classes which consider themselves 'Christian', patronize idealist philosophy, and are firmly convinced that the individuality (their own) is an end-in-itself. As for us, we were never concerned with the Kantian–priestly and vegetarian–Quaker prattle about the 'sacredness of human life'. We were revolutionaries in opposition, and have remained revolutionaries in power. To make the individual sacred we must destroy the social order which crucifies him. And this problem can only be solved by blood and iron.

There is another difference between the White Terror and the Red, which Kautsky today ignores, but which in the eyes of a Marxist is of decisive significance. The White Terror is the weapon of the historically reactionary class. When we exposed the futility of the repressions of the bourgeois state against the proletariat, we never denied that by arrests and executions the ruling class, under certain conditions, might temporarily retard the development of the social revolution. But we were convinced that they would not be able to bring it to a halt. We relied on the fact that the proletariat is the historically rising class, and that bourgeois society could not develop without increasing the forces of the proletariat. The bourgeoisie today is a falling class. It not only no longer plays an essential part in production, but by its imperialist methods of appropriation is destroying the economic structure of the world and human culture generally. Nevertheless, the historical persistence of the bourgeoisie is colossal. It holds to power, and does not wish to abandon it. Thereby it threatens to drag after it into the abyss the whole of society. We are forced to tear it off, to chop it away. The Red Terror is a weapon utilized against a class, doomed to destruction, which does not wish to perish. If the White Terror can only retard the historical rise of the proletariat, the Red Terror hastens the destruction of the bourgeoisie. This hastening – a pure question of acceleration – is at certain periods of decisive importance. Without the Red Terror, the Russian bourgeoisie, together with the world bourgeoisie, would throttle us long before the coming of the revolution in Europe. One must be blind not to see this, or a swindler to deny it.

The man who recognizes the revolutionary historic importance of the very fact of the existence of the Soviet system must also sanction the Red Terror. Kautsky, who, during the last two years, has covered mountains of paper with polemics against communism and terrorism, is obliged, at the end of his pamphlet, to recognize the facts, and unexpectedly to admit that the Russian Soviet government is today the most important factor in the world revolution. 'However one regards the Bolshevik methods,' he writes, 'the fact that a proletarian government in a large country has not only reached power, but has retained it for two years up to the present time, amidst great difficulties, extraordinarily increases the sense of power amongst the proletariat of all countries. For the actual revolution the Bolsheviks have thereby accomplished a great work [*grosses geleistet*]' (p. 233).

This announcement stuns us as a completely unexpected recognition of historical truth from a quarter whence we had long since ceased to await it. The Bolsheviks have accomplished a great historical task by existing for two years against the united capitalist world. But the Bolsheviks held out not only by ideas, but by the sword. Kautsky's admission is an involuntary sanctioning of the methods of the Red Terror, and at the same time the most effective condemnation of his own critical concoction.

THE INFLUENCE OF THE WAR

Kautsky sees one of the reasons for the extremely bloody character of the revolution in the war and in its hardening influence on manners. Quite undeniable. That influence, with all the consequences that follow from it, might have been foreseen earlier − approximately in the period when Kautsky was not certain whether one ought to vote for the war credits or against them.

'Imperialism has violently torn society out of its condition of unstable equilibrium', we wrote five years ago in our book, *The War and the International*. 'It has blown up the sluices with which social democracy held back the current of the revolutionary energy of the proletariat, and has directed that current into its own channels. This monstrous historical experiment, which at one blow has broken the back of the Socialist International, represents a deadly danger for bourgeois society itself. The hammer has been taken from the hand of the worker, and has been replaced by the sword. The worker, bound hand and foot by the mechanism of capitalist society, has suddenly burst out of its midst, and is learning to put the aims of the community higher than his own domestic happiness and than life itself.

'With this weapon, which he himself has forged in his hand, the worker is placed in a position in which the political destiny of the state depends directly on him. Those who in former times oppressed and despised him now flatter and caress him. At the same time he is entering into intimate relations with those same guns which, according to Lassalle, constitute the most important integral part of the constitution. He crosses the boundaries of states, participates in violent requisitions, and under his blows towns pass from hand to hand. Changes take place such as the last generation did not dream of.

'If the most advanced workers were aware that force was the mother of law, their political thought still remained saturated with the spirit of opportunism and self-adaptation to bourgeois legality. Today the worker has learned in practice to despise that legality, and violently to destroy it. The static moments in his psychology are giving place to the dynamic. Heavy guns are knocking into his head the idea that, in cases where it is impossible to avoid an obstacle, there remains the possibility of destroying it. Nearly the whole adult male population is passing through this school of war, terrible in its social realism, which is bringing forth a new type of humanity.

'Over all the criteria of bourgeois society – its law, its morality, its religion – is now raised the fist of iron necessity. "Necessity knows no law" was the declaration of the German Chancellor (4 August 1914). Monarchs come out into the marketplace to accuse one another of lying in the language of fishwives; governments break promises they have solemnly made, while the national church binds its Lord God like a convict to the national cannon. Is it not obvious that these circumstances must create important alterations in the psychology of the working class, radically curing it of that hypnosis of legality which was created by the period of political stagnation? The propertied classes will soon, to their sorrow, have to be convinced of this. The proletariat, after passing through the school of war, at the first serious obstacle within its own country will feel the necessity of speaking with the language of force. "Necessity knows no law" he will throw in the face of those who attempt to stop him by laws of bourgeois legality. And the terrible economic necessity which will arise during the course of this war, and particularly at its end, will drive the masses to spurn very many laws' (pp. 56–7).

All this is undeniable. But to what is said above one must add that the war has exercised no less influence on the psychology of the ruling classes. As the masses become more insistent in their demands, so the bourgeoisie has become more unyielding.

In times of peace, the capitalists used to guarantee their interests by means of the 'peaceful' robbery of hired labour. During the war they served those same interests by means of the destruction of countless human lives. This has imparted to their consciousness as a master class a new 'Napoleonic' trait. The capitalists during the war became accustomed to send to their death millions of slaves – fellow countrymen and colonials – for the sake of coal, railways and other profits.

During the war there emerged from the ranks of the bourgeoisie – large, middle and small – hundreds of thousands of officers, professional fighters, men whose character has received the hardening of battle, and has become freed from all external restraints: qualified soldiers, ready and able to defend the privileged position of the bourgeoisie which produced them with a ferocity which, in its way, borders on heroism.

The revolution would probably be more humane if the proletariat had the possibility of 'buying off all this band', as Marx once put it. But capitalism during the war has imposed upon the toilers too great a load of debt, and has too deeply undermined the foundations of production, for us to be able seriously to contemplate a ransom in return for which the bourgeoisie would silently make its peace with the revolution. The masses have lost too much blood, have suffered too much, have become too savage, to accept a decision which economically would be beyond their capacity.

To this there must be added other circumstances working in the same direction. The bourgeoisie of the conquered countries has been embittered by defeat, the responsibility for which it is inclined to throw on the rank and file – on the workers and peasants who proved incapable of carrying on 'the great national war' to a victorious conclusion. From this point of view, one finds very instructive those explanations, unparalleled for their effrontery, which Ludendorff gave to the Commission of the National Assembly. The bands of Ludendorff are burning with the desire to take revenge for their humiliation abroad on the blood of their own proletariat. As for the bourgeoisie of the victorious countries, it has become inflated with arrogance, and is more than ever ready to defend its social position with the help of the bestial methods which guaranteed its victory. We have seen that the bourgeoisie is incapable of organizing the division of the booty amongst its own ranks without war and destruction. Can it, without a fight, abandon its booty altogether? The experience of the last five years leaves no doubt whatsoever on this score: if even previously it was absolutely utopian to expect that the expropriation of the propertied classes – thanks to 'democracy' – would take place imperceptibly and painlessly, without insurrections, armed conflicts, attempts at counter-revolution and severe repression, the state of affairs we have inherited from the imperialist war predetermines, doubly and trebly, the tense character of the civil war and the dictatorship of the proletariat.

5

THE PARIS COMMUNE AND SOVIET RUSSIA

The short episode of the first revolution carried out by the proletariat
for the proletariat ended in the triumph of its enemy. This episode
– from 18 March to 28 May – lasted seventy-two days.

P.L. Lavrov, *The Paris Commune*, 1919

THE IMMATURITY OF THE SOCIALIST
PARTIES IN THE COMMUNE

The Paris Commune of 1871 was the first, as yet weak, historic
attempt of the working class to impose its supremacy. We cherish
the memory of the Commune in spite of the extremely limited
character of its experience, the immaturity of its participants, the
confusion of its programme, the lack of unity amongst its leaders,
the indecision of their plans, the hopeless panic of its executive organs,
and the terrifying defeat fatally precipitated by all these. We cherish
in the Commune, in the words of Lavrov, 'the first, though still pale,
dawn of the proletarian republic'. Quite otherwise with Kautsky.
Devoting a considerable part of his book to a crudely tendentious
contrast between the Commune and Soviet power, he sees the main
advantages of the Commune in features that we find are its misfortune
and its fault.

Kautsky laboriously proves that the Paris Commune of 1871 was
not 'artificially' prepared, but emerged unexpectedly, taking the revolutionaries by surprise – in contrast to the November revolution,
which was carefully prepared by our party. This is incontestable. Not
daring clearly to formulate his profoundly reactionary ideas, Kautsky

does not say outright whether the Paris revolutionaries of 1871 deserve praise for not having foreseen the proletarian insurrection, and for not having foreseen the inevitable and consciously gone to meet it. However, all Kautsky's picture was built up in such a way as to produce in the reader just this idea: the Communards were simply overtaken by misfortune (the Bavarian philistine Vollmar once expressed his regret that the Communards had not gone to bed instead of taking power into their hands) and, therefore, deserve pity. The Bolsheviks consciously went to meet misfortune (the conquest of power) and, therefore, there is no forgiveness for them either in this or the future world. Such a formulation of the question may seem incredible in its internal inconsistency. Nonetheless, it follows quite inevitably from the position of the Kautskian 'Independents', who draw their heads into their shoulders in order to see and foresee nothing; and, if they do move forward, it is only after having received a preliminary stout blow in the rear.

'To humiliate Paris,' writes Kautsky, 'not to give it self-government, to deprive it of its position as capital, to disarm it in order afterwards to attempt with greater confidence a monarchist coup d'état – such was the most important task of the National Assembly and the chief of the executive power it elected, Thiers. Out of this situation arose the conflict which led to the Paris insurrection.

'It is clear how different from this was the character of the coup d'état carried out by the Bolsheviks, which drew its strength from the yearning for peace; which had the peasantry behind it; which had in the National Assembly against it, not monarchists, but SRs and Menshevik Social Democrats.

'The Bolsheviks came to power by means of a well-prepared coup d'état, which at one blow handed over to them the whole machinery of the State – immediately utilized in the most energetic and merciless manner for the purpose of suppressing their opponents, amongst them their proletarian opponents.

'No one, on the other hand, was more surprised by the insurrection of the Commune than the revolutionaries themselves, and for a considerable number amongst them the conflict was in the highest degree undesirable' (p. 56).

In order more clearly to realize the actual sense of what Kautsky has written here of the Communards, let us bring forward the following evidence.

'On 1 March 1871,' writes Lavrov, in his very instructive book on the Commune, 'six months after the fall of the Empire, and a few days before the explosion of the Commune, the guiding personalities in the Paris International still had no definite political programme' (pp. 64–5).

'After 18 March' writes the same author, 'Paris was in the hands of the proletariat, but its leaders, overwhelmed by their unexpected power, did not take the most elementary measures' (p. 71).

' "Your part is too big for you to play, and your sole aim is to get rid of responsibility", said one member of the Central Committee of the National Guard. In this was a great deal of truth,' writes the Communard and historian of the Commune, Lissagaray. 'But at the moment of action itself the absence of preliminary organization and preparation is very often a reason why parts are assigned to men which are too big for them to play' (*Histoire de la Commune de 1871*; p. 106).

From this one can already see (later on it will become still more obvious) that the absence of a direct struggle for power on the part of the Paris socialists was explained by their theoretical shapelessness and political helplessness, and not at all by higher considerations of tactics.

We have no doubt that Kautsky's own loyalty to the traditions of the Commune will be expressed mainly in that extraordinary surprise with which he will greet the proletarian revolution in Germany as 'a conflict in the highest degree undesirable'. We doubt, however, whether this will be ascribed by posterity to his credit. In reality, one must describe his historical analogy as a combination of confusion, omission and fraudulent suggestion.

The intentions which were entertained by Thiers towards Paris were entertained by Miliukov, who was openly supported by Tsereteli and Chernov, towards Petrograd. All of them, from Kornilov to Potresov, affirmed day after day that Petrograd had alienated itself from the country, had nothing in common with it, was completely corrupted, and was attempting to impose its will upon the community. To overthrow and humiliate Petrograd was the first task of Miliukov and his assistants. And this took place at a period when Petrograd was the true centre of the revolution, which had not yet been able to consolidate its position in the rest of the country. The former president of the Duma, Rodzianko, openly talked about handing over Petrograd to the Germans for educative purposes, as Riga had been handed over. Rodzianko only called by its name what Miliukov was trying to carry out, and what Kerensky assisted by his whole policy.

Miliukov, like Thiers, wished to disarm the proletariat. More than that, thanks to Kerensky, Chernov and Tsereteli, the Petrograd proletariat was to a considerable extent disarmed in July 1917. It was partially rearmed during Kornilov's march on Petrograd in August. And this new arming was a serious element in the preparation of the November insurrection. In this way, it is just the points at which Kautsky contrasts our November revolution to the March revolt of the Paris workers that actually, to a very large extent, coincide.

In what, however, lies the difference between them? First of all, in the fact that Thiers's criminal plans succeeded: Paris was throttled by him, and tens of thousands of workers were destroyed. Miliukov, on the other hand, ended up with a complete fiasco: Petrograd remained an impregnable fortress of the proletariat, and the leader of the bourgeoisie went to the Ukraine to petition that the Kaiser's troops should occupy Russia. For this difference we were to a considerable extent responsible – and we are ready to bear the responsibility. There is a capital difference also in the fact – this told more than once in the further course of events – that, while the Communards began mainly with considerations of patriotism, we were invariably guided by the point of view of the international revolution. The defeat of the Commune led to the practical collapse of the First International. The victory of the Soviet power has led to the creation of the Third International.

But Marx – on the eve of the insurrection – advised the Communards not to revolt, but to create an organization! One might understand Kautsky if he adduced this evidence in order to show that Marx had insufficiently gauged the acuteness of the situation in Paris. But Kautsky attempts to exploit Marx's advice as a proof of his condemnation of insurrection in general. Like all the mandarins of German social democracy, Kautsky sees in organization first and foremost a method of hindering revolutionary action.

But limiting ourselves to the question of organization as such, we must not forget that the November revolution was preceded by nine months of Kerensky's government, during which our party, not without success, devoted itself not only to agitation, but also to organization. The November revolution took place after we had achieved a crushing majority in the Workers' and Soldiers' Councils of Petrograd, Moscow and all the industrial centres in the country, and had transformed the soviets into powerful organizations directed by our party. The Communards did nothing of the kind. Finally, we had behind us the heroic Commune of Paris, from the defeat of which we had drawn the deduction that revolutionaries must foresee events and prepare for them. For this also we are to blame.

Kautsky requires his extensive comparison of the Commune and Soviet Russia only in order to slander and humiliate a living and victorious dictatorship of the proletariat in the interests of an attempted dictatorship, in the already fairly distant past.

Kautsky quotes with extreme satisfaction the statement of the Central Committee of the National Guard on 19 March in connection with the murder of the two generals by the soldiery. 'We say indignantly: the bloody filth with the help of which it is hoped to stain our honour is a pitiful slander. We never organized murder, and never did the National Guard take part in the execution of crime.'

Naturally, the Central Committee had no cause to assume responsibility for murders with which it had no concern. But the sentimental, pathetic tone of the statement very clearly characterizes the political timorousness of these men in the face of bourgeois public opinion. Nor is this surprising. The representatives of the National Guard were men in most cases with a very modest revolutionary past. 'Not one well-known name', writes Lissagaray. 'They were petty bourgeois shopkeepers, strangers to all but limited circles, and, in most cases, strangers hitherto to politics' (p. 70).

'The modest and, to some extent, fearful sense of terrible historical responsibility, and the desire to get rid of it as soon as possible', writes Lavrov of them, 'is evident in all the proclamations of this Central Committee, into the hands of which the destiny of Paris had fallen' (p. 77).

After bringing forward, to our confusion, the declamation concerning bloodshed, Kautsky later on follows Marx and Engels in criticizing the indecision of the Commune. 'If the Parisians [i.e., the Communards] had persistently followed up the tracts of Thiers, they would, perhaps, have managed to seize the government. The troops falling back from Paris would not have shown the least resistance . . . but they let Thiers go without hindrance. They allowed him to lead away his troops and reorganize them at Versailles, to inspire a new spirit in, and strengthen, them' (p. 49).

Kautsky cannot understand that it was the same men, and for the very same reasons, who published the statement of 19 March quoted above, who allowed Thiers to leave Paris with impunity and gather his forces. If the Communards had conquered with the help of resources of a purely moral character, their statement would have acquired great weight. But this did not take place. In reality, their sentimental humaneness was simply the obverse of their revolutionary passivity. The men who, by the will of fate, had received power in Paris, could not understand the necessity of immediately utilizing that power to the end, of hurling themselves after Thiers, and, before he recovered his grasp of the situation, of crushing him, of concentrating the troops in their hands, of carrying out the necessary weeding-out of the officer class, of seizing the provinces. Such men, of course, were not inclined to severe measures with counter-revolutionary elements. The one was closely bound up with the other. Thiers could not be followed up without arresting Thiers's agents in Paris and shooting conspirators and spies. When one considered the execution of counter-revolutionary generals as an indelible 'crime', one could not develop energy in following up troops who were under the direction of counter-revolutionary generals.

In the revolution in the highest degree of energy is the highest degree of humanity. 'Just the men', Lavrov justly remarks, 'who hold human life and human blood dear must strive to organize the possibility for a swift and decisive victory, and then to act with the greatest swiftness and energy, in order to crush the enemy. For only in this way can we achieve the minimum of inevitable sacrifice and the minimum of bloodshed' (p. 225).

The statement of 19 March will, however, be considered with more justice if we examine it, not as an unconditional confession of faith, but as the expression of transient moods the day after an unexpected and bloodless victory. Being an absolute stranger to the understanding of the dynamics of revolution, and the internal limitations of its swiftly developing moods, Kautsky thinks in lifeless schemes, and distorts the perspective of events by arbitrarily selected analogies. He does not understand that soft-hearted indecision is generally characteristic of the masses in the first period of the revolution. The workers pursue the offensive only under the pressure of iron necessity, just as they have recourse to the Red Terror only under the threat of destruction by the White Guards. That which Kautsky represents as the result of the peculiarly elevated moral feeling of the Parisian proletariat in 1871 is, in reality, merely a characteristic of the first stage of the civil war. A similar phenomenon could have been witnessed in our case.

In Petrograd we conquered power in November 1917, almost without bloodshed, and even without arrests. The ministers of Kerensky's government were set free very soon after the revolution. More, the Cossack general, Krasnov, who had advanced on Petrograd together with Kerensky after the power had passed to the soviet, and who had been made prisoner by us at Gatchina, was set free on his word of honour the next day. This was 'generosity' quite in the spirit of the first measures of the Commune. But it was a mistake. Afterwards, General Krasnov, after fighting against us for about a year in the south, and destroying many thousands of Communists, again advanced on Petrograd, this time in the ranks of Yudenich's army. The proletarian revolution assumed a more severe character only after the rising of the junkers in Petrograd, and particularly after the rising of the Czechoslovaks on the Volga organized by the Kadets, the SRs and the Mensheviks, after their mass executions of Communists, the attempt on Lenin's life, the murder of Uritsky, etc., etc.

The same tendencies, only in an embryonic form, we see in the history of the Commune.

Driven by the logic of the struggle, it took its stand in principle on the path of intimidation. The creation of the Committee of Public Safety was dictated, in the case of many of its supporters, by the idea of the Red Terror. The Committee was appointed 'to cut off the heads of traitors' (*Journal Officiel*, no. 123), 'to avenge treachery' (no. 124). Under the head of 'intimidatory' decrees we must class the order to seize the property of Thiers and of his ministers, to destroy Thiers's house, to destroy the Vendôme column, and especially the decree on hostages. For every captured Communard or sympathizer with the Commune shot by the *Versaillais*, three hostages were to be shot. The activity of the Prefecture of Paris controlled by Raoul Rigault had a purely terroristic, though not always a useful, purpose.

The effect of all these measures of intimidation was paralysed by the helpless opportunism of the guiding elements in the Commune, by their striving to reconcile the bourgeoisie with the fait accompli by the help of pitiful phrases, by their vacillations between the fiction of democracy and the reality of dictatorship. The late Lavrov expresses the latter idea splendidly in his book on the Commune.

'The Paris of the rich bourgeois and the poor proletarians, as a political community of different classes, demanded, in the name of liberal principles, complete freedom of speech, of assembly, of criticism of the government, etc. The Paris which had accomplished the revolution in the interests of the proletariat, and had before it the task of realizing this revolution in the shape of institutions, Paris, as the community of the emancipated working-class proletariat, demanded revolutionary – i.e., dictatorial, measures against the enemies of the new order' (pp. 143–4).

If the Paris Commune had not fallen, but had continued to exist in the midst of a ceaseless struggle, there can be no doubt that it would have been obliged to have recourse to more and more severe measures for the suppression of the counter-revolution. True, Kautsky would not then have had the possibility of contrasting the humane Communards with the inhumane Bolsheviks. But in return, probably, Thiers would not have had the possibility of inflicting his monstrous bloodletting upon the proletariat of Paris. History, possibly, would not have been the loser.

THE IRRESPONSIBLE CENTRAL COMMITTEE AND 'DEMOCRATIC' COMMUNE

'On 19 March,' Kautsky informs us, 'in the Central Committee of the National Guard, some demanded a march on Versailles, others an appeal to the electors, and a third party the adoption first of all of revolutionary measures; as if every one of these steps', he proceeds very learnedly to inform us, 'were not equally necessary, and as if one excluded the other' (p. 72). Further on, Kautsky, in connection with these disputes in the Commune, presents us with various warmed-up platitudes as to the mutual relations of reform and revolution. In reality, the following was the situation. If it were decided to march on Versailles, and to do this without losing an hour it was necessary immediately to reorganize the National Guard, to place at its head the best fighting elements of the Paris proletariat, and thereby temporarily to weaken Paris from the revolutionary point of view. But to organize elections in Paris, while at the same time sending out of its walls the flower of the working class, would have been senseless from the point of view of the revolutionary party. Theoretically, a march on Versailles and elections to the Commune, of course, did not exclude each other in the slightest degree, but in practice they did exclude each other: for the success of the elections, it was necessary to postpone the attack; for the attack to succeed, the elections had to be put off. Finally, leading the proletariat out to the field and thereby temporarily weakening Paris, it was essential to obtain some guarantee against the possibility of counter-revolutionary attempts in the capital; for Thiers would not have hesitated at any measures to raise a White revolt in the rear of the Communards. It was essential to establish a more military – i.e., a more stringent regime in the capital. 'They had to fight', writes Lavrov, 'against many internal foes with whom Paris was full, who only yesterday had been rioting around the Exchange and the Place Vendôme, who had their representatives in the administration and in the National Guard, who possessed their press, and their meetings, who almost openly maintained contact with the *Versaillais*, and who became more determined and more audacious at every piece of carelessness, at every check of the Commune' (p. 87).

It was necessary, side by side with this, to carry out revolutionary measures of a financial and generally of an economic character: first and foremost, for the equipment of the revolutionary army. All these most necessary measures of revolutionary dictatorship could with difficulty be reconciled with an extensive electoral campaign. But Kautsky has not the least idea of what a revolution is in practice. He thinks that theoretically to reconcile is the same as practically to accomplish.

The Central Committee appointed 22 March as the day of elections for the Commune; but, not sure of itself, frightened at its own illegality, striving to act in unison with more 'legal' institutions, it entered into ridiculous and endless negotiations with a quite helpless assembly of mayors and deputies of Paris, showing its readiness to divide power with them if only an agreement could be arrived at. Meanwhile precious time was slipping by.

Marx, on whom Kautsky, through old habit, tries to rely, did not under any circumstances propose that, at one and the same time, the Commune should be elected and the workers should be led out into the field for the war. In his letter to Kugelmann, Marx wrote, on 12 April 1871, that the Central Committee of the National Guard had too soon given up its power in favour of the Commune. Kautsky, in his own words, 'does not understand' this opinion of Marx. It is quite simple. Marx at any rate understood that the problem was not one of chasing legality, but of inflicting a fatal blow upon the enemy. 'If the Central Committee had consisted of real revolutionaries,' says Lavrov, and rightly, 'it ought to have acted differently. It would have been quite unforgivable for it to have given the enemy ten days' respite before the election and assembly of the Commune, while the leaders of the proletariat refused to carry out their duty and did not recognize that they had the right immediately to lead the proletariat. As it was, the feeble immaturity of the popular parties created a committee which considered those ten days of inaction incumbent upon it' (p. 78).

The yearning of the Central Committee to hand over power as soon as possible to a 'legal' government was dictated, not so much by the superstitions of former democracy, of which, by the way, there was no lack, as by fear of responsibility. Under the plea that it was a temporary institution, the Central Committee avoided the taking of the most necessary and absolutely pressing measures, in spite of the fact that all the material apparatus of power was centred in its hands. But the Commune itself did not take over political power in full from the Central Committee, and the latter continued to interfere in all business quite unceremoniously. This created a dual government, which was extremely dangerous, particularly under military conditions.

On 3 May the Central Committee sent deputies to the Commune demanding that the Ministry for War should be placed under its control. Again there arose, as Lissagaray writes, the question as to whether 'the Central Committee should be dissolved, or arrested, or entrusted with the administration of the Ministry for War'.

Here was a question, not of the principles of democracy, but of the absence, in the case of both parties, of a clear programme of action, and of the readiness, both of the irresponsible revolutionary organizations in the shape of the Central Committee and of the 'democratic' organization of the Commune, to shift the responsibility onto the other's shoulders, while at the same time not entirely renouncing power.

These were political relations which it might seem no one could call worthy of imitation.

'But the Central Committee', Kautsky consoles himself, 'never attempted to infringe the principle in virtue of which the supreme power must belong to the delegates elected by universal suffrage. In this respect the Paris Commune was the direct antithesis of the Soviet

Republic' (p. 74). There was no unity of government, there was no revolutionary decision, there existed a division of power, and, as a result, there came swift and terrible destruction. But to counterbalance this – is it not comforting? – there was no infringement of the 'principle' of democracy.

THE DEMOCRATIC COMMUNE AND
THE REVOLUTIONARY DICTATORSHIP

Comrade Lenin has already pointed out to Kautsky that attempts to depict the Commune as the expression of formal democracy constitute a piece of absolute theoretical swindling. The Commune, in its tradition and in the conception of its leading political party – the Blanquists – was the expression of the dictatorship of the revolutionary city over the country. So it was in the great French Revolution; so it would have been in the revolution of 1871 if the Commune had not fallen in the first days. The fact that in Paris itself a government was elected on the basis of universal suffrage does not exclude a much more significant fact – namely, that of the military operations carried on by the Commune, one city, against peasant France, that is the whole country. To satisfy the great democrat Kautsky, the revolutionaries of the Commune ought, as a preliminary, to have consulted, by means of universal suffrage, the whole population of France as to whether it permitted them to carry on a war with Thiers's bands.

Finally, in Paris itself the elections took place after the bourgeoisie, or at least its most active elements, had fled, and after Thiers's troops had been evacuated. The bourgeoisie that remained in Paris, in spite of all its impudence, was still afraid of the revolutionary battalions, and the elections took place under the auspices of that fear, which was the forerunner of what in the future would have been inevitable – namely, of the Red Terror. But to console oneself with the thought that the Central Committee of the National Guard, under the dictatorship of which – unfortunately a very feeble and formalist dictatorship – the elections to the Commune were held, did not infringe the principle of universal suffrage, is truly to brush with the shadow of a broom.

Amusing himself by barren analogies, Kautsky benefits by the circumstance that his reader is not acquainted with the facts. In Petrograd, in

November 1917, we also elected a Commune (town council) on the basis of the most 'democratic' voting, without limitations for the bourgeoisie. These elections, being boycotted by the bourgeoisie parties, gave us a crushing majority. The 'democratically' elected council voluntarily submitted to the Petrograd soviet – i.e., placed the fact of the dictatorship of the proletariat higher than the 'principle' of universal suffrage, and, after a short time, dissolved itself altogether by its own act, in favour of one of the sections of the Petrograd soviet. Thus the Petrograd soviet – that true father of the Soviet regime – has upon itself the seal of a formal 'democratic' benediction in no way less than the Paris Commune.[1]

'At the elections of 26 March, eighty members were elected to the Commune. Of these, fifteen were members of the government party (Thiers), and six were bourgeois radicals who were in opposition to the government, but condemned the rising (of the Paris workers).

'The Soviet Republic', Kautsky teaches us, 'would never have allowed such counter-revolutionary elements to stand as candidates, let alone be elected. The Commune, on the other hand, out of respect for democracy, did not place the least obstacle in the way of the election of its bourgeois opponents' (p. 74).

We have already seen above that here Kautsky completely misses the mark. First of all, at a similar stage of development of the Russian Revolution, there did take place democratic elections to the Petrograd commune, in which the Soviet government placed no obstacle in the way of the bourgeois parties; and if the Kadets, the SRs and the Mensheviks, who had their press which was openly calling for the overthrow of the Soviet government, boycotted the elections, it was only because at that time they still hoped soon to make an end of us with the help of armed force. Secondly, no democracy expressing all classes was actually to be found in the Paris Commune. The bourgeois deputies – Conservatives, Liberals, Gambettists – found no place in it.

'Nearly all these individuals,' says Lavrov, 'either immediately or very soon, left the council of the Commune. They might have been representatives of Paris as a free city under the rule of the bourgeoisie, but were quite out of place in the council of the Commune, which, willy-nilly, consistently or inconsistently, completely or incompletely, did represent the revolution of the proletariat, and an attempt, feeble though it might be, of building up forms of society corresponding to that revolution' (pp. 111–12). If the Petrograd bourgeoisie had not boycotted the municipal elections, its representatives would have entered the Petrograd council. They would have remained there up to the first Social Revolutionary and Kadet rising, after which – with the permission or without the permission of Kautsky – they would probably have been arrested if they did not leave the council in good time, as at a certain moment did the bourgeois members of the Paris Commune. The course of events would have remained the same: only on their surface would certain episodes have worked out differently.

In supporting the democracy of the Commune, and at the same time accusing it of an insufficiently decisive note in its attitude to Versailles, Kautsky does not understand that the Communal elections, carried out with the ambiguous help of the 'lawful' mayors and deputies, reflected the hope of a peaceful agreement with Versailles. This is the whole point. The leaders were anxious for a compromise, not for a struggle. The masses had not yet outlived their illusions. Undeserved revolutionary reputations had not yet had time to be exposed. Everything taken together was called democracy.

'We must rise above our enemies by moral force', preached Vermorel. 'We must not infringe liberty and individual life. . .' Striving to avoid fratricidal war, Vermorel called upon the liberal bourgeoisie, whom hitherto he had so mercilessly exposed, to set up 'a lawful government, recognized and respected by the whole population of Paris'. The *Journal Officiel*, published under the editorship of the internationalist Longuet, wrote: 'The sad misunderstanding, which in the June days (1848) armed two classes of society against each other, cannot be renewed . . . Class antagonism has ceased to exist' (30 March). And, further: 'Now all conflicts will be appeased, because all are inspired with a feeling of solidarity, because never yet was there so little social hatred and social antagonism' (3 April).

At the session of the Commune of 25 April, Jourdé, and not without foundation, congratulated himself on the fact that the Commune had 'never yet infringed the principle of private property'. By this means they hoped to win over bourgeois public opinion and find the path to compromise.

'Such a doctrine', says Lavrov, and rightly, 'did not in the least disarm the enemies of the proletariat, who understood excellently with what its success threatened them, and only sapped the proletarian energy and, as it were, deliberately blinded it in the face of its irreconcilable enemies' (p. 137). But this enfeebling doctrine was inextricably bound up with the fiction of democracy. The form of mock legality it was that allowed them to think that the problem would be solved without a struggle. 'As far as the mass of the population is concerned,' writes Arthur Arnould, a member of the Commune, 'it was to a certain extent justified in the belief in the existence of, at the very least, a hidden agreement with the government.' Unable to attract the bourgeoisie, the compromisers, as always, deceived the proletariat.

The clearest evidence of all that, in the conditions of the inevitable and already beginning civil war, democratic parliamentarism expressed only the compromising helplessness of the leading groups, was the senseless procedure of the supplementary elections to the Commune of 6 April. At this moment, 'it was no longer a question of voting,' writes Arthur Arnould. 'The situation had become so tragic that there was not either the time or the calmness necessary for the correct functioning of the elections. . . . All persons devoted to the Commune were on the fortifications, in the forts, in the foremost detachments. . . . The people attributed no importance whatever to these supplementary elections. The elections were in reality merely parliamentarism. What was required was not to count voters, but to have soldiers: not to discover whether we had lost or gained in the Commune of Paris, but to defend Paris from the *Versaillais*.' From these words Kautsky might have observed why in practice it is not so simple to combine class war with inter-class democracy.

'The Commune is not a constituent assembly,' wrote in his book, Milliard, one of the best brains of the Commune. 'It is a military council. It must have one aim, victory; one weapon, force; one law, the law of social salvation.'

'They could never understand', Lissagaray accuses the leaders, 'that the Commune was a barricade, and not an administration.'

They began to understand it in the end, when it was too late. Kautsky has not understood it to this day. There is no reason to believe that he will ever understand it.

The Commune was the living negation of formal democracy, for in its development it signified the dictatorship of working-class Paris over the peasant country. It is this fact that dominates all the rest. However much the political doctrinaires, in the midst of the

Commune itself, clung to the appearances of democratic legality, every action of the Commune, though insufficient for victory, was sufficient to reveal its illegal nature. The Commune – that is to say, the Paris city council – repealed the national law concerning conscription. It called its official organ *The Official Journal of the French Republic*. Though cautiously, it still laid hands on the state bank. It proclaimed the separation of church and state, and abolished the church budgets. It entered into relations with various embassies. And so on, and so on. It did all this in virtue of the revolutionary dictatorship. But Clemenceau, young democrat as he was then, would not recognize that virtue.

At a conference with the Central Committee, Clemenceau said: 'The rising had an unlawful beginning. Soon the Committee will become ridiculous, and its decrees will be despised. Besides, Paris has not the right to rise against France, and must unconditionally accept the authority of the Assembly.'

The problem of the Commune was to dissolve the National Assembly. Unfortunately it did not succeed in doing so. Today Kautsky seeks to discover for its criminal intentions some mitigating circumstances.

He points out that the Communards had as their opponents in the National Assembly the monarchists, while we in the Constituent Assembly had against us socialists, in the persons of the SRs, and the Mensheviks. A complete mental eclipse! Kautsky talks about the Mensheviks and the SRs, but forgets our sole serious foe – the Kadets. It was they who represented our Russian Thiers party – i.e., a bloc of property-owners in the name of property: and Professor Miliukov did his utmost to imitate the 'little great man'. Very soon indeed – long before the October Revolution – Miliukov began to seek his Galliffet in the generals Kornilov, Alexeiev, then Kaledin, Krasnov, in turn. And after Kolchak had thrown aside all political parties, and had dissolved the Constituent Assembly, the Kadet Party, the sole serious bourgeois party, in its essence monarchist through and through, not only did not refuse to support him, but on the contrary devoted more sympathy to him than before.

The Mensheviks and the SRs played no independent role amongst us – just like Kautsky's party during the revolutionary events in Germany. They based their whole policy upon a coalition with the Kadets, and thereby put the Kadets in a position to dictate quite irrespective of the balance of political forces. The Social Revolutionary and Menshevik parties were only an intermediary apparatus for the purpose of collecting, at meetings and elections, the political confidence of the masses awakened by the revolution, and for handing it over for disposal by the counter-revolutionary imperialist party of the Kadets – independently of the issue of the elections.

The purely vassal-like dependence of the SRs and Menshevik majority on the Kadet minority itself represented a very thinly veiled insult to the idea of 'democracy'. But this is not all.

In all districts of the country where the regime of 'democracy' lived too long, it inevitably ended in an open coup d'état of the counter-revolution. So it was in the Ukraine, where the democratic Rada, having sold the Soviet government to German imperialism, found itself overthrown by the monarchist Skoropadsky. So it was in the Kuban, where the democratic Rada found itself under the heel of Denikin. So it was – and this was the most important experiment of our 'democracy' – in Siberia, where the Constituent Assembly, with the formal supremacy of the SRs and the Mensheviks, in the absence of the Bolsheviks, and the de facto guidance of the Kadets, led in the end to the dictatorship of the tsarist Admiral Kolchak. So it was, finally, in the north, where the Constituent Assembly government of the Socialist Revolutionary Chaikovsky became merely a tinsel decoration for the rule of counter-revolutionary generals, Russian and British. So it was, or is, in all the small border states – in Finland, Estonia, Latvia, Lithuania, Poland, Georgia, Armenia – where, under the formal banner of 'democracy', there is being consolidated the supremacy of the landlords, the capitalists and the foreign militarists.

THE PARIS WORKER OF 1871 AND THE PETROGRAD PROLETARIAN OF 1917

One of the most coarse, unfounded and politically disgraceful comparisons which Kautsky makes between the Commune and Soviet Russia is touching the character of the Paris worker in 1871 and the Russian proletarian of 1917–19. The first Kautsky depicts as a revolutionary enthusiast capable of a high measure of self-sacrifice; the second, as an egoist and a coward, an irresponsible anarchist.

The Parisian worker has behind him too definite a past to need revolutionary recommendations – or protection from the praises of the present Kautsky. Nonetheless, the Petrograd proletarian has not, and cannot have, any reason for avoiding a comparison with his heroic elder brother. The continuous three years' struggle of the Petrograd workers – first for the conquest of power, and then for its maintenance and consolidation – represents an exceptional story of collective heroism and self-sacrifice, amidst unprecedented tortures in the shape of hunger, cold and constant perils.

Kautsky, as we can discover in another connection, takes for contrast with the flower of the Communards the most sinister elements of the Russian proletariat. In this respect also he is in no way different from the bourgeois sycophants, to whom dead Communards always appear infinitely more attractive than the living.

The Petrograd proletariat seized power four and a half decades after the Parisian. This period has told enormously in our favour. The petty-bourgeois craft character of old and partly of new Paris is quite foreign to Petrograd, the centre of the most concentrated industry in the world. The latter circumstance has extremely facilitated our tasks of agitation and organization, as well as the setting up of the soviet system.

Our proletariat did not have even a faint measure of the rich revolutionary traditions of the French proletariat. But, instead, there was still very fresh in the memory of the older generation of our workers, at the beginning of the present revolution, the great experiment of 1905, its failure, and the duty of vengeance it had handed down.

The Russian workers had not, like the French, passed through a long school of democracy and parliamentarism which at a certain epoch represented an important factor in the political education of the proletariat. But, on the other hand, the Russian working class had not had seared into its soul the bitterness of dissolution and the poison of scepticism, which up to a certain, and – let us hope – not very distant moment, still restrain the revolutionary will of the French proletariat.

The Paris Commune suffered a military defeat before economic problems had arisen before it in their full magnitude. In spite of the splendid fighting qualities of the Paris workers, the military fate of the Commune was at once determined as hopeless. Indecision and compromise-mongering above brought about collapse below.

The pay of the National Guard was issued on the basis of the existence of 162,000 rank and file and 6,000 officers; the number of those who actually went into battle, especially after the unsuccessful sortie of 3 April, varied between 20,000 and 30,000.

These facts do not in the least compromise the Paris workers, and do not give us the right to consider them cowards and deserters – although, of course, there was no lack of desertion. For a fighting army there must be, first of all, a centralized and accurate apparatus of administration. Of this the Commune had not even a trace.

The War Department of the Commune, was, in the expression of one writer, as it were a dark room, in which all collided. The office of the Ministry was filled with officers and ordinary guards, who demanded military supplies and food, and complained that they were not relieved. They were sent to the garrison.

'One battalion remained in the trenches for twenty and thirty days, while others were constantly in reserve. . . . This carelessness soon killed any discipline. Courageous men soon determined to rely only on themselves; others avoided service. In the same way did officers behave. One would leave his post to go to the help of a neighbour who was under fire; others went away to the city' (Lavrov, p. 100).

Such a regime could not remain unpunished; the Commune was drowned in blood. But in this connection Kautsky has a marvellous solution.

'The waging of war', he says, sagely shaking his head, 'is, after all, not a strong side of the proletariat' (p. 76).

This aphorism, worthy of Pangloss, is fully on a level with the other great remark of Kautsky, namely, that the International is not a suitable weapon to use in wartime, being in its essence an 'instrument of peace'.

In these two aphorisms, in reality, may be found the present Kautsky, complete, in his entirety – i.e., just a little over a round zero.

The waging of war, do you see, is on the whole, not a strong side of the proletariat, the more that the International itself was not created for wartime. Kautsky's ship was built for lakes and quiet harbours, not at all for the open sea, and not for a period of storms. If that ship has sprung a leak, and has begun to fill, and is now comfortably going to the bottom, we must throw all the blame upon the storm, the unnecessary mass of water, the extraordinary size of the waves, and a series of other unforeseen circumstances for which Kautsky did not build his marvellous instrument.

The international proletariat put before itself as its problem the conquest of power. Independently of whether civil war, 'generally', belongs to the inevitable attributes of revolution, 'generally', this fact remains unquestioned – that the advance of the proletariat, at any rate in Russia, Germany and parts of former Austro-Hungary, took the form of an intense civil war not only on internal but also on external fronts. If the waging of war is not the strong side of the proletariat, while the workers' International is suited only for peaceful epochs, then we may as well erect a cross over the revolution and over socialism; for the waging of war is a fairly strong side of the capitalist state, which without a war will not admit the workers to supremacy. In that case there remains only to proclaim the so-called 'socialist' democracy to be merely the accompanying feature of capitalist society and bourgeois parliamentarism – i.e., openly to sanction what the Eberts, Scheidemanns and Renaudels carry out in practice and what Kautsky still, it seems, protests against in words.

The waging of war was not a strong side of the Commune. Quite so; that was why it was crushed. And how mercilessly crushed!

'We have to recall the proscriptions of Sulla, Antony, and Octavius', wrote in his time the very moderate liberal Fiaux, 'to meet such massacres in the history of civilized nations. The religious wars under the last Valois, the night of St Bartholomew, the Reign of Terror were, in comparison with it, child's play. In the last week of May alone, in Paris, 17,000 corpses of the insurgent Federals were picked up . . . the killing was still going on about 15 June.'

'The waging of war, after all, is not the strong side of the proletariat.'

It is not true! The Russian workers have shown that they are capable of wielding the 'instrument of war' as well. We see here a gigantic step forward in comparison with the Commune. It is not a renunciation of the Commune – for the traditions of the Commune consist not at all in its helplessness – but the continuation of its work. The Commune was weak. To complete its work we have become strong. The Commune was crushed. We are inflicting blow after blow upon the executioners of the Commune. We are taking vengeance for the Commune, and we shall avenge it.

Out of 167,000 National Guards who received pay, only 20,000 or 30,000 went into battle. These figures serve as interesting material for conclusions as to the role of formal democracy in a revolutionary epoch. The vote of the Paris Commune was decided, not at the elections, but in the battles with the troops of Thiers. One hundred and sixty-seven thousand National Guards represented the great mass of the electorate. But in reality, in the battles, the fate of the Commune was decided by 20,000 or 30,000 persons; the most devoted fighting minority. This minority did not stand alone: it simply expressed, in a more courageous and self-sacrificing manner, the will of the majority. But nonetheless it was a minority. The others who hid at the critical moment were not hostile to the Commune; on the contrary, they actively or passively supported it, but they were less politically conscious, less decisive. On the arena of political democracy, their lower level of political consciousness afforded the possibility of their being deceived by adventurers, swindlers, middle-class cheats and honest dullards who really deceived themselves. But, at the moment of open class war, they, to a greater or lesser degree, followed the self-sacrificing minority. It was this that found its expression in the organization of the National Guard. If the existence of the Commune had been prolonged, this relationship between the advance guard and the mass of the proletariat would have grown more and more firm.

The organization which would have been formed and consolidated in the process of the open struggle, as the organization of the labouring masses, would have become the organization of their dictatorship – the Council of Deputies of the armed proletariat.

6

MARX ... AND KAUTSKY

Kautsky loftily sweeps aside Marx's views on terror, expressed by him in the *Neue Rheinische Zeitung* – as at that time, do you see, Marx was still very 'young', and consequently his views had not yet had time to arrive at that condition of complete enfeeblement which is so clearly to be observed in the case of certain theoreticians in the seventh decade of their life. As a contrast to the green Marx of 1848–49 (the author of the *Communist Manifesto*!) Kautsky quotes the mature Marx of the epoch of the Paris Commune – and the latter, under the pen of Kautsky, loses his great lion's mane, and appears before us as an extremely respectable reasoner, bowing before the holy places of democracy, declaiming on the sacredness of human life, and filled with all due reverence for the political charms of Scheidemann, Vandervelde, and particularly of his own physical grandson, Jean Longuet. In a word, Marx, instructed by the experience of life, proves to be a well-behaved Kautskian.

From the immortal *Civil War in France,* the pages of which have been filled with a new and intense life in our own epoch, Kautsky has quoted only those lines in which the mighty theoretician of the social revolution contrasted the generosity of the Communards with the bourgeois ferocity of the *Versaillais.* Kautsky has devastated these lines and made them commonplace. Marx, as the preacher of detached humanity, as the apostle of general love of mankind! Just as if we were talking about Buddha or Leo Tolstoy . . . It is more than natural that, against the international campaign which represented the Communards as *souteneurs* and the women of the Commune as prostitutes, against the vile slanders which attributed to the conquered fighters ferocious features drawn from the degenerate imagination of the victorious bourgeoisie, Marx should emphasize and underline those features of tenderness and nobility which not infrequently were merely the reverse side of indecision. Marx was Marx. He was neither an empty pedant, nor, all the more, the legal defender of the revolution: he combined a scientific analysis of the Commune with its revolutionary apology. He not only explained and criticized – he defended and struggled. But, emphasizing the mildness of the Commune which failed, Marx left no doubt possible concerning the measures which the Commune ought to have taken in order not to fail.

The author of the *Civil War* accuses the Central Committee – i.e., the then Council of National Guards' Deputies, of having too soon given up its place to the elective Commune. Kautsky 'does not understand' the reason for such a reproach. This conscientious non-understanding is one of the symptoms of Kautsky's mental decline in connection with questions of the revolution generally. The first place, according to Marx, ought to have been filled by a purely fighting organ, a centre of the insurrection and of military operations against Versailles, and not the organized self-government of the labour democracy. For the latter the turn would come later.

Marx accuses the Commune of not having at once begun an attack against the Versailles, and of having entered upon the defensive, which always appears 'more humane', and gives more possibilities of appealing to moral law and the sacredness of human life, but in conditions of civil war never leads to victory. Marx, on the other hand, first and foremost wanted a revolutionary victory. Nowhere, by one word, does he put forward the principle of democracy as something standing above the class struggle. On the contrary, with the concentrated contempt of the revolutionary and the Communist, Marx – not the young editor of the Rhine paper, but the mature author of *Capital*: our genuine Marx with the mighty leonine mane, not as yet fallen under the hands of the hairdressers of the Kautsky school – with what concentrated contempt he speaks about the 'artificial atmosphere of parliamentarism' in which physical and spiritual dwarfs like Thiers seem giants! The *Civil War*, after the barren and pedantic pamphlet of Kautsky, acts like a storm that clears the air.

In spite of Kautsky's slanders, Marx had nothing in common with the view of democracy as the last, absolute, supreme product of history.

The development of bourgeois society itself, out of which contemporary democracy grew up, in no way represents that process of gradual democratization which figured before the war in the dreams of the greatest socialist illusionist of democracy – Jean Jaurès – and now in those of the most learned of pedants, Karl Kautsky. In the empire of Napoleon III, Marx sees 'the only possible form of government in the epoch in which the bourgeoisie has already lost the possibility of governing the people, while the working class has not yet acquired it'. In this way, not democracy, but Bonapartism, appears in Marx's eyes as the final form of bourgeois power. Learned men may say that Marx was mistaken, as the Bonapartist empire gave way for half a century to the 'democratic republic'. But Marx was not mistaken. In essence he was right. The Third Republic has been the period of the complete decay of democracy. Bonapartism has found in the Stock Exchange Republic of Poincaré and of Clemenceau, a more finished expression than in the Second Empire. True, the Third Republic was not crowned by the imperial diadem; but in return there loomed over it the shadow of the Russian tsar.

In his estimate of the Commune, Marx carefully avoids using the worn currency of democratic terminology. 'The Commune was', he writes, 'not a parliament, but a working institution, and united in itself both executive and legislative power.' In the first place, Marx puts forward, not the particular democratic form of the Commune, but its class essence. The Commune, as is known, abolished the regular army and the police, and decreed the confiscation of church property. It did this in the right of the revolutionary dictatorship of Paris, without the permission of the general democracy of the state, which at that moment formally had found a much more 'lawful' expression in the National Assembly of Thiers. But a revolution is not decided by votes. 'The National Assembly', says Marx, 'was nothing more nor less than one of the episodes of that revolution, the true embodiment of which was, nevertheless, armed Paris.' How far this is from formal democracy!

'It only required that the Communal order of things', says Marx, 'should be set up in Paris and in the secondary centres, and the old central government would in the provinces also have yielded to the self-government of the producers.' Marx, consequently, sees the problem of revolutionary Paris, not in appealing from its victory to the frail will of the Constituent Assembly, but in covering the whole of France with a centralized organization of communes, built up not on the external principles of democracy but on the genuine self-government of the producers.

Kautsky has cited as an argument against the Soviet constitution the indirectness of elections, which contradicts the fixed laws of bourgeois democracy. Marx characterizes the proposed structure of workers' France in the following words: 'The management of the general affairs of the village communes of every district was to devolve on the assembly of plenipotentiary delegates meeting in the chief town of the district; while the district assemblies were in turn to send delegates to the National Assembly sitting in Paris.'

Marx, as we can see, was not in the least degree disturbed by the many degrees of indirect election, in so far as it was a question of the state organization of the proletariat itself. In the framework of bourgeois democracy, indirectness of election confuses the demarcation line of parties and classes but in the 'self-government of the producers' – i.e., in the class proletarian state, indirectness of election is a question not of politics, but of the technical requirements of self-government, and within certain limits may present the same advantages as in the realm of trade union organization.

The Philistines of democracy are indignant at the inequality in representation of the workers and peasants which, in the Soviet constitution, reflects the difference in the revolutionary roles of the town and the country. Marx writes: 'The Commune desired to bring the rural producers under the intellectual leadership of the central towns of their districts, and there to secure to them, in the workmen of the towns, the natural guardians of their interests.' The question was not one of making the peasant equal to the worker on paper, but of spiritually raising the peasant to the level of the worker. All questions of the proletarian state Marx decides according to the revolutionary dynamics of living forces, and not according to the play of shadows upon the marketplace screen of parliamentarism.

In order to reach the last confines of mental collapse, Kautsky denies the universal authority of the workers' councils on the ground that there is no legal boundary between the proletariat and the bourgeoisie. In the indeterminate nature of the social divisions Kautsky sees the source of the arbitrary authority of the Soviet dictatorship. Marx sees directly the contrary. 'The Commune was an extremely elastic form of the state, while all former forms of government had suffered from narrowness. Its secret consists in this, that in its very essence it was the government of the working class, the result of the struggle between the class of producers and the class of appropriators, the political form, long sought, under which there could be accomplished the economic emancipation of labour.' The secret of the Commune consisted in the fact that by its very essence it was a government of the working class. This secret, explained by Marx, has remained, for Kautsky, even to this day, a mystery sealed with seven seals.

The Pharisees of democracy speak with indignation of the repressive measures of the Soviet government, of the closing of newspapers, of arrests and shooting. Marx replies to 'the vile abuse of the lackeys of the press' and to the reproaches of the 'well-intentioned bourgeois doctrinaires', in connection with the repressive measures of the Commune in the following words: 'Not satisfied with their open waging of a most bloodthirsty war against Paris, the *Versaillais* strove secretly to gain an entry by corruption and conspiracy. Could the Commune at such a time without shamefully betraying its trust, have observed the customary forms of liberalism, just as if profound peace reigned around it? Had the government of the Commune been akin in spirit to that of Thiers, there would have been no more occasion to suppress newspapers of the party of order in Paris than there was to suppress newspapers of the Commune at Versailles.' In this way, what Kautsky demands in the name of the sacred foundations of democracy Marx brands as a shameful betrayal of trust.

Concerning the destruction of which the Commune is accused, and of which now the Soviet government is accused, Marx speaks as of 'an inevitable and comparatively insignificant episode in the titanic struggle of the newborn order with the old in its collapse'. Destruction and cruelty are inevitable in any war. Only sycophants can consider them a crime 'in the war of the slaves against their oppressors, the only just war in history' (Marx). Yet our dread accuser Kautsky, in his whole book, does not breathe a word of the fact that we are in a condition of perpetual revolutionary self-defence, that we are waging an intensive war against the oppressors of the world, the 'only just war in history'.

Kautsky yet again tears his hair because the Soviet government, during the civil war, has made use of the severe method of taking hostages. He once again brings forward pointless and dishonest comparisons between the fierce Soviet government and the humane Commune. Clear and definite in this connection sounds the opinion of Marx. 'When Thiers, from the very beginning of the conflict, had enforced the humane practice of shooting down captured Communards, the Commune, to protect the lives of those prisoners, had nothing left for it but to resort to the Prussian custom of taking hostages. The lives of the hostages had been forfeited over and over again by the continued shooting of the prisoners on the part of the *Versaillais*. How could their lives be spared any longer after the bloodbath with which MacMahon's Pretorians celebrated their entry into Paris?' How otherwise, we shall ask together with Marx, can one act in conditions of civil war, when the counter-revolution, occupying a considerable portion of the national territory, seizes wherever it can the unarmed workers, their wives, their mothers, and shoots or hangs them: how otherwise can one act than to seize as hostages the beloved or the trusted of the bourgeoisie, thus placing the whole bourgeois class under the Damocles sword of mutual responsibility?

It would not be difficult to show, day by day through the history of the civil war, that all the severe measures of the Soviet government were forced upon it as measures of revolutionary self-defence. We shall not here enter into details. But, to give though it be but a partial criterion for valuing the conditions of the struggle, let us remind the reader that, at the moment when the White Guards, in company with their Anglo-French allies, shoot every Communist without exception who falls into their hands, the Red Army spares all prisoners without exception, including even officers of high rank.

'Fully grasping its historical task, filled with the heroic decision to remain equal to that task,' Marx wrote, 'the working class may reply with a smile of calm contempt to the vile abuse of the lackeys of the press and to the learned patronage of well-intentioned bourgeois doctrinaires, who utter their ignorant stereotyped commonplaces, their characteristic nonsense, with the profound tone of oracles of scientific immaculateness.'

If the well-intentioned bourgeois doctrinaires sometimes appear in the guise of retired theoreticians of the Second International, this in no way deprives their characteristic nonsense of the right of remaining nonsense.

7

THE WORKING CLASS
AND ITS SOVIET POLICY

THE RUSSIAN PROLETARIAT

The initiative in the social revolution proved, by the force of events, to be imposed, not upon the old proletariat of Western Europe, with its mighty economic and political organization, with its ponderous traditions of parliamentarism and trade unionism, but upon the young working class of a backward country. History, as always, moved along the line of least resistance. The revolutionary epoch burst upon us through the least barricaded door. Those extraordinary, truly super-human, difficulties which were thus flung upon the Russian proletariat have prepared, hastened, and to a considerable extent assisted the revolutionary work of the West European proletariat which still lies before us.

Instead of examining the Russian Revolution in the light of the revolutionary epoch that has arrived throughout the world, Kautsky discusses the theme of whether or not the Russian proletariat has taken power into its hands too soon.

'For socialism,' he explains, 'there is necessary a high development of the people, a high morale amongst the masses, strongly developed social instincts, sentiments of solidarity, etc. Such a form of morale', Kautsky further informs us, 'was very highly developed amongst the proletariat of the Paris Commune. It is absent amongst the masses which at the present time set the tone amongst the Bolshevik proletariat' (p. 177).

For Kautsky's purpose, it is not sufficient to fling mud at the

Bolsheviks as a political party before the eyes of his readers. Knowing that Bolshevism has become amalgamated with the Russian proletariat, Kautsky makes an attempt to fling mud at the Russian proletariat as a whole, representing it as an ignorant, greedy mass, without any ideals, which is guided only by the instincts and impulses of the moment.

Throughout his brochure Kautsky returns many times to the question of the intellectual and moral level of the Russian workers, and every time only to deepen his characterization of them as ignorant, stupid and barbarous. To bring about the most striking contrasts, Kautsky adduces the example of how a workshop committee in one of the war industries during the Commune decided upon compulsory night duty in the works for one worker so that it might be possible to distribute repaired arms by night. 'As under present circumstances it is absolutely necessary to be extremely economical with the resources of the Commune,' the regulation read, 'the night duty will be rendered without payment . . .' 'Truly,' Kautsky concludes, 'these working men did not regard the period of their dictatorship as an opportune moment for the satisfaction of their personal interests' (p. 90). Quite otherwise is the case with the Russian working class. That class has no intelligence, no stability, no ideals, no steadfastness, no readiness for self-sacrifice, and so on. 'It is just as little capable of choosing suitable plenipotentiary leaders for itself', Kautsky jeers, 'as Münchausen was able to drag himself from the swamp by means of his own hair.' This comparison of the Russian proletariat with the impostor Munchausen dragging himself from the swamp is a striking example of the brazen tone in which Kautsky speaks of the Russian working class.

He brings extracts from various speeches and articles of ours in which undesirable phenomena amongst the working class are shown up, and attempts to represent matters in such a way as if the life of the Russian proletariat between 1917 and 1920 – in the greatest of revolutionary epochs – is fully described by passivity, ignorance and egotism.

Kautsky, forsooth, does not know, has never heard, cannot guess, may not imagine, that during the civil war the Russian proletariat had more than one occasion of freely giving its labour, and even of establishing 'unpaid' guard duties – not of one worker for the space of one night, but of tens of thousands of workers for the space of a long series of disturbed nights. In the days and weeks of Yudenich's advance on Petrograd, one telephonogram of the Soviet was sufficient to ensure that many thousands of workers should spring to their posts in all the factories, in all the wards of the city. And this not in the first days of the Petrograd commune, but after a two years' struggle in cold and hunger.

Two or three times a year our party mobilizes a high proportion of its numbers for the front. Scattered over a distance of 8,000 *versts*, they die and teach others to die. And when, in hungry and cold Moscow, which has given the flower of its workers to the front, a Party Week is proclaimed, there pour into our ranks from the proletarian masses, in the space of seven days, 15,000 persons. And at what moment? At the moment when the danger of the destruction of the Soviet government had reached its most acute point. At the moment when Orel had been taken, and Denikin was approaching Tula and Moscow, when Yudenich was threatening Petrograd. At that most painful moment, the Moscow proletariat, in the course of a week, gave to the ranks of our party 15,000 men, who waited only for a new mobilization for the front. And it can be said with certainty that never yet, with the exception of the week of the November rising in 1917, was the Moscow proletariat so single-minded in its revolutionary enthusiasm, and in its readiness for devoted struggle, as in those most difficult days of peril and self-sacrifice.

When our party proclaimed the watchword of *Subbotniks* and *Voskresniks* (Communist Saturdays and Sundays), the revolutionary idealism of the proletariat found for itself a striking expression in the shape of voluntary labour. At first tens and hundreds, later thousands, and now tens and hundreds of thousands of workers every week give up several hours of their labour without reward, for the sake of the economic reconstruction of the country. And this is done by half-starved people, in torn boots, in dirty linen – because the country has neither boots nor soap. Such, in reality, is that Bolshevik proletariat to whom Kautsky recommends a course of self-sacrifice. The facts of the situation, and their relative importance, will appear still more vividly before us if we recall that all the egoist, bourgeois, coarsely selfish elements of the proletariat – all those who avoid service at the front and in the *Subbotniks*, who engage in speculation and in weeks of starvation incite the workers to strikes – all of them vote at the soviet elections for the Mensheviks; that is, for the Russian Kautskys.

Kautsky quotes our words to the effect that even before the

November revolution, we clearly realized the defects in education of the Russian proletariat, but, recognizing the inevitability of the transference of power to the working class, we considered ourselves justified in hoping that during the struggle itself, during its experience, and with the ever-increasing support of the proletariat of other countries, we should deal adequately with our difficulties, and be able to guarantee the transition of Russia to the socialist order. In this connection, Kautsky asks: 'Would Trotsky undertake to get on a locomotive and set it going, in the conviction that he would during the journey have time to learn and to arrange everything? One must preliminarily have acquired the qualities necessary to drive a locomotive before deciding to set it going. Similarly the proletariat ought beforehand to have acquired those necessary qualities which make it capable of administering industry, once it had to take it over' (p. 173).

This instructive comparison would have done honour to any village clergyman. Nonetheless, it is stupid. With infinitely more foundation one could say 'Will Kautsky dare to mount a horse before he has learned to sit firmly in the saddle, and to guide the animal in all its steps?' We have foundations for believing that Kautsky would not make up his mind to such a dangerous, purely Bolshevik experiment. On the other hand, we fear that, through not risking to mount the horse, Kautsky would have considerable difficulty in learning the secrets of riding on horseback. For the fundamental Bolshevik prejudice is precisely this: that one learns to ride on horseback only when sitting on the horse.

Concerning the driving of the locomotive, this principle is at first sight not so evident; but nonetheless it is there. No one yet has learned to drive a locomotive sitting in his study. One has to get up on to the engine, to take one's stand in the tender, to take into one's hands the regulator, and to turn it. True, the engine allows training manoeuvres only under the guidance of an old driver. The horse allows of instructions in the riding school only under the guidance of experienced trainers. But in the sphere of state administration such artificial conditions cannot be created. The bourgeoisie does not build for the proletariat academies of state administration, and does not place at its disposal, for preliminary practice, the helm of the state. And besides, the workers and peasants learn even to ride on horseback not in the riding school, and without the assistance of trainers.

To this we must add another consideration, perhaps the most important. No one gives the proletariat the opportunity of choosing whether it will or will not mount the horse, whether it will take power immediately or postpone the moment. Under certain conditions the working class is bound to take power, under the threat of political self-annihilation for a whole historical period.

Once having taken power, it is impossible to accept one set of consequences at will and refuse to accept others. If the capitalist bourgeoisie consciously and malignantly transforms the disorganization of production into a method of political struggle, with the object of restoring power to itself, the proletariat is obliged to resort to socialization, independent of whether this is beneficial or otherwise at the given moment.

And, once having taken over production, the proletariat is obliged, under the pressure of iron necessity, to learn by its own experience a most difficult art – that of organizing socialist economy. Having mounted the saddle, the rider is obliged to guide the horse – on the peril of breaking his neck.

To give his high-souled supporters, male and female, a complete picture of the moral level of the Russian proletariat, Kautsky adduces, on page 172 of his brochure, the following mandate, issued, it is alleged, by the Murzilovka soviet: 'The soviet hereby empowers Comrade Gregory Sareiev, in accordance with his choice and instructions, to requisition and lead to the barracks, for the use of the Artillery Division stationed in Murzilovka, Briansk region, sixty women and girls from the bourgeois and speculating class, 16 September 1918.' (*What Are the Bolshevists Doing?* Published by Dr Nath. Wintch-Malejeff. Lausanne 1919, p. 10.)

Without having the least doubt of the forged character of this document and the lying nature of the whole communication, I gave instructions, however, that careful inquiry should be made, in order to discover what facts and episodes lay at the root of this invention. A carefully carried out investigation showed the following:

1. In the Briansk region there is absolutely no village by the name of Murzilovka. There is no such village in the neighbouring regions either. The most similar in name is the village of Muraviovka, Briansk region; but no artillery division has ever been stationed

there, and altogether nothing ever took place which might be in any way connected with the above 'document'.

2. The investigation was also carried on along the line of the artillery units. Absolutely nowhere were we able to discover even an indirect allusion to a fact similar to that adduced by Kautsky from the words of his inspirer.

3. Finally the investigation dealt with the question of whether there had been any rumours of this kind on the spot. Here, too, absolutely nothing was discovered; and no wonder. The very contents of the forgery are in too brutal a contrast with the morals and public opinion of the foremost workers and peasants who direct the work of the soviets, even in the most backward regions.

In this way, the document must be described as a pitiful forgery, which might be circulated only by the most malignant sycophants in the most yellow of the gutter press.

While the investigation described above was going on, Comrade Zinoviev showed me a number of a Swedish paper (*Svenska Dagbladet*) of 9 November 1919, in which was printed the facsimile of a mandate running as follows: 'Mandate. The bearer of this, Comrade Raraseiev, has the right of socializing in the town of Ekaterinodar (obliterated) girls aged from sixteen to thirty-six at his pleasure. – Glavkom Ivashcheff.'

This document is even more stupid and impudent that that quoted by Kautsky. The town of Ekaterinodar – the centre of the Kuban – was, as is well known, for only a very short time in the hands of the Soviet government. Apparently the author of the forgery, not very well up in his revolutionary chronology, rubbed out the date on this document, lest by some chance it should appear that 'Glavkom Ivashcheff' 'socialized' the Ekaterinodar women during the reign of Denikin's militarism there. That the document might lead into error the thick-witted Swedish bourgeois is not at all amazing. But for the Russian reader it is only too clear that the document is not merely a forgery, but drawn up by a foreigner, dictionary in hand. It is extremely curious that the names of both the socializers of women, 'Gregory Sareiev' and 'Karaseiev' sound absolutely non-Russian. The ending -*eiev* in Russian names is found rarely, and only in definite combinations. But the accuser of the Bolsheviks himself, the author of the English pamphlet on whom Kautsky bases his evidence, has a name that does actually end in -*eiev*. It seems obvious that this Anglo-Bulgarian police agent, sitting in Lausanne, creates socializers of women, in the fullest sense of the word, after his own likeness and image.

Kautsky, at any rate, has original inspirers and assistants!

SOVIETS, TRADE UNIONS AND THE PARTY

The soviets, as a form of the organization of the working class, represent for Kautsky, 'in relation to the party and professional organizations of more developed countries, not a higher form of organization, but first and foremost a substitute [*Notbehelf*], arising out of the absence of political organizations' (p. 68).

Let us grant that this is true in connection with Russia. But then, why have soviets sprung up in Germany? Ought one not absolutely to repudiate them in the Ebert Republic? We note, however, that Hilferding, the nearest sympathizer of Kautsky, proposes to include the soviets in the constitution. Kautsky is silent.

The estimate of soviets as a 'primitive' organization is true to the extent that the open revolutionary struggle is more 'primitive' than parliamentarism. But the artificial complexity of the latter embraces only the upper strata, insignificant in their size. On the other hand, revolution is only possible where the masses have their vital interests at stake. The November revolution raised onto their feet such deep layers as pre-revolutionary social democracy could not even dream of. However wide were the organizations of the party and the trade unions in Germany, the revolution immediately proved incomparably wider than they. The revolutionary masses found their direct representation in the most simple and generally comprehensive delegate organization – in the soviet. One may admit that the Council of Deputies falls behind both the party and the trade union in the sense of the clearness of its programme, or the exactness of its organization. But it is far and away in front of the party and the trade unions in the size of the masses drawn by it into the organized struggle; and this superiority in quality gives the soviet undeniable revolutionary preponderance.

The soviet embraces workers of all undertakings, of all professions, of all stages of cultural development, all stages of political consciousness

– and thereby objectively is forced to formulate the general interests of the proletariat.

The *Communist Manifesto* viewed the problem of the Communist just in this sense – namely, the formulating of the general historical interests of the working class as a whole.

'The Communists are only distinguished from other proletarian parties', in the words of the *Manifesto*, 'by this: that in the different national struggles of the proletariat they point out, and bring to the fore, the common interests of the proletariat, independently of nationality; and again that, in the different stages of evolution through which the struggle between the proletariat and bourgeoisie passes, they constantly represent the interests of the movement taken as a whole.'

In the form of the all-embracing class organization of the soviets, the movement takes itself 'as a whole'. Hence it is clear why the Communists could and had to become the guiding party in the soviets. But hence also is seen all the narrowness of the estimate of soviets as 'substitutes for the party' (Kautsky), and all the stupidity of the attempt to include the soviets, in the form of an auxiliary lever, in the mechanism of bourgeois democracy (Hilferding).

The soviets are the organization of the proletarian revolution, and have purpose either as an organ of the struggle for power or as the apparatus of power of the working class.

Unable to grasp the revolutionary role of the soviets, Kautsky sees their root defects in that which constitutes their greatest merit. 'The demarcation of the bourgeois from the worker', he writes, 'can never be actually drawn. There will always be something arbitrary in such demarcation, which fact transforms the soviet idea into a particularly suitable foundation for dictatorial and arbitrary rule, but renders it unfitted for the creation of a clear, systematically built-up constitution' (p. 170).

Class dictatorship, according to Kautsky, cannot create for itself institutions answering to its nature, because there do not exist lines of demarcation between the classes. But in that case, what happens to the class struggle altogether? Surely it was just, in the existence of numerous transitional stages between the bourgeoisie and the proletariat, that the lower-middle-class theoreticians always found their principal argument against the 'principle' of the class struggle? For Kautsky, however, doubts as to principle begin just at the point where the proletariat, having overcome the shapelessness and unsteadiness of the intermediate class, having brought one part of them over to its side and thrown the remainder into the camp of the bourgeoisie, has actually organized its dictatorship in the Soviet constitution.

The very reason why the soviets are absolutely irreplaceable apparatus in the proletarian state is that their framework is elastic and yielding, with the result that not only social but political changes in the relationship of classes and sections can immediately find their expression in the soviet apparatus. Beginning with the largest factories and works, the soviets then draw into their organization the workers of private workshops and shop assistants, proceed to enter the village, organize the peasants against the landowners, and finally the lower and middle-class sections of the peasantry against the richest.

The labour state collects numerous staffs of employees, to a considerable extent from the ranks of the bourgeoisie and the bourgeois educated classes. To the extent that they become disciplined under the Soviet regime, they find representation in the soviet system. Expanding – and at certain moments contracting – in harmony with the expansion and contraction of the social positions conquered by the proletariat, the soviet system remains the state apparatus of the social revolution, in its internal dynamics, its ebbs and flows, its mistakes and successes. With the final triumph of the social revolution, the soviet system will expand and include the whole population, in order thereby to lose the characteristics of a form of state, and melt away into a mighty system of producing and consuming cooperation.

If the party and the trade unions were organizations of preparation for the revolution, the soviets are the weapon of the revolution itself. After its victory, the soviets become the organs of power. The role of the party and the unions, without decreasing, is nevertheless essentially altered.

In the hands of the party is concentrated the general control. It does not immediately administer, since its apparatus is not adapted for this purpose. But it has the final word in all fundamental questions. Further, our practice has led to the result that, in all moot questions, generally – conflicts between departments and personal conflicts within departments – the last word belongs to the Central Committee of the party. This affords extreme economy of time and energy. And in the most difficult and complicated circumstances gives a guarantee for the necessary unity of action. Such a regime is possible only in the presence of the unquestioned authority of the party, and the faultlessness of its discipline. Happily for the revolution, our party does possess in an equal measure both of these qualities. Whether in other countries which have not received from their past a strong revolutionary organization, with a great hardening in conflict, there will be created just as authoritative a Communist Party by the time of the proletarian revolution, it is difficult to foretell; but it is quite obvious that on this question, to a very large extent, depends the progress of the socialist revolution in each country.

The exclusive role of the Communist Party under the conditions of a victorious proletarian revolution is quite comprehensible. The question is of the dictatorship of a class. In the composition of that class there enter various elements, heterogeneous moods, different levels of development. Yet the dictatorship presupposes unity of will, unity of direction, unity of action. By what other path then can it be attained? The revolutionary supremacy of the proletariat presupposes within the proletariat itself the political supremacy of a party, with a clear programme of action and a faultless internal discipline.

The policy of coalitions contradicts internally the regime of the revolutionary dictatorship. We have in view, not coalitions with bourgeois parties, of which of course there can be no talk, but a coalition of Communists with other 'socialist' organizations, representing different stages of backwardness and prejudice of the labouring masses.

The revolution swiftly reveals all that is unstable, wears out all that is artificial; the contradictions glossed over in a coalition are swiftly revealed under the pressure of revolutionary events. We have had an example of this in Hungary, where the dictatorship of the proletariat assumed the political form of the coalition of the Communists with disguised opportunists. The coalition soon broke up. The Communist Party paid heavily for the revolutionary instability and the political treachery of its companions. It is quite obvious that for the Hungarian Communists it would have been more profitable to have come to power later, after having afforded to the left opportunists the possibility of compromising themselves once and for all. It is quite another question as to how far this was possible. In any case, a coalition with the opportunists, only temporarily hiding the relative weakness of the Hungarian Communists, at the same time prevented them from growing stronger at the expense of the opportunists; and brought them to disaster.

The same idea is sufficiently illustrated by the example of the

Russian Revolution. The coalition of the Bolsheviks with the left Social Revolutionists, which lasted for several months, ended with a bloody conflict. True, the reckoning for the coalition had to be paid, not so much by us Communists as by our disloyal companions. Apparently, such a coalition, in which we were the stronger side and, therefore, were not taking too many risks in the attempt, at one definite stage in history, to make use of the extreme left wing of bourgeois democracy, tactically must be completely justified. But, nonetheless, the left SR episode quite clearly shows that the regime of compromises, agreements, mutual concessions – for that is the meaning of the regime of coalition – cannot last long in an epoch in which situations alter with extreme rapidity, and in which supreme unity in point of view is necessary in order to render possible unity of action.

We have more than once been accused of having substituted for the dictatorship of the soviets the dictatorship of our party. Yet it can be said with complete justice that the dictatorship of the soviets became possible only by means of the dictatorship of the party. It is thanks to the clarity of its theoretical vision and its strong revolutionary organization that the party has afforded to the soviets the possibility of becoming transformed from shapeless parliaments of labour into the apparatus of the supremacy of labour. In this 'substitution' of the power of the party for the power of the working class there is nothing accidental, and in reality there is no substitution at all. The Communists express the fundamental interests of the working class. It is quite natural that, in the period in which history brings up those interests, in all their magnitude, on to the order of the day, the Communists have become the recognized representatives of the working class as a whole.

But where is your guarantee, certain wise men ask us, that it is just your party that expresses the interests of historical development? Destroying or driving underground the other parties, you have thereby prevented their political competition with you, and consequently you have deprived yourselves of the possibility of testing your line of action.

This idea is dictated by a purely liberal conception of the course of the revolution. In a period in which all antagonisms assume an open character, and the political struggle swiftly passes into a civil war, the ruling party has sufficient material standard by which to test its line of action, without the possible circulation of Menshevik papers. Noske crushes the Communists, but they grow. We have suppressed the Mensheviks and the SRs – and they have disappeared. This criterion is sufficient for us. At all events, our problem is not at every given moment statistically to measure the grouping of tendencies; but to render victory for our tendency secure. For that tendency is the tendency of the revolutionary dictatorship; and in the course of the latter, in its internal friction, we must find a sufficient criterion for self-examination.

The continuous 'independence' of the trade union movement, in the period of the proletarian revolution, is just as much an impossibility as the policy of coalition. The trade unions become the most important economic organs of the proletariat in power. Thereby they fall under the leadership of the Communist Party. Not only questions of principle in the trade union movement, but serious conflicts of organization within it, are decided by the Central Committee of our party.

The Kautskians attack the Soviet government as the dictatorship of a 'section' of the working class. 'If only', they say, 'the dictatorship was carried out by the whole class!' It is not easy to understand what actually they imagine when they say this. The dictatorship of the proletariat, in its very essence, signifies the immediate supremacy of the revolutionary vanguard, which relies upon the heavy masses, and, where necessary, obliges the backward tail to dress by the head. This refers also to the trade unions. After the conquest of power by the proletariat, they acquire a compulsory character. They must include all industrial workers. The party, on the other hand, as before, includes in its ranks only the most class-conscious and devoted; and only in a process of careful selection does it widen its ranks. Hence follows the guiding role of the Communist minority in the trade unions, which answers to the supremacy of the Communist Party in the soviets, and represents the political expression of the dictatorship of the proletariat.

The trade unions become the direct organizers of social production. They express not only the interests of the industrial workers, but the interests of industry itself. During the first period, the old currents in trade unionism more than once raised their head, urging the unions to haggle with the Soviet state, lay down conditions for it, and demand from it guarantees. The further we go, however, the more do the unions recognize that they are organs of production of the Soviet state, and assume responsibility for its fortunes – not opposing themselves to it, but identifying themselves with it. The unions become the organizers of labour discipline. They demand from the workers intensive labour under the most difficult conditions, to the extent that the labour state is not yet able to alter those conditions.

The unions become the apparatus of revolutionary repression against undisciplined, anarchical, parasitic elements in the working class. From the old policy of trade unionism, which at a certain stage is inseparable from the industrial movement within the framework of capitalist society, the unions pass along the whole line onto the new path of the policy of revolutionary communism.

THE PEASANT POLICY

The Bolsheviks 'hoped', Kautsky thunders, 'to overcome the substantial peasants in the villages by granting political rights exclusively to the poorest peasants. They then again granted representation to the substantial peasantry' (p. 216).

Kautsky enumerates the external 'contradictions' of our peasant policy, not dreaming to inquire into its general direction, and into the internal contradictions visible in the economic and political situation of the country.

In the Russian peasantry as it entered the Soviet order there were three elements: the poor, living to a considerable extent by the sale of their labour-power, and forced to buy additional food for their requirements; the middle peasants, whose requirements were covered by the products of their farms, and who were able to a limited extent to sell their surplus; and the upper layer – i.e., the rich peasants, the vulture (kulak) class, which systematically bought labour-power and sold their agricultural produce on a large scale. It is quite unnecessary to point out that these groups are not distinguished by definite symptoms or by homogeneousness throughout the country.

Still, on the whole, and generally speaking, the peasant poor represented the natural and undeniable allies of the town proletariat, whilst the vulture class represented its just as undeniable and irreconcilable enemies. The most hesitation was principally to be observed amongst the widest, the middle section of the peasantry.

Had not the country been so exhausted, and if the proletariat had had the possibility of offering to the peasant masses the necessary quantity of commodities and cultural requirements, the adaptation of the toiling majority of the peasantry to the new regime would have taken place much less painfully. But the economic disorder of the country, which was not the result of our land or food policy, but was generated by the causes which preceded the appearance of that policy, robbed the town for a prolonged period of any possibility of giving the village the products of the textile and metal-working industries, imported goods, and so on. At the same time, industry could not entirely cease drawing from the village all, albeit the smallest quantity, of its food resources. The proletariat demanded of the peasantry the granting of food credits, economic subsidies in respect of values which it is only now about to create. The symbol of those future values was the credit symbol, now finally deprived of all value. But the peasant mass is not very capable of historical detachment. Bound up with the Soviet government by the abolition of landlordism, and seeing in it a guarantee against the restoration of tsarism, the peasantry at the same time not infrequently opposes the collection of corn, considering it a bad bargain so long as it does not itself receive printed calico, nails and kerosene.

The Soviet government naturally strove to impose the chief weight of the food tax upon the upper strata of the village. But, in the unformed social conditions of the village, the influential peasantry, accustomed to lead the middle peasants in its train, found scores of methods of passing on the food tax from itself to the wide masses of the peasantry, thereby placing them in a position of hostility and opposition to Soviet power. It was necessary to awaken in the lower ranks of the peasantry suspicion and hostility towards the speculating upper strata. This purpose was served by the Committees of the Poor. They were built up of the rank and file, of elements who in the last epoch were oppressed, driven into a dark corner, deprived of their rights. Of course, in their midst there turned out to be a certain number of semi-parasitic elements. This served as the chief text for the demagogues amongst the populist 'socialists', whose speeches found a grateful echo in the hearts of the village vultures. But the mere fact of the transference of power to the village poor had an immeasurable revolutionary significance. For the guidance of the village, semi-prole- tarians there were dispatched from the towns' parties from amongst the foremost workers, who accomplished invaluable work in the villages. The Committees of the Poor became shock battalions against the vulture class. Enjoying the support of the state, they thereby obliged the middle section of the peasantry to choose, not only between Soviet power and the power of the landlords, but between the dictatorship of the proletariat and the semi-proletarian elements of the village on the one hand, and the yoke of the rich speculators on the other. By a series of lessons, some of which were very severe, the middle peasantry was obliged to become convinced that the Soviet regime, which had driven away the landlords and bailiffs, in its turn imposes new duties upon the peasantry, and demands sacrifices from them. The political education of tens of millions of the middle peasantry did not take place as easily and smoothly as in the schoolroom, and it did not give immediate and unquestionable results. There were risings of the middle peasants, uniting with the speculators, and always in such cases falling under the leadership of White Guard landlords; there were abuses committed by local agents of the Soviet government, particularly by those of the Committees of the Poor. But the fundamental political end was attained. The powerful class of rich peasantry, if it was not finally annihilated, proved to be shaken to its foundations, with its self-reliance undermined. The middle peasantry, remaining politically shapeless, just as it is economically shapeless, began to learn to find its representative in the foremost worker, as before it found it in the noisy village speculator. Once this fundamental result was achieved, the Committees of the Poor, as temporary institutions, as a sharp wedge driven into the village masses, had to yield their place to the soviets, in which the village poor are represented side by side with the middle peasantry.

The Committees of the Poor existed for about six months, from June to December 1918. In their institution, as in their abolition, Kautsky sees nothing but the 'waverings' of Soviet policy. Yet at the same time he himself has not even a suspicion of any practical lessons to be drawn. And after all, how should he think of them? Experience such as we are acquiring in this respect knows no precedent; and questions and problems such as the Soviet government is now solving in practice have no solution in books. What Kautsky calls contradictions in policy are, in reality, the active manoeuvring of the proletariat in the spongy, undivided, peasant mass. The sailing ship has to manoeuvre before the wind; yet no one will see contradictions in the manoeuvres which finally bring the ship to harbour.

In questions as to agricultural communes and soviet farms, there could also be found not a few 'contradictions', in which, side by side with individual mistakes, there are expressed various stages of the revolution. What quantity of land shall the Soviet state leave for itself in the Ukraine, and what quantity shall it hand over to the peasants; what policy shall it lay down for the agricultural communes; in what form shall it give them support, so as not to make them the nursery for parasitism; in what form is control to be organized over them – all these are absolutely new problems of socialist economic construction, which have been settled beforehand neither theoretically nor practically, and in the settling of which the general principles of our programme have even yet to find their actual application and their testing in practice, by means of inevitable temporary deviations to right or left.

But even the very fact that the Russian proletariat has found support in the peasantry Kautsky turns against us. 'This has introduced into the Soviet regime an economically reactionary element which was spared [!] the Paris Commune, as its dictatorship did not rely on peasant soviets.'

As if in reality we could accept the heritage of the feudal and bourgeois order with the possibility of excluding from it at will 'an economically reactionary element'! Nor is this all. Having poisoned the Soviet regime by its 'reactionary element', the peasantry has deprived us of its support. Today it 'hates' the Bolsheviks. All this Kautsky knows very certainly from the radios of Clemenceau and the squibs of the Mensheviks.

In reality, what is true is that wide masses of the peasantry are suffering from the absence of the essential products of industry. But it is just as true that every other regime – and there were not a few of them, in various parts of Russia, during the last three years – proved infinitely more oppressive for the shoulders of the peasantry. Neither monarchical nor democratic governments were able to increase their stores of manufactured goods. Both of them found themselves in need of the peasant's corn and the peasant's horses. To carry out their policy, the bourgeois governments – including the Kautskian–Menshevik variety – made use of a purely bureaucratic apparatus, which reckons with the requirements of the peasant's farm to an infinitely lesser degree than the soviet apparatus, which consists of workers and peasants. As a result, the middle peasant, in spite of his waverings, his dissatisfaction, and even his risings, ultimately always comes to the conclusion that, however difficult it is for him at present under the

Bolsheviks, under every other regime it would be infinitely more difficult for him. It is quite true that the Commune was 'spared' peasant support. But in return the Commune was not spared annihilation by the peasant armies of Thiers, whereas our army, four-fifths of whom are peasants, is fighting with enthusiasm and with success for the Soviet republic. And this one fact, controverting Kautsky and those inspiring him, gives the best possible verdict on the peasant policy of the Soviet government.

THE SOVIET GOVERNMENT AND THE EXPERTS

'The Bolsheviks at first thought they could manage without the intelligentsia, without the experts,' Kautsky narrates to us (p. 191). But then, becoming convinced of the necessity of the intelligentsia, they abandoned their severe repressions, and attempted to attract them to work by all sorts of measures, incidentally by giving them extremely high salaries. 'In this way,' Kautsky says ironically, 'the true path, the true method of attracting experts consists in first of all giving them a thorough good hiding' (p. 192). Quite so. With all due respect to all philistines, the dictatorship of the proletariat does just consist in 'giving a hiding' to the classes that were previously supreme, before forcing them to recognize the new order and to submit to it.

The professional intelligentsia, brought up with a prejudice about the omnipotence of the bourgeoisie, long would not, could not, and did not believe that the working class is really capable of governing the country; that it seized power not by accident; and that the dictatorship of the proletariat is an insurmountable fact. Consequently, the bourgeois intelligentsia treated its duties to the labour state extremely lightly, even when it entered its service; and it considered that to receive money from Wilson, Clemenceau or Mirbach for anti-Soviet agitation, or to hand over military secrets and technical resources to White Guards and foreign imperialists, is a quite natural and obvious course under the regime of the proletariat. It became necessary to show it in practice, and to show it severely, that the proletariat had not seized power in order to allow such jokes to be played at its expense.

In the severe penalties adopted in the case of the intelligentsia, our bourgeois idealist sees the 'consequence of a policy which strove to attract the educated classes, not by means of persuasion, but by means of kicks from before and behind' (p. 193). In this way, Kautsky seriously imagines that it is possible to attract the bourgeois intelligentsia to the work of socialist construction by means of mere persuasion – and this in conditions when, in all other countries, there is still supreme the bourgeoisie which hesitates at no methods of terrifying, flattering, or buying over the Russian intelligentsia and making it a weapon for the transformation of Russia into a colony of slaves.

Instead of analyzing the course of the struggle, Kautsky, when dealing with the intelligentsia, gives once again merely academic recipes. It is absolutely false that our party had the idea of managing without the intelligentsia, not realizing to the full its importance for the economic and cultural work that lay before us. On the contrary. When the struggle for the conquest and consolidation of power was in full blast, and the majority of the intelligentsia was playing the part of a shock battalion of the bourgeoisie, fighting against us openly or sabotaging our institutions, Soviet power fought mercilessly with the experts, precisely because it knew their enormous importance from the point of view of organization so long as they do not attempt to carry on an independent 'democratic' policy and execute the orders of one of the fundamental classes of society. Only after the opposition of the intelligentsia had been broken by a severe struggle did the possibility open before us of enlisting the assistance of the experts. We immediately entered that path. It proved not as simple as it might have seemed at first. The relations which existed under capitalist conditions between the working man and the director, the clerk and the manager, the soldier and the officer, left behind a very deep class distrust of the experts; and that distrust had become still more acute during the first period of the civil war, when the intelligentsia did its utmost to break the labour revolution by hunger and cold. It was not easy to outlive this frame of mind, and to pass from the first violent antagonism to peaceful collaboration. The labouring masses had gradually to become accustomed to see in the engineer, the agricultural expert, the officer, not the oppressor of yesterday but the useful worker of today – a necessary expert, entirely under the orders of the workers' and peasants' government.

We have already said that Kautsky is wrong when he attributes to the Soviet government the desire to replace experts by proletarians. But that such a desire was bound to spring up in wide circles of the proletariat cannot be denied. A young class which had proved to its own satisfaction that it was capable of overcoming the greatest obstacles in its path, which had torn to pieces the veil of mystery which had hitherto surrounded the power of the propertied classes, which had realized that all good things on the earth were not the direct gift of heaven – that a revolutionary class was naturally inclined, in the person of the less mature of its elements, at first to overestimate its capacity for solving each and every problem, without having recourse to the aid of experts educated by the bourgeoisie.

It was not merely yesterday that we began the struggle with such tendencies, in so far as they assumed a definite character.

'Today, when the power of the soviets has been set on a firm footing,' we said at the Moscow City Conference on 28 March 1918, 'the struggle with sabotage must express itself in the form of transforming the saboteurs of yesterday into the servants, executive officials, technical guides, of the new regime, wherever it requires them. If we do not grapple with this, if we do not attract all the forces necessary to us and enlist them in the Soviet service, our struggle of yesterday with sabotage would thereby be condemned as an absolutely vain and fruitless struggle.

'Just as in dead machines, so into those technical experts – engineers, doctors, teachers, former officers – there is sunk a certain portion of our national capital, which we are obliged to exploit and utilize if we want to solve the root problems standing before us.

'Democratization does not at all consist – as every Marxist learns in his ABC – in abolishing the meaning of skilled forces, the meaning of persons possessing special knowledge, and in replacing them every-where and anywhere by elective boards.

'Elective boards, consisting of the best representatives of the working class, but not equipped with the necessary technical knowledge, cannot replace one expert who has passed through the technical school, and who knows how to carry out the given technical work. That flood-tide of the collegiate principle which is at present to be observed in all spheres is the quite natural reaction of a young, revolutionary, only yesterday oppressed class, which is throwing out the one-man principle of its rulers of yesterday – the landlords and the generals – and everywhere is appointing its elected representatives. This, I say, is quite a natural and, in its origin, quite a healthy revolutionary reaction; but it is not the last word in the economic constructive work of the proletarian class.

'The next step must consist in the self-limitation of the collegiate principle, in a healthy and necessary act of self-limitation by the working class, which knows where the decisive word can be spoken by the elected representatives of the workers themselves, and where it is necessary to give way to a technical specialist, who is equipped with certain knowledge, on whom a great measure of responsibility must be laid, and who must be kept under careful political control. But it is necessary to allow the expert freedom to act, freedom to create; because no expert, be he ever so little gifted or capable, can work in his department when subordinate in his own technical work to a board of men who do not know that department. Political, collegiate and soviet control everywhere and anywhere; but for the executive functions, we must appoint technical experts, put them in responsible positions, and impose responsibility upon them.

'Those who fear this are quite unconsciously adopting an attitude of profound internal distrust towards the Soviet regime. Those who think that the enlisting of the saboteurs of yesterday in the administration of technically expert posts threatens the very foundations of the Soviet regime, do not realize that it is not through the work of some engineer or of some general of yesterday that the Soviet regime may stumble – in the political, in the revolutionary, in the military sense, the Soviet regime is unconquerable. But it may stumble through its own incapacity to grapple with the problems of creative organization. The Soviet regime is bound to draw from the old institutions all that was vital and valuable in them, and harness it on to the new work. If, comrades, we do not accomplish this, we shall not deal successfully with our principal problems; for it would be absolutely impossible for us to bring forth from our masses, in the shortest possible time, all the necessary experts, and throw aside all that was accumulated in the past.

'As a matter of fact, it would be just the same as if we said that all the machines which hitherto had served to exploit the workers were now to be thrown aside. It would be madness. The enlisting of scientific experts is for us just as essential as the administration of the resources of production and transport, and all the wealth of the country generally. We must, and in addition we must immediately, bring under our control all the technical experts we possess, and introduce in practice for them the principle of compulsory labour; at the same time leaving them a wide margin of activity, and maintaining over them careful political control'.[3]

The question of experts was particularly acute, from the very beginning, in the War Department. Here, under the pressure of iron necessity, it was solved first.

In the sphere of administration of industry and transport, the necessary forms of organization are very far from being attained, even to this day. We must seek the reason in the fact that during the first two years we were obliged to sacrifice the interests of industry and transport to the requirements of military defence. The extremely changeable course of the civil war, in its turn, threw obstacles in the way of the establishment of regular relations with the experts. Qualified technicians of industry and transport, doctors, teachers, professors, either went away with the retreating armies of Kolchak and Denikin, or were compulsorily evacuated by them.

Only now, when the civil war is approaching its conclusion, is the intelligentsia in its mass making its peace with the Soviet government, or bowing before it. Economic problems have acquired first-class importance. One of the most important amongst them is the problem of the scientific organization of production. Before the experts there opens a boundless field of activity. They are being accorded the independence necessary for creative work. The general control of industry on a national scale is concentrated in the hands of the party of the proletariat.

THE INTERNAL POLICY OF THE SOVIET GOVERNMENT

'The Bolsheviks', Kautsky mediates, 'acquired the force necessary for the seizure of political power through the fact that, amongst the political parties in Russia, they were the most energetic in their demands for peace – peace at any price, a separate peace – without interesting themselves as to the influence this would have on the general international situation, as to whether this would assist the victory and world domination of the German military monarchy, under the protection of which they remained for a long time, just like Indian or Irish rebels or Italian anarchists' (p. 53).

Of the reasons for our victory, Kautsky knows only the one that we stood for peace. He does not explain the Soviet government has continued to exist now that it has again mobilized a most important proportion of the soldiers of the imperial army, in order for two years successfully to combat its political enemies.

The watchword of peace undoubtedly played an enormous part in our struggle; but precisely because it was directed against the imperialist war. The idea of peace was supported most strongly of all, not by the tired soldiers, but by the foremost workers, for whom it had the import, not for a rest, but of a pitiless struggle against the exploiters. It was those same workers who, under the watchword of peace, later laid down their lives on the Soviet fronts.

The affirmation that we demanded peace without reckoning on the effect it would have on the international situation is a belated echo of Kadet and Menshevik slanders. The comparison of us with the Germanophile nationalists of India and Ireland seeks its justification in the fact that German imperialism did actually attempt to make use of us as it did the Indians and the Irish. But the chauvinists of France spared no efforts to make use of Liebknecht and Luxemburg – even of Kautsky and Bernstein – in their own interests. The whole question is, Did we allow ourselves to be utilized? Did we, by our conduct, give the European workers even the shadow of a ground to place us in the same category as German imperialism? It is sufficient to remember the course of the Brest negotiations,[7] their breakdown, and the German advance of February 1918, to reveal all the cynicism of Kautsky's accusation. In reality, there was no peace for a single day between ourselves and German imperialism. On the Ukrainian and Caucasian fronts, we, in the measure of our then extremely feeble energies, continued to wage war without openly calling it such. We were too weak to organize war along the whole Russo-German front. We maintained persistently the fiction of peace, utilizing the fact that the chief German forces were drawn away to the west. If German imperialism did prove sufficiently powerful, in 1917–18, to impose upon us the Treaty of Brest-Litovsk, after all our efforts to tear that noose from our necks, one of the principal reasons was the disgraceful behaviour of the German Social Democratic Party, of which Kautsky remained an integral and essential part. The Treaty of Brest-Litovsk was predetermined on 4 August 1914. At that moment, Kautsky not only did not declare war against German militarism, as he later demanded from the Soviet government, which was in 1918 still powerless from a military point of view; Kautsky actually proposed voting for the war credits, 'under certain conditions'; and generally behaved in such a way that for months it was impossible to discover whether he stood for the war or against it. And this political coward, who at the decisive moment gave up the principal positions of socialism, dares to accuse us of having found ourselves obliged, at a certain moment, to retreat – not in principle, but materially. And why? Because we were betrayed by the German Social Democracy, corrupted by Kautskianism – i.e., by political prostitution disguised by theories.

We did concern ourselves with the international situation! In reality, we had a much more profound criterion by which to judge the international situation; and it did not deceive us. Already before the February revolution the Russian army no longer existed as a fighting force. Its final collapse was predetermined. If the February revolution had not taken place, tsarism would have come to an agreement with the German monarchy. But the February revolution which prevented that finally destroyed the army built on a monarchist basis, precisely because it was a revolution. A month sooner or later the army was bound to fall to pieces. The military policy of Kerensky was the policy of an ostrich. He closed his eyes to the decomposition of the army, spoke sounding phrases and uttered verbal threats against German imperialism.

In such conditions, we had only one way out: to take our stand on the platform of peace, as the inevitable conclusion from the military powerlessness of the revolution, and to transform that watchword into the weapon of revolutionary influence on all the peoples of Europe. That is, instead of, together with Kerensky, peacefully awaiting the final military catastrophe – which might bury the revolution in its ruins – we proposed to take possession of the watchword of peace and to lead after it the proletariat of Europe – and first and foremost the workers of Austro-Germany. It was in the light of this view that we carried on our peace negotiations with the central empires, and it was in the light of this that we drew up our notes to the governments of the Entente. We drew out the negotiations as long as we could, in order to give the European working masses the possibility of realizing the meaning of the Soviet government and its policy. The January strike of 1918 in Germany and Austria showed that out efforts had not been in vain. That strike was the first serious premonition of the German revolution. The German imperialists understood then that it was just we who represented for them a deadly danger. This is very strikingly shown in Ludendorff's book. True, they could not risk any longer coming out against us in an open crusade. But wherever they could fight against us secretly deceiving the German workers with the help of the German Social Democracy, they did so; in the Ukraine, on the Don, in the Caucasus. In central Russia, in Moscow, Count Mirbach from the very first day of his arrival stood as the centre of counter-revolutionary plots against the Soviet government – just as Comrade Joffe in Berlin was in the closest possible touch with the revolution. The extreme left group of the German revolutionary move-ment, the party of Karl Liebknecht and Rosa Luxemburg, all the time went hand in hand with us. The German revolution at once took on the form of soviets, and the German proletariat, in spite of the Treaty of Brest-Litovsk, did not for a moment entertain any doubts as to whether we were with Liebknecht or Ludendorff. In his evidence before the Reichstag Commission in November, 1919, Ludendorff explained how 'the High Command demanded the creation of an institution with the object of disclosing the connection of revolutionary tendencies in Germany with Russia. Joffe arrived in Berlin, and in various towns there were set up Russian consulates. This had the most painful consequences in the army and navy.' Kautsky, however, has the audacity to write that 'if matters did come to a German revolution, truly it is not the Bolsheviks who are responsible for it' (p. 162).

Even if we had had the possibility in 1917–18, by means of revo-lutionary abstention, of supporting the old imperial army instead of hastening its destruction, we should have merely been assisting the Entente, and would have covered up by our aid its brigands' peace with Germany, Austria and all the countries of the world generally. With such a policy we should at the decisive moment have proved absolutely disarmed in the face of the Entente – still more disarmed than Germany is today. Whereas, thanks to the November revolution and the Treaty of Brest-Litovsk we are today the only country which opposes the Entente rifle in hand. By our international policy, we not only did not assist the Hohenzollern to assume a position of world domination; on the contrary, by our November revolution we did more than anyone else to prepare his overthrow. At the same time, we gained a military breathing space, in the course of which we created a large and strong army, the first army of the proletariat in history, with which today not all the unleashed hounds of the Entente can cope.

The most critical moment in our international situation arose in the autumn of 1918, after the destruction of the German armies. In the place of two mighty camps, more or less neutralizing each other, there stood before us the victorious Entente, at the summit of its world power, and there lay broken Germany, whose Junker blackguards would have considered it a happiness and an honour to spring at the throat of the Russian proletariat for a bone from the kitchen of Clemenceau. We proposed peace to the Entente, and were again ready – for we were obliged – to sign the most painful conditions. But Clemenceau, in whose imperialist rapacity there have remained in their full force all the characteristics of lower-middle-class thick-headedness, refused the Junkers their bone, and at the same time decided at all costs to decorate the Invalides with the scalps of the leaders of the Soviet Republic. By this policy Clemenceau did us no small service. We defended ourselves successfully, and held out.

What, then, was the guiding principle of our external policy, once the first months of existence of the Soviet government had made clear the considerable vitality as yet of the capitalist governments of Europe? Just that which Kautsky accepts today uncomprehendingly as an accidental result – to hold out!

We realized too clearly that the very fact of the existence of the Soviet government is an event of the greatest revolutionary importance; and this realization dictated to us our concessions and our temporary retirements – not in principle but in practical conclusions from a sober estimate of our own forces. We retreated like an army which gives up to the enemy a town, and even a fortress, in order, having retreated, to concentrate its forces not only for defence but for an advance. We retreated like strikers amongst whom today energies and resources have been exhausted, but who, clenching their teeth, are preparing for a new struggle. If we were not filled with an unconquerable belief in the world significance of the Soviet dictatorship, we should not have accepted the most painful sacrifices at Brest-Litovsk. If our faith had proved to be contradicted by the actual course of events, the Treaty of Brest-Litovsk would have gone down to history as the futile capitulation of a doomed regime. That is how the situation was judged then, not only by the Kühlmanns but also by the Kautskys of all countries. But we proved right in our estimate, as of our weakness then, so of our strength in the future. The existence of the Ebert Republic, with its universal suffrage, its parliamentary swindling, its 'freedom' of the press, and its murder of labour leaders, is merely a necessary link in the historical chain of slavery and scoundrelism. The existence of the Soviet government is a fact of immeasurable revolutionary significance. It was necessary to retain it, utilizing the conflict of the capitalist nations, the as yet unfinished imperialist war, the self-confident effrontery of the Hohenzollern bands, the thickwittedness of the world-bourgeoisie as far as the fundamental questions of the revolution were concerned, the antagonism of America and Europe, the complication of relations within the Entente. We had to lead our yet unfinished Soviet ship over the stormy waves, amid rocks and reefs, completing its building and armament en route.

Kautsky has the audacity to repeat the accusation that we did not, at the beginning of 1918, hurl ourselves unarmed against our mighty foe. Had we done this we would have been crushed. The first great attempt of the proletariat to seize power would have suffered defeat. The revolutionary wing of the European proletariat would have been dealt the severest possible blow. The Entente would have made peace with the Hohenzollerns over the corpse of the Russian Revolution, and the world capitalist reaction would have received a respite for a number of years. When Kautsky says that, concluding the Treaty of Brest-Litovsk, we did not think of its influence on the fate of the German revolution, he is uttering a disgraceful slander. We considered the question from all sides, and our sole criterion was the interests of the international revolution.

We came to the conclusion that those interests demanded that the only Soviet government in the world should be preserved. And we were proved right. Whereas Kautsky awaited our fall, if not with impatience, at least with certainty; and on this expected fall built up his whole international policy.

The minutes of the session of the coalition government of 19 November 1918, published by the Bauer Ministry, run: 'First, a continuation of the discussion as to the relations of Germany and the Soviet Republic. Haase advises a policy of procrastination. Kautsky agrees with Haase: decision must be postponed. The Soviet government will not last long. It will inevitably fail in the course of a few weeks.'

In this way, at the time when the situation of the Soviet government was really extremely difficult – for the destruction of German militarism had given the Entente, it seemed, the full possibility of finishing with us 'in the course of a few weeks' – at that moment Kautsky not only does not hasten to our aid, and even does not merely wash his hands of the whole affair; he participates in active treachery against revolutionary Russia. To aid Scheidemann in his role of watchdog of the bourgeoisie, instead of the 'programme' role assigned to him of its 'grave-digger', Kautsky himself hastens to become the grave-digger of the Soviet government. But the Soviet government is alive. It will outlive all its grave-diggers.

8

PROBLEMS OF THE
ORGANIZATION OF LABOUR

If, in the first period of the Soviet revolution, the principal ire of the bourgeois world was directed against our savagery and bloodthirstiness, later, when that argument, from frequent use, had become blunted, and had lost its force, we were made responsible chiefly for the economic disorganization of the country. In harmony with his present mission, Kautsky methodically translates into the language of pseudo-Marxism all the bourgeois charges against the Soviet government of destroying the industrial life of Russia. The Bolsheviks began socialization without a plan. They socialized what was not ready for socialization. The Russian working class, altogether, is not yet prepared for the administration of industry; and so on, and so on.

Repeating and combining these accusations, Kautsky, with dull obstinacy, hides the real cause for our economic disorganization: the imperialist slaughter, the civil war and the blockade.

Soviet Russia, from the first months of its existence, found itself deprived of coal, oil, metal and cotton. First the Austro-German and then the Entente imperialisms, with the assistance of the Russian White Guards, tore away from Soviet Russia the Donetz coal and metal-working region, the oil districts of the Caucasus, Turkestan with its cotton, Ural with its richest deposits of metals, Siberia with its bread and meat. The Donetz area had usually supplied our industry with 94 per cent of its coal and 74 per cent of its crude ore. The Ural supplied the remaining 20 per cent of the ore and 4 per cent of the coal. Both these regions, during the civil war, were cut off from us. We were deprived of half a milliard *poods* of coal imported from abroad. Simultaneously, we were left without oil: the oilfields, one and all, passed into the hands of our enemies. One needs to have a truly brazen forehead to speak, in the face of these facts, of the destructive influence of 'premature', 'barbarous', etc., socialization. An industry which is completely deprived of fuel and raw materials – whether that industry belongs to a capitalist trust or to the labour state, whether its factories be socialized or not – its chimneys will not smoke in either case without coal or oil. Something might be learned about this, say, in Austria; and for that matter in Germany itself. A weaving factory administered according to the best Kautskian methods – if we admit that anything at all can be administered by Kautskian methods, except one's own inkstand – will not produce prints if it is not supplied with cotton. And we were simultaneously deprived both of Turkestan and American cotton. In addition, as has been pointed out, we had no fuel.

Of course, the blockade and the civil war came as the result of the proletarian revolution in Russia. But it does not at all follow from this that the terrible devastation caused by the Anglo-American–French blockade and the robber campaigns of Kolchak and Denikin have to be put down to the discredit of the Soviet methods of economic organization.

The imperialist war that preceded the revolution, with its all-devouring material and technical demands, imposed a much greater strain on our young industry than on the industry of more powerful capitalist countries. Our transport suffered particularly severely. The exploitation of the railways increased considerably; the wear and tear correspondingly; while repairs were reduced to a strict minimum. The inevitable hour of Nemesis was brought nearer by the fuel crisis. Our almost simultaneous loss of the Donetz coal, foreign coal and the oil of the Caucasus, obliged us in the sphere of transport to have recourse to wood. And, as the supplies of wood fuel were not in the least calculated with a view to this, we had to stoke our boilers with recently stored raw wood, which has an extremely destructive effect on the mechanism of locomotives that are already worn out. We see, in consequence, that the chief reasons for the collapse of transport preceded November 1917. But even those reasons which are directly or indirectly bound up with the November revolution fall under the heading of political consequences of the revolution; and in no circumstances do they affect socialist economic methods.

The influence of political disturbances in the economic sphere was not limited only to questions of transport and fuel. If world industry, during the last decade, was more and more becoming a single organism, the more directly does this apply to national industry. On the other hand, the war and the revolution were mechanically breaking up and tearing asunder Russian industry in every direction. The industrial ruin of Poland, the Baltic fringe, and later of Petrograd, began under tsarism and continued under Kerensky, embracing ever newer regions. Endless evacuations simultaneous with the destruction of industry, of necessity meant the destruction of transport also. During the civil war, with its changing fronts, evacuations assumed a more feverish and consequently a still more destructive character. Each side temporarily or permanently evacuated this or that industrial centre, and took all possible steps to ensure that the most important industrial enterprises could not be utilized by the enemy: all valuable machines were carried off, or at any rate their most delicate parts, together with the technical and best workers. The evacuation was followed by a re-evacuation, which not infrequently completed the destruction both of the property transferred and of the railways. Some of the most important industrial areas – especially in the Ukraine and in the Urals – changed hands several times.

To this it must be added that, at the time when the destruction of technical equipment was being accomplished on an unprecedented scale, the supply of machines from abroad, which hitherto played a decisive part in our industry, had completely ceased.

But not only did the dead elements of production – buildings, machines, rails, fuel and raw material – suffer terrible losses under the combined blows of the war and the revolution. Not less, if not more, did the chief factor of industry, its living creative force – the proletariat – suffer. The proletariat was consolidating the November revolution, building and defending the apparatus of Soviet power, and carrying on a ceaseless struggle with the White Guards. The skilled workers are, as a rule, at the same time the most advanced. The civil war tore away many tens of thousands of the best workers for a long time from productive labour, swallowing up many thousands of them for ever. The socialist revolution placed the chief burden of its sacrifices upon the proletarian vanguard, and consequently on industry.

All the attention of the Soviet state has been directed, for the two and a half years of its existence, to the problem of military defence. The best forces and its principal resources were given to the front.

In any case, the class struggle inflicts blows upon industry. That accusation, long before Kautsky, was levelled at it by all the philosophers of the social harmony. During simple economic strikes the workers consume, and do not produce. Still more powerful, therefore, are the blows inflicted upon economic life by the class struggle in its severest form – in the form of armed conflicts. But it is quite clear that the civil war cannot be classified under the heading of socialist economic methods.

The reasons enumerated above are more than sufficient to explain the difficult economic situation of Soviet Russia. There is no fuel, there is no metal, there is no cotton, transport is destroyed, technical equipment is in disorder, living labour-power is scattered over the face of the country, and a high percentage of it has been lost to the front – is there any need to seek supplementary reasons in the economic utopianism of the Bolsheviks in order to explain the fall of our industry? On the contrary, each of the reasons quoted alone is sufficient to evoke the question: How is it possible at all that, under such conditions, factories and workshops should continue to function?

And yet they do continue principally in the shape of war industry, which is at present living at the expense of the rest. The Soviet government was obliged to re-create it, just like the army, out of fragments. War industry, set up again under these conditions of unprecedented difficulty, has fulfilled and is fulfilling its duty: the Red Army is clothed, shod, equipped with its rifle, its machine gun, its cannon, its bullet, its shells, its aeroplane and all else that it requires.

As soon as the dawn of peace made its appearance – after the destruction of Kolchak, Yudenich and Denikin – we placed before ourselves the problem of economic organization in the fullest possible way. And already, in the course of three or four months of intensive work in this sphere, it has become clear beyond all possibility of doubt that, thanks to its most intimate connection with the popular masses, the elasticity of its apparatus, and its own revolutionary initiative, the Soviet government disposes of such resources and methods for economic reconstruction as no other government ever had or has today.

True, before us there arose quite new questions and new difficulties in the sphere of the organization of labour. Socialist theory had no answers to these questions, and could not have them. We had to find the solution in practice, and test it in practice. Kautskianism is a whole epoch behind the gigantic economic problems being solved at present by the Soviet government. In the form of Menshevism, it constantly throws obstacles in our way, opposing the practical measures of our economic reconstruction by bourgeois prejudices and bureaucratic-intellectual scepticism.

To introduce the reader to the very essence of the questions of the organization of labour, as they stand at present before us, we quote below the report of the author of this book at the Third All-Russian Congress of Trade Unions. With the object of the fullest possible elucidation of the question, the text of the speech is supplemented by considerable extracts from the author's reports at the All-Russian Congress of Economic Councils and at the Ninth Congress of the Communist Party.

REPORT ON THE ORGANIZATION OF LABOUR

'Comrades, the internal civil war is coming to an end. On the western front, the situation remains undecided. It is possible that the Polish bourgeoisie will hurl a challenge at its fate ... But even in this case – we do not seek it – the war will not demand of us that all-devouring concentration of forces which the simultaneous struggle on four fronts imposed upon us. The frightful pressure of the war is becoming weaker. Economic requirements and problems are more and more coming to the fore. History is bringing us, along the whole line, to our fundamental problem – the organization of labour on new social foundations. The organization of labour is in its essence the organization of the new society: every historical form of society is in its foundation a form of organization of labour. While every previous form of society was an organization of labour in the interests of a minority, which organized its state apparatus for the oppression of the overwhelming majority of the workers, we are making the first attempt in world history to organize labour in the interests of the labouring majority itself. This, however, does not exclude the element of compulsion in all its forms, both the most gentle and the extremely severe. The element of state compulsion not only does not disappear from the historical arena, but on the contrary will still play, for a considerable period, an extremely prominent part.

'As a general rule, man strives to avoid labour. Love for work is not at all an inborn characteristic: it is created by economic pressure and social education. One may even say that man is a fairly lazy animal. It is on this quality, in reality, that is founded to a considerable extent all human progress; because if man did not strive to expend his energy economically, did not seek to receive the largest possible quantity of products in return for a small quantity of energy, there would have been no technical development or social culture. It would appear, then, from this point of view that human laziness is a progressive force. Old Antonio Labriola, the Italian Marxist, even used to picture the man of the future as a 'happy and lazy genius'. We must not, however, draw the conclusion from this that the party and the trade unions must propagate this quality in their agitation as a moral duty. No, no. We have sufficient of it as it is. The problem before the social organization is just to bring 'laziness' within a definite framework, to discipline it, and to pull mankind together with the help of methods and measures invented by mankind itself.

COMPULSORY LABOUR SERVICE

'The key to economic organization is labour-power, skilled, elementarily trained, semi-trained, untrained, or unskilled. To work out methods for its accurate registration, mobilization, distribution and productive application means practically to solve the problem of economic construction. This is a problem for a whole epoch – a gigantic problem. Its difficulty is intensified by the fact that we have to reconstruct labour on socialist foundations in conditions of hitherto unknown poverty and terrifying misery.

'The more our machine equipment is worn out, the more disordered our railways grow, the less hope there is for us of receiving machines to any significant extent from abroad in the near future, the greater is the importance acquired by the question of living labour-power. At first sight it would seem that there is plenty of it. But how are we to get at it? How are we to apply it? How are we productively to organize it? Even with the clearing of snow drifts from the railway tracks, we were brought face to face with very big difficulties. It was absolutely impossible to meet those difficulties by means of buying labour-power on the market, with the present insignificant purchasing power of money, and in the most complete absence of manufactured products. Our fuel requirements cannot be satisfied, even partially, without a mass application on a scale hitherto unknown, of labour-power to work on wood, fuel, peat and combustible slate. The civil war has played havoc with our railways, our bridges, our buildings, our stations. We require at once tens and hundreds of thousands of hands to restore order to all this. For production on a large scale in our timber, peat and other enterprises, we require housing for our workers, if they be only temporary huts. Hence, again, the necessity of devoting a considerable amount of labour-power to building work. Many workers are required to organize river navigation; and so on, and so forth . . .

'Capitalist industry utilizes auxiliary labour-power on a large scale, in the shape of peasants employed on industry for only part of the year. The village, throttled by the grip of landlessness, always threw a certain surplus of labour-power onto the market. The state obliged it to do this by its demand for taxes. The market offered the peasant manufactured goods. Today, we have none of this. The village has acquired more land; there is not sufficient agricultural machinery; workers are required for the land; industry can at present give practically nothing to the village; and the market no longer has an attractive influence on labour-power.

'Yet labour-power is required – required more than at any time before. Not only the worker, but the peasant also, must give to the Soviet state his energy, in order to ensure that labouring Russia, and with it the labouring masses, should not be crushed. The only way to attract the labour-power necessary for our economic problems is to introduce compulsory labour service.

'The very principle of compulsory labour service is for the Communist quite unquestionable. "He who works not, neither shall he eat." And as all must eat, all are obliged to work. Compulsory labour service is sketched in our constitution and in our labour code. But hitherto it has always remained a mere principle. Its application has always had an accidental, impartial, episodic character. Only now, when along the whole line we have reached the question of the economic rebirth of the country, have problems of compulsory labour service arisen before us in the most concrete way possible. The only solution of economic difficulties that is correct from the point of view both of principle and of practice is to treat the population of the whole country as the reservoir of the necessary labour-power – an almost inexhaustible reservoir – and to introduce strict order into the work of its registration, mobilization and utilization.

'How are we practically to begin the utilization of labour-power on the basis of compulsory military service?

'Hitherto only the War Department has had any experience in the sphere of the registration, mobilization, formation and transference from one place to another of large masses. These technical methods and principles were inherited by our War Department, to a considerable extent, from the past.

'In the economic sphere there is no such heritage; since in that sphere there existed the principle of private property, and labour-power entered each factory separately from the market. It is consequently natural that we should be obliged, at any rate during the first period, to make use of the apparatus of the War Department on a large scale for labour mobilizations.

'We have set up special organizations for the application of the principle of compulsory labour service in the centre and in the districts: in the provinces the regions, and the rural districts, we have already compulsory labour committees at work. They rely for the most part on the central and local organs of the War Department. Our economic centres – the Supreme Economic Council, the People's Commissariat for Agriculture, the People's Commissariat for Ways and Communications, the People's Commissariat for Food – work out estimates of the labour-power they require. The Chief Committee for Compulsory Labour Service receives these estimates, coordinates them, brings them into agreement with the local resources of labour-power, gives corresponding directions to its local organs, and through them carries out labour mobilizations. Within the boundaries of regions, provinces and regions, the local bodies carry out this work independently, with the object of satisfying local economic requirements.

'All this organization is at present only in the embryo stage. It is still very imperfect. But the course we have adopted is unquestionably the right one.

'If the organization of the new society can be reduced fundamentally to the reorganization of labour, the organization of labour signifies in its turn the correct introduction of general labour service. This problem is in no way met by measures of a purely departmental and administrative character. It touches the very foundations of economic life and the social structure. It finds itself in conflict with the most powerful psychological habits and prejudices. The introduction of compulsory labour service presupposes, on the one hand, a colossal work of education, and, on the other, the greatest possible care in the practical method adopted.

'The utilization of labour-power must be to the last degree economical. In our labour mobilizations we have to reckon with the economic and social conditions of every region, and with the requirements of the principal occupation of the local population – i.e., of agriculture. We have, if possible, to make use of the previous auxiliary occupations and part-time industries of the local population. We have to see that the transference of mobilized labour-power should take place over the shortest possible distances – i.e., to the nearest sectors of the labour front. We must see that the number of workers mobilized corresponds to the breadth of our economic problem. We must see that the workers mobilized be supplied in good time with the necessary implements of production, and with food. We must see that at their head be placed experienced and businesslike instructors. We must see that the workers mobilized become convinced on the spot that their labour-power is being made use of cautiously and economically and is not being expended haphazardly. Wherever it is possible, direct mobilization must be replaced by the labour task – i.e., by the imposition on the rural district of an obligation to supply, for example, in such a time such a number of cubic *sazhens* of wood, or to bring up by carting to such a station so many *poods* of cast iron, etc. In this sphere, it is essential to study experience as it accumulates with particular care, to allow a great measure of elasticity to the economic apparatus, to show more attention to local interests and social peculiarities of tradition. In a word, we have to complete, ameliorate, perfect, the system, methods and organs for the mobilization of labour-power. But at the same time it is necessary once and for all to make clear to ourselves that the principle itself of compulsory labour service has just so radically and permanently replaced the principle of free hiring as the socialization of the means of production has replaced capitalist property.

THE MILITARIZATION OF LABOUR

'The introduction of compulsory labour service is unthinkable without the application, to a greater or less degree, of the methods of militarization of labour. This term at once brings us into the region of the greatest possible superstitions and outcries from the opposition.

'To understand what militarization of labour in the workers' state means, and what its methods are, one has to make clear to oneself in what way the army itself was militarized – for, as we all know, in its first days the army did not at all possess the necessary 'military' qualities. During these two years we mobilized for the Red Army nearly as many soldiers as there are members in our trade unions. But the members of the trade unions are workers, while in the army the workers constitute about 15 per cent, the remainder being a peasant mass. And, nonetheless, we can have no doubt that the true builder and 'militarizer' of the Red Army has been the foremost worker, pushed forward by the party and the trade union organization. Whenever the situation at the front was difficult, whenever the recently mobilized peasant mass did not display sufficient stability, we turned on the one hand to the Central Committee of the Communist Party, and on the other to the All-Russian Council of Trade Unions. From both these sources the foremost workers were sent to the front, and there built the Red Army after their own likeness and image – educating, hardening and militarizing the peasant mass.

'This fact must be kept in mind today with all possible clearness because it throws the best possible light on the meaning of militarization in the workers' and peasants' state. The militarization of labour has more than once been put forward as a watchword and realized in separate branches of economic life in the bourgeois countries, both in the West and in Russia under tsarism. But our militarization is distinguished from those experiments by its aims and methods, just as much as the class-conscious proletariat organized for emancipation is distinguished from the class-conscious bourgeoisie organized for exploitation.

'From the confusion, semi-unconscious and semi-deliberate, of two different historical forms of militarization – the proletarian or socialist and the bourgeois – there spring the greater part of the prejudices, mistakes, protests and outcries on this subject. It is on such a confusion of meanings that the whole position of the Mensheviks, our Russian Kautskys, is founded, as it was expressed in their theoretical resolution moved at the present Congress of Trade Unions.

'The Mensheviks attacked not only the militarization of labour, but general labour service also. They reject these methods as 'compulsory'. They preach that general labour service means a low productivity of labour, while militarization means senseless scattering of labour-power.

'"Compulsory labour always is unproductive labour" – such is the exact phrase in the Menshevik resolution. This affirmation brings us right up to the very essence of the question. For, as we see, the question is not at all whether it is wise or unwise to proclaim this or that factory militarized, or whether it is helpful or otherwise to give the military revolutionary tribunal powers to punish corrupt workers who steal materials and instruments, so precious to us, or who sabotage their work. No, the Mensheviks have gone much further into the question. Affirming that compulsory labour is always unproductive, they thereby attempt to cut the ground from under the feet of our economic reconstruction in the present transitional epoch. For it is beyond question that to step from bourgeois anarchy to socialist economy without a revolutionary dictatorship, and without compulsory forms of economic organization, is impossible.

'In the first paragraph of the Menshevik resolution we are told that we are living in the period of transition from the capitalist method of production to the socialist. What does this mean? And, first of all, whence does this come? Since what time has this been admitted by our Kautskians? They accused us – and this formed the foundation of our differences – of socialist utopianism; they declared – and this constituted the essence of their political teaching – that there can be no talk about the transition to socialism in our epoch, and that our revolution is a bourgeois revolution, and that we Communists are only destroying capitalist economy, and that we are not leading the country forward but are throwing it back. This was the root difference – the most profound, the most irreconcilable – from which all the others followed. Now the Mensheviks tell us incidentally, in the introductory paragraph of their resolution, as something that does not require proof, that we are in the period of transition from capitalism to socialism. And this quite unexpected admission, which, one might think, is extremely like a complete capitulation, is made the more lightly and carelessly that, as the whole resolution shows, it imposes no revolutionary obligations on the Mensheviks. They remain entirely captive to the bourgeois ideology. After recognizing that we are on the road to socialism, the Mensheviks with all the greater ferocity attack those methods without which, in the harsh and difficult conditions of the present day, the transition to socialism cannot be accomplished.

'Compulsory labour, we are told, is always unproductive. We ask what does compulsory labour mean here, that is, to what kind of labour is it opposed? Obviously, to free labour. What are we to understand, in that case, by free labour? That phrase was formulated by the progressive philosophers of the bourgeoisie, in the struggle against unfree, i.e., against the serf labour of peasants, and against the standardized and regulated labour of the craft guilds. Free labour meant labour which might be 'freely' bought in the market; freedom was reduced to a legal fiction, on the basis of freely hired slavery. We know of no other form of free labour in history. Let the very few representatives of the Mensheviks at this congress explain to us what they mean by free, non-compulsory labour, if not the market of labour-power.

'History has known slave labour. History has known serf labour. History has known the regulated labour of the medieval craft guilds. Throughout the world there now prevails hired labour, which the yellow journalists of all countries oppose, as the highest possible form of liberty, to Soviet 'slavery'. We, on the other hand, oppose capitalist slavery by socially regulated labour on the basis of an economic plan, obligatory for the whole people and consequently compulsory for each worker in the country. Without this we cannot even dream of a transition to socialism. The element of material, physical, compulsion may be greater or less; that depends on many conditions – on the degree of wealth or poverty of the country, on the heritage of the past, on the general level of culture, on the condition of transport, on the admin-istrative apparatus, etc., etc. But obligation, and, consequently, compul-sion, are essential conditions in order to bind down the bourgeois anarchy, to secure socialization of the means of production and labour, and to reconstruct economic life on the basis of a single plan.

'For the liberal, freedom in the long run means the market. Can or cannot the capitalist buy labour-power at a moderate price – that is for him the sole measure of the freedom of labour. That measure is false, not only in relation to the future but also in connection with the past.

'It would be absurd to imagine that, during the time of bondage-right, work was carried entirely under the stick of physical compulsion, as if an overseer stood with a whip behind the back of every peasant. Medieval forms of economic life grew up out of definite conditions of production, and created definite forms of social life, with which the peasant grew accustomed, and which he at certain periods considered just, or at any rate unalterable. Whenever he, under the influence of a change in material conditions, displayed hostility, the State descended upon him with its material force, thereby displaying the compulsory character of the organization of labour.

'The foundations of the militarization of labour are those forms of state compulsion without which the replacement of capitalist economy by the socialist will forever remain an empty sound. Why do we speak of militarization? Of course, this is only an analogy – but an analogy very rich in content. No social organization except the army has ever considered itself justified in subordinating citizens to itself in such a measure, and to control them by its will on all sides to such a degree, as the state of the proletarian dictatorship considers itself justified in doing, and does. Only the army – just because in its way it used to decide questions of the life or death of nations, states, and ruling classes – was endowed with powers of demanding from each and all complete submission to its problems, aims, regulations and orders. And it achieved this to the greater degree, the more the problems of military organization coincided with the requirements of social development.

'The question of the life or death of Soviet Russia is at present being settled on the labour front; our economic, and together with them our professional and productive organizations, have the right to demand from their members all that devotion, discipline, and executive thoroughness, which hitherto only the army required.

'On the other hand, the relation of the capitalist to the worker is not at all founded merely on the "free" contract, but includes the very powerful elements of state regulation and material compulsion.

'The competition of capitalist with capitalist imparted a certain very limited reality to the fiction of freedom of labour; but this competition, reduced to a minimum by trusts and syndicates, we have finally eliminated by destroying private property in the means of production. The transition to socialism, verbally acknowledged by the Mensheviks, means the transition from anarchical distribution of labour-power – by means of the game of buying and selling, the movement of market prices and wages – to systematic distribution of the workers by the economic organizations of the region, the province and the whole country. Such a form of planned distribution presupposes the subordination of those distributed to the economic plan of the state. And this is the essence of compulsory labour service, which inevitably enters into the programme of the socialist organization of labour, as its fundamental element.

'If organized economic life is unthinkable without compulsory labour service, the latter is not to be realized without the abolition of the fiction of the freedom of labour, and without the substitution for it of the obligatory principle, which is supplemented by real compulsion.

'That free labour is more productive than compulsory labour is quite true when it refers to the period of transition from feudal society to bourgeois society. But one needs to be a liberal or – at the present day – a Kautskian, to make that truth permanent, and to transfer its application to the period of transition from the bourgeois to the socialist order. If it were true that compulsory labour is unproductive always and under every condition, as the Menshevik resolution says, all our constructive work would be doomed to failure. For we can have no way to socialism except by the authoritative regulation of the economic forces and resources of the country, and the centralized distribution of labour-power in harmony with the general state plan. The labour state considers itself empowered to send every worker to the place where his work is necessary. And not one serious socialist will begin to deny to the labour state the right to lay its hand upon the worker who refuses to execute his labour duty. But the whole point is that the Menshevik path of transition to 'socialism' is a milky way, without the bread monopoly, without the abolition of the market, without the revolutionary dictatorship, and without the militarization of labour.

'Without general labour service, without the right to order and demand fulfilment of orders, the trade unions will be transformed into a mere form without a reality; for the young socialist state requires trade unions, not for a struggle for better conditions of labour – that is the task of the social and state organizations as a whole – but to organize the working class for the ends of production, to educate, discipline, distribute, group, retain certain categories and certain workers at their posts for fixed periods – in a word, hand in hand with the state to exercise their authority in order to lead the workers into the framework of a single economic plan. To defend, under such conditions, the 'freedom' of labour means to defend fruitless, helpless, absolutely unregulated searches for better conditions, unsystematic, chaotic changes from factory to factory, in a hungry country, in conditions of terrible disorganization of the transport and food apparatus . . . What except the complete collapse of the working class and complete economic anarchy could be the result of the stupid attempt to reconcile bourgeois freedom of labour with proletarian socialization of the means of production?

'Consequently, Comrades, militarization of labour, in the root sense indicated by me, is not the invention of individual politicians or an invention of our War Department, but represents the inevitable method of organization and disciplining of labour-power during the period of transition from capitalism to socialism. And if the compulsory distribution of labour-power, its brief or prolonged retention at particular industries and factories, its regulation within the framework of the general state economic plan – if these forms of compulsion lead always and everywhere, as the Menshevik resolution states, to the lowering of productivity, then you can erect a monument over the grave of socialism. For we cannot build socialism on decreased production. Every social organization is in its foundation an organization of labour, and if our new organization of labour leads to a lowering of its productivity, it thereby most fatally leads to the destruction of the socialist society we are building, whichever way we twist and turn, whatever measures of salvation we invent.

'That is why I stated at the very beginning that the Menshevik argument against militarization leads us to the root question of general labour service and its influence on the productivity of labour. Is it true that compulsory labour is always unproductive? We have to reply that that is the most pitiful and worthless liberal prejudice. The whole question is: Who applies the principle of compulsion, over whom, and for what purpose? What state, what class, in what conditions, by what methods? Even the serf organization was in certain conditions a step forward, and led to the increase in the productivity of labour. Production has grown enormously under capitalism, that is, in the epoch of the free buying and selling of labour-power on the market. But free labour, together with the whole of capitalism, entered the stage of imperialism and blew itself up in the imperialist war. The whole economic life of the world entered a period of bloody anarchy, monstrous perturbations, the impoverishment, dying out, and destruction of masses of the people. Can we, under such conditions, talk about the productivity of free labour, when the fruits of that labour are destroyed ten times more quickly than they are created? The imperialistic war, and that which followed it, displayed the impossibility of society existing any longer on the foundation of free labour. Or perhaps someone possesses the secret of how to separate free labour from the delirium tremens of imperialism, that is, of turning back the clock of social development half a century or a century?

'If it were to turn out that the planned, and consequently compulsory, organization of labour which is arising to replace imperialism led to the lowering of economic life, it would mean the destruction of all our culture, and a retrograde movement of humanity back to barbarism and savagery.

'Happily, not only for Soviet Russia but for the whole of humanity, the philosophy of the low productivity of compulsory labour – "everywhere and under all conditions" – is only a belated echo of ancient liberal melodies. The productivity of labour is the total productive meaning of the most complex combination of social conditions, and is not in the least measured or predetermined by the legal form of labour.

'The whole of human history is the history of the organization and education of collective man for labour, with the object of attaining a higher level of productivity. Man, as I have already permitted myself to point out, is lazy; that is, he instinctively strives to receive the largest possible quantity of products for the least possible expenditure of energy. Without such a striving, there would have been no economic development. The growth of civilization is measured by the productivity of human labour, and each new form of social relations must pass through a test on such lines.

'"Free", that is, freely hired labour, did not appear all at once upon the world, with all the attributes of productivity. It acquired a high level of productivity only gradually, as a result of a prolonged application of methods of labour organization and labour education. Into that education there entered the most varying methods and practices, which in addition changed from one epoch to another. First of all the bourgeoisie drove the peasant from the village to the high road with its club, having preliminarily robbed him of his land, and when he would not work in the factory it branded his forehead with red-hot irons, hung him, sent him to the gallows; and in the long run it taught the tramp who had been shaken out of his village to stand at the lathe in the factory. At this stage, as we see, "free" labour is little different as yet from convict labour, both in its material conditions and in its legal aspect.

'At different times the bourgeoisie combined the red-hot irons of repression in different proportions with methods of moral influence, and, first of all, the teaching of the priest. As early as the sixteenth century, it reformed the old religion of Catholicism, which defended the feudal order, and adapted for itself a new religion in the form of the Reformation, which combined the free soul with free trade and free labour. It found for itself new priests, who became the spiritual shop assistants, pious counter-jumpers of the bourgeoisie. The school, the press, the marketplace and parliament were adapted by the bourgeoisie for the moral fashioning of the working class. Different forms of wages – day-wages, piece wages, contract and collective bargaining – all these are merely changing methods in the hands of the bourgeoisie for the labour mobilization of the proletariat. To this there are added all sorts of forms for encouraging labour and exciting ambition. Finally, the bourgeoisie learned how to gain possession even of the trade unions – i.e., the organizations of the working class itself; and it made use of them on a large scale, particularly in Great Britain, to discipline the workers. It domesticated the leaders, and with their help inoculated the workers with the fiction of the necessity for peaceful organic labour, for a faultless attitude to their duties, and for a strict execution of the laws of the bourgeois state. The crown of all this work is Taylorism, in which the elements of the scientific organization of the process of production are combined with the most concentrated methods of the system of sweating.

'From all that has been said above, it is clear that the productivity of freely hired labour is not something that appeared all at once, perfected, presented by history on a salver. No, it was the result of a long and stubborn policy of repression, education, organization and encouragement, applied by the bourgeoisie in its relations with the working class. Step by step it learned to squeeze out of the workers ever more and more of the products of labour; and one of the most powerful weapons in its hand turned out to be the proclamation of free hiring as the sole free, normal, healthy, productive and saving form of labour.

'A legal form of labour which would of its own virtue guarantee its productivity has not been known in history, and cannot be known. The legal superstructure of labour corresponds to the relations and current ideas of the epoch. The productivity of labour is developed, on the basis of the development of technical forces, by labour education, by the gradual adaptation of the workers to the changed methods of reduction and the new form of social relations.

'The creation of socialist society means the organization of the workers on new foundations, their adaptation to those foundations, and their labour re-education, with the one unchanging end of the increase in the productivity of labour. The working class, under the leadership of its vanguard, must itself re-educate itself on the foundations of socialism. Whoever has not understood this is ignorant of the ABC of socialist construction.

'What methods have we, then, for the re-education of the workers? Infinitely wider methods than the bourgeoisie has – and, in addition, honest, direct, open methods, infected neither by hypocrisy nor by lies. The bourgeoisie had to have recourse to deception, representing its labour as free, when in reality it was not merely socially imposed, but actually slave labour. For it was the labour of the majority in the interests of the minority. We, on the other hand, organize labour in the interests of the workers themselves, and therefore we can have no motives for hiding or masking the socially compulsory character of our labour organization. We need the fairy stories neither of the priests, nor of the liberals, nor of the Kautskians. We say directly and openly to the masses that they can save, rebuild and bring to a flourishing condition a socialist country only by means of hard work, unquestioning discipline and exactness in execution on the part of every worker.

'The chief of our resources is moral influence – propaganda not only in word but in deed. General labour service has an obligatory character; but this does not mean at all that it represents violence done to the working class. If compulsory labour came up against the opposition of the majority of the workers it would turn out a broken reed, and with it the whole of the Soviet order. The militarization of labour, when the workers are opposed to it, is the state slavery of Arakeheyev. The militarization of labour by the will of the workers themselves is the socialist dictatorship. That compulsory labour service and the militarization of labour do not force the will of the workers, as 'free' labour used to do, is best shown by the flourishing, unprecedented in the history of humanity, of labour voluntarism in the form of *Subbotniks* (Communist Saturdays). Such a phenomenon there never was before, anywhere or at any time. By their own voluntary labour, freely given – once a week and oftener – the workers clearly demonstrate not only their readiness to bear the yoke of 'compulsory' labour but their eagerness to give the state besides that a certain quantity of additional labour. The *Subbotniks* are not only a splendid demonstration of Communist solidarity, but also the best possible guarantee for the successful introduction of general labour service. Such truly communist tendencies must be shown up in their true light, extended, and developed with the help of propaganda.

'The chief spiritual weapon of the bourgeoisie is religion; ours is the open explanation to the masses of the exact position of things, the extension of scientific and technical knowledge, and the initiation of the masses into the general economic plan of the state, on the basis of which there must be brought to bear all the labour-power at the disposal of the Soviet regime.

'Political economy provided us with the principal substance of our agitation in the period we have just left: the capitalist social order was a riddle, and we explained that riddle to the masses. Today, social riddles are explained to the masses by the very mechanism of the Soviet order, which draws the masses into all branches of administration. Political economy will more and more pass into the realms of history. There move forward into the foreground the sciences which study nature and the methods of subordinating it to man.

'The trade unions must organize scientific and technical educational work on the widest possible scale, so that every worker in his own branch of industry should find the impulses for theoretical work of the brain, while the latter should again return him to labour, perfecting it and making him more productive. The press as a whole must fall into line with the economic problems of the country – not in that sense alone in which this is being done at present – i.e., not in the sense of a mere general agitation in favour of a revival of labour – but in the sense of the discussion and the weighing of concrete economic problems and plans, ways and means of their solution, and, most important of all, the testing and criticism of results already achieved. The newspapers must from day to day follow the production of the most important factories and other enterprises, registering their successes and failures encouraging some and pillorying others . . .

'Russian capitalism, in consequence of its lateness, its lack of independence, and its resulting parasitic features, has had much less time than European capitalism technically to educate the labouring masses, to train and discipline them for production. That problem is now in its entirety imposed upon the industrial organizations of the proletariat. A good engineer, a good mechanic and a good carpenter must have in the Soviet Republic the same publicity and fame as hitherto was enjoyed by prominent agitators, revolutionary fighters and, in the most recent period, the most courageous and capable commanders and commissars. Greater and lesser leaders of technical development must occupy the central position in the public eye. Bad workers must be made ashamed of doing their work badly.

'We still retain, and for a long time will retain, the system of wages. The further we go, the more will its importance become simply to guarantee to all members of society all the necessaries of life; and thereby it will cease to be a system of wages. But at present we are not sufficiently rich for this. Our main problem is to raise the quantity of products turned out, and to this problem all the remainder must be subordinated. In the present difficult period the system of wages is for us, first and foremost, not a method for guaranteeing the personal existence of any separate worker, but a method of estimating what that individual worker brings by his labour to the labour republic.

'Consequently, wages, in the form both of money and of goods, must be brought into the closest possible touch with the productivity of individual labour. Under capitalism, the system of piecework and of grading, the application of the Taylor system, etc., have as their object to increase the exploitation of the workers by the squeezing-out of surplus-value. Under socialist production, piecework, bonuses, etc., have as their problem to increase the volume of social product, and consequently to raise the general well-being. Those workers who do more for the general interest than others receive the right to a greater quantity of the social product than the lazy, the careless and the disorganizers.

'Finally, when it rewards some, the labour state cannot but punish others – those who are clearly infringing labour solidarity, undermining the common work, and seriously impairing the socialist renaissance of the country. Repression for the attainment of economic ends is a necessary weapon of the socialist dictatorship.

'All the measures enumerated above – and together with them a number of others – must assist the development of rivalry in the sphere of production. Without this we shall never rise above the average, which is a very unsatisfactory level. At the bottom of rivalry lies the vital instinct – the struggle for existence – which in the bourgeois order assumes the character of competition. Rivalry will not disappear even in the developed socialist society; but with the growing guarantee of the necessary requirements of life rivalry will acquire an ever less selfish and purely idealist character. It will express itself in a striving to perform the greatest possible service for one's village, region, town, or the whole of society, and to receive in return renown, gratitude, sympathy, or, finally, just internal satisfaction from the consciousness of work well done. But in the difficult period of transition, in conditions of the extreme shortage of material goods, and the as yet insufficiently developed state of social solidarity, rivalry must inevitably be to a greater or less degree bound up with a striving to guarantee for oneself one's own requirements.

'This, Comrades, is the sum of resources at the disposal of the labour state in order to raise the productivity of labour. As we see, there is no ready-made solution here. We shall find it written in no book. For there could not be such a book. We are now only beginning, together with you, to write that book in the sweat and the blood of the workers. We say: Working Men and Women, you have crossed to the path of regulated labour. Only along that road will you build the socialist society. Before you there lies a problem which no one will settle for you: the problem of increasing production on new social foundations. Unless you solve that problem, you will perish. If you solve it, you will raise humanity by a whole head.

LABOUR ARMIES

'The question of the application of armies to labour purposes, which has acquired amongst us an enormous importance from the point of view of principle, was approached by us by the path of practice, not at all on the foundations of theoretical consideration. On certain borders of Soviet Russia, circumstances had arisen which had left considerable military forces free for an indefinite period. To transfer them to other active fronts, especially in the winter, was difficult in consequence of the disorder of railway transport. Such, for example, proved the position of the Third Army, distributed over the provinces of the Urals and the Ural area. The leading workers of that army, understanding that as yet it could not be demobilized, themselves raised the question of its transference to labour work. They sent to the centre a more or less worked-out draft decree for a labour army.

'The problem was novel and difficult. Would the Red soldiers work? Would their work be sufficiently productive? Would it pay for itself? In this connection there were doubts even in our own ranks. Needless to say, the Mensheviks struck up a chorus of opposition. The same Abramovich, at the Congress of Economic Councils called in January or the beginning of February – that is to say, when the whole affair was still in draft stage – foretold that we should suffer an inevitable failure, for the whole undertaking was senseless, an Arakcheev utopia, etc., etc. We considered the matter otherwise. Of course the difficulties were great, but they were not distinguishable in principle from many other difficulties of Soviet constructive work.

'Let us consider in fact what was the organism of the Third Army. Taken all in all, one rifle division and one cavalry division – a total of fifteen regiments – and, in addition, special units. The remaining military formations had already been transformed to other armies and fronts. But the apparatus of military administration had remained untouched as yet, and we considered it probable that in the spring we should have to transfer it along the Volga to the Caucasus front, against Denikin, if by that time he were not finally broken. On the whole, in the Third Army there remained about 120,000 Red soldiers in administrative posts, institutions, military units, hospitals, etc. In this general mass, mainly peasant in its composition, there were reckoned about 16,000 Communists and members of the organization of sympathizers – to a considerable extent workers of the Urals. In this way, in its composition and structure, the Third Army represented a peasant mass bound together into a military organization under the leadership of the foremost workers. In the army there worked a considerable number of military specialists, who carried out important military functions while remaining under the general control of the Communists. If we consider the Third Army from this general point of view, we shall see that it represents in miniature the whole of Soviet Russia. Whether we take the Red Army as a whole, or the organization of the Soviet regime in the region, province, or the whole Republic, including the economic organs, we shall find everywhere the same scheme of organization: millions of peasants drawn into new forms of political, economic and social life by the organized workers, who occupy a controlling position in all spheres of Soviet construction. To posts requiring special knowledge, we send experts of the bourgeois school. They are given the necessary independence, but control over their work remains in the hands of the working class, in the person of its Communist Party. The introduction of general labour service is again only conceivable for us as the mobilization of mainly peasant labour-power under the guidance of the most advanced workers. In this way there were not, and could not be, any obstacles in principle in the way of application of the army to labour. In other words, the opposition in principle to labour armies, on the part of those same Mensheviks, was in reality opposition to "compulsory" labour generally, and consequently against general labour service and against Soviet methods of economic reconstruction as a whole. This opposition did not trouble us a great deal.

'Naturally, the military apparatus as such is not adapted directly to the process of labour. But we had no illusions about that. Control had to remain in the hands of the appropriate economic organs; the army supplied the necessary labour-power in the form of organized, compact units, suitable in the mass for the execution of the simplest homogeneous types of work: the freeing of roads from snow, the storage of fuel, building work, organization of cartage, etc., etc.

'Today we have already had considerable experience in the work of the labour application of the army, and can give not merely a preliminary or hypothetical estimate. What are the conclusions to be drawn from that experience? The Mensheviks have hastened to draw them. The same Abramovich, again, announced at the Miners' Congress that we had become bankrupt, that the labour armies represent parasitic formations, in which there are a hundred officials for every ten workers. Is this true? No. This is the irresponsible and malignant criticism of men who stand on one side, do not know the facts, collect only fragments and rubbish, and are concerned in any way and every way either to declare our bankruptcy or to prophesy it. In reality, the labour armies have not only not gone bankrupt, but, on the contrary, have had important successes, have displayed their fidelity, are developing and are becoming stronger and stronger. Just those prophets have gone bankrupt who foretold that nothing would come of the whole plan, that nobody would begin to work, and that the Red soldiers would not go to the labour front but would simply scatter to their homes.

'These criticisms were dictated by a philistine scepticism, lack of faith in the masses, lack of faith in bold initiative and organization. But did we not hear exactly the same criticism, at bottom, when we had recourse to extensive mobilizations for military problems? Then too we were frightened, we were terrified by stories of mass desertion, which was absolutely inevitable, it was alleged, after the imperialist war. Naturally, desertion there was, but considered by the test of experience it proved not at all on such a mass scale as was foretold; it did not destroy the army; the bond of morale and organization – Communist voluntarism and state compulsion combined – allowed us to carry out mobilizations of millions to carry through numerous formations and redistributions, and to solve the most difficult military problems. In the long run, the army was victorious. In relation to labour problems, on the foundation of our military experience, we awaited the same results; and we were not mistaken. The Red soldiers did not scatter when they were transformed from military to labour service, as the sceptics prophesied. Thanks to our splendidly organized agitation, the transference itself took place amidst great enthusiasm. True, a certain portion of the soldiers tried to leave the army, but this always happens when a large military formation is transferred from one front to another, or is sent from the rear to the front – in general when it is shaken up – and when potential desertion becomes active. But immediately the political sections, the press, the organs of struggle with desertion, etc., entered into their rights; and today the percentage of deserters from our labour armies is in no way higher than in our armies on active service.

'The statement that the armies in view of their internal structure can produce only a small percentage of workers is true only to a certain extent. As far as the Third Army is concerned, I have already pointed out that it retained its complete apparatus of administration side by side with an extremely insignificant number of military units. While we – owing to military and not economic considerations – retained untouched the staff of the army and its administrative apparatus, the percentage of workers produced by the army was actually extremely low. From the general number of 120,000 Red soldiers, 21 per cent proved to be employed in administrative and economic work; 16 per cent were engaged in daily detail work (guards etc.) in connection with the large number of army institutions and stores; the number of sick, mainly typhus cases, together with the medico–sanitary personnel, was about 13 per cent; about 25 per cent were not available for various reasons (detachment, leave, absence without leave, etc.). In this way, the total personnel available for work constitutes no more than 23 per cent; this is the maximum of what can be drawn for labour from the given army. Actually, at first, there worked only about 14 per cent, mainly drawn from the two divisions, rifle and cavalry, which still remained with the army.

'But as soon as it was clear that Denikin had been crushed, and that we should not have to send the Third Army down the Volga in the spring to assist the forces on the Caucasus front, we immediately entered upon the disbanding of the clumsy army apparatus and a more regular adaptation of the army institutions to problems of labour. Although this work is not yet complete, it has already had time to give some very significant results. At the present moment (March 1920), the former Third Army gives about 38 per cent of its total composition as workers. As for the military units of the Ural military area working side by side with it, they already provide 49 per cent of their number as workers. This result is not so bad, if we compare it with the amount of work done in factories and workshops, amongst which in the case of many quite recently, in the case of some even today, absence from work for legal and illegal reasons reached 50 per cent and over.[1] To this one must add that workers in factories and workshops are not infrequently assisted by the adult members of their family, while the Red soldiers have no auxiliary force but themselves.

'If we take the case of the nineteen-year-olds, who have been mobilized in the Ural with the help of the military apparatus − principally for wood-fuel work − we shall find that, out of their general number of over 30,000, over 75 per cent attend work. This is already a very great step forward. It shows that, using the military apparatus for mobilization and formation, we can introduce such alterations in the construction of purely labour units as guarantee an enormous increase in the percentage of those who participate directly in the material process of production.

'Finally, in connection with the productivity of military labour, we can also now judge on the basis of experience. During the first days, the productivity of labour in the principal departments of work, in spite of the great moral enthusiasm, was in reality very low, and might seem completely discouraging when one read the first labour communiqués. Thus, for the preparation of a cubic *sazhen* of wood, at first, one had to reckon thirteen to fifteen labour days; whereas the standard − true, rarely attained at the present day − is reckoned at three days. One must add, in addition, that artistes in this sphere are capable, under favourable conditions, of producing one cubic *sazhen* per day per man. What happened in reality? The military units were quartered far from the forest to be felled. In many cases it was necessary to march to and from work six to eight *versts*, which swallowed up a considerable portion of the working day. There were not sufficient axes and saws on the spot. Many Red soldiers, born in the plains, did not know the forests, had never felled trees, had never chopped or sawed them up. The provincial and region Timber Committees were very far from knowing at first how to use the military units, how to direct them where they were required, how to equip them as they should be equipped. It is not wonderful that all this had as its result an extremely low level of productivity. But after the most crying defects in organization were eliminated, results were achieved that were much more satisfactory. Thus, according to the most recent data, in that same First Labour Army, four and a half working days are now devoted to one *sazhen* of wood, which is not so far from the present standard. What is most comforting, however, is the fact that the productivity of labour systematically increases, in the measure of the improvement of its conditions.

'While as to what can be achieved in this respect, we have a brief but very rich experience in the Moscow Engineer Regiment. The Chief Board of Military Engineers, which controlled this experiment, began with fixing the standard of production as three working days for a cubic *sazhen* of wood. This standard soon proved to be surpassed. In January there were spent on a cubic *sazhen* of wood two and one-third working days; in February, 2.1; in March, 1.5; which represents an exclusively high level of productivity. This result was achieved by moral influence, by the exact registration of the individual work of each man, by the awakening of labour pride, by the distribution of bonuses to the workers who produced more than the average result – or, to speak in the language of the trade unions, by a sliding scale adaptable to all individual changes in the productivity of labour. This experiment, carried out almost under laboratory conditions, clearly indicates the path along which we have to go in future.

'At present we have functioning a series of labour armies – the First, the Petrograd, the Ukrainian, the Caucasian, the South Volga, the Reserve. The latter, as is known, assisted considerably to raise the traffic capacity of the Kazan–Ekaterinburg railway; and, wherever the experiment of the adaptation of military units for labour problems was carried out with any intelligence at all, the results showed that this method is unquestionably live and correct.

'The prejudice concerning the inevitably parasitic nature of military organization – under each and every condition – proves to be shattered. The Soviet army reproduces within itself the tendencies of the Soviet social order. We must not think in the petrifying terms of the last epoch: "militarism", "military organization", "the unproductiveness of compulsory labour". We must approach the phenomena of the new epoch without any prejudices, and with eyes wide open; and we must remember that Saturday exists for man, and not vice versa; that all forms of organization, including the military, are only weapons in the hands of the working class in power, which has both the right and the possibility of adapting, altering, refashioning, those weapons, until it has achieved the requisite result.

THE SINGLE ECONOMIC PLAN

'The widest possible application of the principle of general labour service, together with measures for the militarization of labour, can play a decisive part only in case they are applied on the basis of a single economic plan covering the whole country and all branches of productive activity. This plan must be drawn up for a number of years, for the whole epoch that lies before us. It is naturally broken up into separate periods or stages, corresponding to the inevitable stages in the economic rebirth of the country. We shall have to begin with the most simple and at the same time most fundamental problems.

'We have first of all to afford the working class the very possibility of living – though it be in the most difficult conditions – and thereby to preserve our industrial centres and save the towns. This is the point of departure. If we do not wish to melt the town into agriculture, and transform the whole country into a peasant state, we must support our transport, even at the minimum level, and secure bread for the towns, fuel and raw materials for industry, fodder for the cattle. Without this we shall not make one step forward. Consequently, the first part of the plan comprises the improvement of transport, or, in any case, the prevention of its further deterioration and the preparation of the most necessary supplies of food, raw materials and fuel. The whole of the next period will be in its entirety filled with the concentration and straining of labour-power to solve these root problems; and only in this way shall we lay the foundations for all that is to come. It was such a problem, incidentally, that we put before our labour armies. Whether the first or the following periods will be measured by months or by years, it is fruitless at present to guess. This depends on many reasons, beginning with the international situation and ending with the degree of single-mindedness and steadfastness of the working class.

'The second period is the period of machine-building in the interests of transport and the storage of raw material and fuel. Here the core is in the locomotive.

'At the present time the repairing of locomotives is carried on in too haphazard a fashion, swallowing up energy and resources beyond all measure. We must reorganize the repairing of our rolling-stock, on the basis of the mass production of spare parts. Today, when the whole network of the railways and the factories is in the hands of one master, the labour state, we can and must fix single types of locomotives and trucks for the whole country, standardize their constituent parts, draw all the necessary factories into the work of the mass production of spare parts, reduce repairing to the simple replacing of worn-out parts by new, and thereby make it possible to build new locomotives on a mass scale out of spare parts.

'Now that the sources of fuel and raw material are again open to us, we must concentrate our exclusive attention on the building of locomotives.

'The third period will be one of machine-building in the interests of the production of articles of primary necessity.

'Finally, the fourth period, reposing on the conquests of the first three, will allow us to begin the production of articles of personal or secondary significance on the widest possible scale.

'This plan has great significance, not only as a general guide for the practical work of our economic organs, but also as a line along which propaganda amongst the labouring masses in connection with our economic problems is to proceed. Our labour mobilization will not enter into real life, will not take root, if we do not excite the living interest of all that is honest, class-conscious and inspired in the working class. We must explain to the masses the whole truth as to our situation and as to our views for the future; we must tell them openly that our economic plan, with the maximum of exertion on the part of the workers, will neither tomorrow nor the day after give us a land flowing with milk and honey: for during the first period our chief work will consist in preparing the conditions for the production of the means of production. Only after we have secured, though on the smallest possible scale, the possibility of rebuilding the means of transport and production, shall we pass on to the production of articles for general consumption. In this way the fruit of their labour, which is the direct object of the workers, in the shape of articles for personal consumption, will arrive only in the last, the fourth, stage of our economic plan; and only then shall we have a serious improvement in our life. The masses, who for a prolonged period will still bear all the weight of labour and of privation, must realize to the full the inevitable internal logic of this economic plan if they are to prove capable of carrying it out.

'The sequence of the four economic periods outlined above must not be understood too absolutely. We do not, of course, propose to bring completely to a standstill our textile industry: we could not do this for military considerations alone. But in order that our attention and our forces should not be distracted under the pressure of requirements and needs crying to us from all quarters, it is essential to make use of the economic plan as the fundamental criterion, and separate the important and the fundamental from the auxiliary and secondary. Needless to say, under no circumstances are we striving for a narrow 'national' communism: the raising of the blockade, and the European revolution all the more, would introduce the most radical alterations in our economic plan, cutting down the stages of its development and bringing them together. But we do not know when these events will take place; and we must act in such a way that we can hold out and become stronger under the most unfavourable circumstances – that is to say, in face of the slowest conceivable development of the European and the world revolution. In case we are able actually to establish trading relations with the capitalist countries, we shall again be guided by the economic plan sketched above. We shall exchange part of our raw material for locomotives or for necessary machines, but under no circumstances for clothing, boots, or colonial products: our first item is not articles of consumption, but the implements of transport and production.

'We should be short-sighted sceptics, and the most typical bourgeois curmudgeons, if we imagined that the rebirth of our economic life will take the form of a gradual transition from the present economic collapse to the conditions that preceded that collapse, i.e., that we shall reascend the same steps by which we descended, and only after a certain, quite prolonged, period will be able to raise our socialist economy to the level at which it stood on the eve of the imperialist war. Such a conception would not only not be consoling; it would be absolutely incorrect. Economic collapse, which destroyed and broke up in its path an incalculable quantity of values, also destroyed a great deal that was poor and rotten, that was absolutely senseless; and thereby it cleared the path for a new method of reconstruction, corresponding to that technical equipment which world economy now possesses.

'If Russian capitalism developed not from stage to stage, but leaping over a series of stages, and instituted American factories in the midst of primitive steppes, the more is such a forced march possible for socialist economy. After we have conquered our terrible misery, have accumulated small supplies of raw material and food, and have improved our transport, we shall be able to leap over a whole series of intermediate stages, benefiting by the fact that we are not bound by the chains of private property, and that therefore we are able to subordinate all undertakings and all the elements of economic life to a single state plan.

'Thus, for example, we shall undoubtedly be able to enter the period of electrification, in all the chief branches of industry and in the sphere of personal consumption, without passing through 'the age of steam'. The programme of electrification is already drawn up in a series of logically consequent stages, corresponding to the fundamental stages of the general economic plan.

'A new war may slow down the realization of our economic intentions; our energy and persistence can and must hasten the process of our economic rebirth. But, whatever be the rate at which economic events unfold themselves in the future, it is clear that at the foundation of all our work – labour mobilization, militarization of labour, *Subbotniks* and other forms of Communist labour voluntarism – there must lie the single economic plan. And the period that is upon us requires from us the complete concentration of all our energies on the first elementary problems: food, fuel, raw material, transport. Not to allow our attention to be distracted, not to dissipate our forces, not to waste our energies. Such is the sole road to salvation.

COLLEGIATE AND ONE-MAN MANAGEMENT

'The Mensheviks attempt to dwell on yet another question which seems favourable to their desire once again to ally themselves with the working class. This is the question of the method of administration of industrial enterprises – the question of the collegiate (board) or the one-man principle. We are told that the transference of factories to single directors instead of to a board is a crime against the working class and the socialist revolution. It is remarkable that the most zealous defenders of the socialist revolution against the principle of one-man management are those same Mensheviks who quite recently still considered that the idea of a socialist revolution was an insult to history and a crime against the working class.

'The first who must plead guilty in the face of the socialist revolution is our party congress, which expressed itself in favour of the principle of one-man management in the administration of industry and, above all, in the lowest grades, in the factories and plants. It would be the greatest possible mistake, however, to consider this decision as a blow to the independence of the working class. The independence of the workers is determined and measured not by whether three workers or one are placed at the head of a factory, but by factors and phenomena of a much more profound character – the construction of the economic organs with the active assistance of the trade unions; the building up of all Soviet organs by means of the Soviet congresses, representing tens of millions of workers; the attraction into the work of administration, or control of administration, of those who are administered. It is in such things that the independence of the working class can be expressed. And if the working class, on the foundation of its existence, comes though its congresses, Soviet party and trade union, to the conclusion that it is better to place one person at the head of a factory, and not a board, it is making a decision dictated by the independence of the working class. It may be correct or incorrect from the point of view of the technique of administration, but it is not imposed upon the proletariat, it is dictated by its own will and pleasure. It would consequently be a most crying error to confuse the question as to the supremacy of the proletariat with the question of boards of workers at the head of factories. The dictatorship of the proletariat is expressed in the abolition of private property in the means of production, in the supremacy over the whole Soviet mechanism of the collective will of the workers, and not at all in the form in which individual economic enterprises are administered.

'Here it is necessary to reply to another accusation directed against the defenders of the one-man principle. Our opponents say: "This is the attempt of the Soviet militarists to transfer their experience in the military sphere to the sphere of economics. Possibly in the army the one-man principle is satisfactory, but it does not suit economical work." Such a criticism is incorrect in every way. It is untrue that in the army we began with the one-man principle: even now we are far from having completely adopted it. It is also untrue that in defence of one-man forms of administration of our economic enterprises with the attraction of experts, we took our stand only on the foundation of our military experience. In reality, in this question we took our stand, and continue to do so on purely Marxist views of the revolutionary problems and creative duties of the proletariat when it has taken power into its own hands. The necessity of making use of technical knowledge and methods accumulated in the past, the necessity of attracting experts and of making use of them on a wide scale, in such a way that our technique should go not backwards but forwards – all this was understood and recognized by us, not only from the very beginning of the revolution, but even long before October. I consider that if the civil war had not plundered our economic organs of all that was strongest, most independent, most endowed with initiative, we should undoubtedly have entered the path of one-man management in the sphere of economic administration much sooner, and much less painfully.

'Some comrades look on the apparatus of industrial administration first and foremost as on a school. This is, of course, absolutely erroneous. The task of administration is to administer. If a man desires and is able to learn administration, let him go to school, to the special courses of instruction: let him go as an assistant, watching and acquiring experience; but a man who is appointed to control a factory is not going to school, but to a responsible post of economic administration. And, even if we look at this question in the limited, and therefore incorrect light of a "school", I will say that when the one-man principle prevails the school is ten times better: because just as you cannot replace one good worker by three immature workers, similarly, having placed a board of three immature workers in a responsible post, you deprive them of the possibility of realizing their own defects. Each looks to the others when decisions are being made, and blames the others when success is not forthcoming.

'That this is not a question of principle for the opponents of the one-man principle is shown best of all by their not demanding the collegiate principle for the actual workshops, jobs and pits. They even say with indignation that only a madman can demand that a board of three or five should manage a workshop. There must be one manager, and one only. Why? If collegiate administration is a "school", why do we not require an elementary school? Why should we not introduce boards into the workshops? And, if the collegiate principle is not a sacred gospel for the workshops, why is it compulsory for the factories?

'Abramovich said here that, as we have few experts – thanks to the Bolsheviks, he repeats after Kautsky – we shall replace them by boards of workers. That is nonsense. No board of persons who do not know the given business can replace one man who knows it. A board of lawyers will not replace one switchman. A board of patients will not replace the doctor. The very idea is incorrect. A board in itself does not give knowledge to the ignorant. It can only hide the ignorance of the ignorant. If a person is appointed to a responsible administrative post, he is under the watch, not only of others but of himself, and sees clearly what he knows and what he does not know. But there is nothing worse than a board of ignorant, badly prepared workers appointed to a purely practical post, demanding expert knowledge. The members of the board are in a state of perpetual panic and mutual dissatisfaction, and by their helplessness introduce hesitation and chaos into all their work. The working class is very deeply interested in raising its capacity for administration, that is, in being educated; but this is attained in the sphere of industry by the periodical report of the administrative body of a factory before the whole factory, and the discussion of the economic plan for the year or for the current month. All the workers who display serious interest in the work of industrial organization are registered by the directors of the undertaking, or by special commissions; are taken through appropriate courses closely bound up with the practical work of the factory itself; and are then appointed, first to less responsible, and then to more responsible posts. In such a way we shall embrace many thousands, and, in the future, tens of thousands. But the question of "threes" and "fives" interests not the labouring masses but the more backward, weaker, less fitted for independent work, section of the Soviet labour bureaucracy. The foremost, intelligent, determined administrator naturally strives to take the factory into his hands as a whole, and to show both to himself and to others that he can carry out his work. While if that administrator is a weakling, who does not stand very steadily on his feet, he attempts to associate another with himself, for in the company of another his own weakness will be unnoticed. In such a collegiate principle there is a very dangerous foundation – the extinction of personal responsibility. If a worker is capable but not experienced, he naturally requires a guide: under his control he will learn, and tomorrow we shall appoint him the foreman of a little factory. That is the way by which he will go forward. In an accidental board, in which the strength and the weakness of each are not clear, the feeling of responsibility inevitably disappears.

'Our resolution speaks of a systematic approach to the one-man principle – naturally, not by one stroke of the pen. Variants and combinations are possible here. Where the worker can manage alone, let us put him in charge of the factory and give him an expert as an assistant. Where there is a good expert, let us put him in charge and give him as assistants two or three of the workers. Finally, where a "board" has in practice shown its capacity for work, let us preserve it. This is the sole serious attitude to take up, and only in such a way shall we reach the correct organization of production.

'There is another consideration of a social and educational character which seems to me most important. Our guiding layer of the working class is too thin. That layer which knew underground work, which long carried on the revolutionary struggle, which was abroad, which read much in prisons and in exile, which had political experience and a broad outlook, is the most precious section of the working class. Then there is a younger generation which has consciously been making the revolution, beginning with 1917. This is a very valuable section of the working class. Wherever we cast our eye – on Soviet construction, on the trade unions, on the front of the civil war – everywhere we find the principal part being played by this upper layer of the proletariat. The chief work of the Soviet government during these two and a half years consisted in manoeuvring and throwing the foremost section of the workers from one front to another. The deeper layers of the working class, which emerged from the peasant mass, are revolutionarily inclined, but are still too poor in initiative. The disease of our Russian peasant is the herd instinct, the absence of personality: in other words, the same quality that used to be extolled by our reactionary populists, and that Leo Tolstoy extolled in the character of Platon Karatayev: the peasant melting into his village community, subjecting himself to the land. It is quite clear that socialist economy is founded not on Platon Karatayev, but on the thinking worker endowed with initiative. That personal initiative it is necessary to develop in the worker. The personal basis under the bourgeoisie meant selfish individualism and competition. The personal basis under the working class is in contradiction neither to solidarity nor to brotherly cooperation. Socialist solidarity can rely neither on absence of personality nor on the herd instinct. And it is just absence of personality that is frequently hidden behind the collegiate principle.

'In the working class there are many forces, gifts and talents. They must be brought out and displayed in rivalry. The one-man principle in the administrative and technical sphere assists this. That is why it is higher and more fruitful than the collegiate principle.

CONCLUSION OF THE REPORT

'Comrades, the arguments of the Menshevik orators, particularly of Abramovich, reflect first of all their complete detachment from life and its problems. An observer stands on the bank of a river which he has to swim over, and deliberates on the qualities of the water and on the strength of the current. He has to swim over: that is his task! But our Kautskian stands first on one foot and then on the other. "We do not deny", he says, "the necessity of swimming over, but at the same time, as realists, we see the danger — and not only one, but several: the current is swift, there are submerged stones, people are tired, etc., etc. But when they tell you that we deny the very necessity of swimming over, that is not true — no, not under any circumstances. Twenty-three years ago we did not deny the necessity of swimming over . . ."

'And on this is built all, from beginning to end. First, say the Mensheviks, we do not deny, and never did deny, the necessity of self-defence, consequently we do not repudiate the army. Secondly, we do not repudiate in principle general labour service. But, after all, where is there anyone in the world, with the exception of small religious sects, who denies self-defence "in principle"! Nevertheless, the matter does not move one step forward as a result of your abstract admission. When it came to a real struggle, and to the creation of a real army against the real enemies of the working class, what did you do then? You opposed, you sabotaged — while not repudiating self-defence in principle. You said and wrote in your papers: "Down with the civil war!" at the time when we were surrounded by White Guards, and the knife was at our throat. Now you, approving our victorious self-defence after the event, transfer your critical gaze to new problems, and attempt to teach us. "In general, we do not repudiate the principle of general labour service," you say, "but . . . without legal compulsion." Yet in these very words there is a monstrous internal contradiction! The idea of "obligatory service" itself includes the element of compulsion. A man is obliged, he is bound to do something. If he does not do it, obviously he will suffer compulsion, a penalty. Here we approach the question of what penalty. Abramovich says: "Economic pressure, yes; but not legal compulsion." Comrade Holtzman, the representative of the Metal Workers' Union, excellently demonstrated all the scholasticism of this idea. Even under capitalism, that is to say under the regime of "free" labour, economic pressure is inseparable from legal compulsion. Still more so now.

'In my report I have attempted to explain that the adaptation of the workers on new social foundations to new forms of labour, and the attainment of a higher level of productivity of labour, are possible only by means of the simultaneous application of various methods – economic interest, legal compulsion, the influence of an internally coordinated economic organization, the power of repression, and, first and last, moral influence, agitation, propaganda, and the general raising of the cultural level,

'Only by the combination of all these methods can we attain a high level of socialist economy.

'If even under capitalism economic interest is inevitably combined with legal compulsion, behind which stands the material force of the state, in the Soviet state – that is, the state of transition to socialism – we can draw no watertight compartment at all between economic and legal compulsion. All our most important industries are in the hands of the state. When we say to the turner Ivanov, "You are bound at once to work at the Sormovo factory; if you refuse, you will not receive your ration," what are we to call it? Economic pressure or legal compulsion? He cannot go to another factory, for all factories are in the hands of the state, which will not allow such a change. Consequently, economic pressure melts here into the pressure of state compulsion. Abramovich apparently would like us, as regulators of the distribution of labour-power, to make use only of such means as the raising of wages, bonuses, etc., in order to attract the necessary workers to our most important factories. Apparently that comprises all his thoughts on the subject. But if we put the question in this way, every serious worker in the trade union movement will understand it is pure utopia. We cannot hope for a free influx of labour-power from the market, for to achieve this the State would need to have in its hands sufficiently extensive "reserves of manoeuvre," in the form of food, housing and transport, i.e., precisely those conditions which we have yet only to create. Without systematically organized transference of labour-power on a mass scale, according to the demands of the economic organization, we shall achieve nothing. Here the moment of compulsion arises before us in all its force of economic necessity. I read you a telegram from Ekaterinburg dealing with the work of the First Labour Army. It says that there have passed through the Ural Committee for Labour Service over 4,000 workers. Whence have they appeared? Mainly from the former Third Army. They were not allowed to go to their homes, but were sent where they were required. From the army they were handed over to the Committee for Labour Service, which distributed them according to their categories and sent them to the factories. This, from the liberal point of view, is "violence" to the freedom of the individual. Yet an overwhelming majority of the workers went willingly to the labour front, as hitherto to the military, realizing that the common interest demanded this. Part went against their will. These were compelled.

'Naturally, it is quite clear that the state must, by means of the bonus system, give the better workers better conditions of existence. But this not only does not exclude, but on the contrary presupposes, that the state and the trade unions without which the Soviet state will not build up industry acquire new rights of some kind over the worker. The worker does not merely bargain with the Soviet state: no, he is subordinated to the Soviet state, under its orders in every direction – for it is his state.

'"If", Abramovich says, "we were simply told that it is a question of industrial discipline, there would be nothing to quarrel about; but why introduce militarization?" Of course, to a considerable extent, the question is one of the discipline of the trade unions; but of the new discipline of new, production-oriented trade unions. We live in a Soviet country, where the working class is in power – a fact which our Kautskians do not understand. When the Menshevik Rubtzov said that there remained only the fragment of the trade union movement in my report, there was a certain amount of truth in it. Of the trade unions, as he understands them – that is to say, trade unions of the old craft type – there in reality has remained very little; but the industrial production-oriented organization of the working class, in the conditions of Soviet Russia, has the very greatest tasks before it. What tasks? Of course not the tasks involved in a struggle with the state, in the name of the interests of labour; but tasks involved in the construction, side by side with the state, of socialist economy. Such a form of union is in principle a new organization, which is distinct, not only from the trade unions, but also from the revolutionary industrial unions in bourgeois society, just as the supremacy of the proletariat is distinct from the supremacy of the bourgeoisie. The production-oriented union of the ruling working class no longer has the problems, the methods, the discipline, of the union for struggle of an oppressed class. All our workers are obliged to enter the unions. The Mensheviks are against this. This is quite comprehensible, because in reality they are against the dictatorship of the proletariat. It is to this, in the long run, that the whole question is reduced. The Kautskians are against the dictatorship of the proletariat, and are thereby against all its consequences. Both economic and political compulsion are only forms of the expression of the dictatorship of the working class in two closely connected regions. True, Abramovich demonstrated to us most learnedly that under socialism there will be no compulsion, that the principle of compulsion contradicts socialism, that under socialism we shall be moved by the feeling of duty, the habit of working, the attractiveness of labour, etc., etc. This is unquestionable. Only this unquestionable truth must be a little extended. In point of fact, under socialism there will not exist the apparatus of compulsion itself, namely, the state: for it will have melted away entirely into a producing and consuming commune. Nonetheless, the road to socialism lies through a period of the highest possible intensification of the principle of the state. And you and I are just passing through that period. Just as a lamp, before going out, shoots up in a brilliant flame, so the state, before disappearing, assumes the form of the dictatorship of the proletariat, i.e., the most ruthless form of state, which embraces the life of the citizens authoritatively in every direction. Now just that insignificant little fact – that historical step of the state dictatorship – Abramovich, and in his person the whole of Menshevism, did not notice; and consequently, he has fallen over it.

'No organization except the army has ever controlled man with such severe compulsion as does the state organization of the working class in the most difficult period of transition. It is just for this reason that we speak of the militarization of labour. The fate of the Mensheviks is to drag along at the tail of events, and to recognize those parts of the revolutionary programme which have already had time to lose all practical significance. Today the Mensheviks, albeit with reservations, do not deny the lawfulness of stern measures with the White Guards and with deserters from the Red Army: they have been forced to recognize this after their own lamentable experiments with "democracy". They have to all appearances understood – very late in the day – that, when one is face to face with the counter-revolutionary bands, one cannot live by phrases about the great truth that under socialism we shall need no Red Terror. But in the economic sphere, the Mensheviks still attempt to refer us to our sons, and particularly to our grandsons. Nonetheless, we have to rebuild our economic life today, without waiting, under circumstances of a very painful heritage from bourgeois society and a yet-unfinished civil war.

'Menshevism, like all Kautskianism generally, is drowned in democratic analogies and socialist abstractions. Again and again it has been shown that for it there do not exist the problems of the transitional period, i.e., of the proletarian revolution. Hence the lifelessness of its criticism, its advice, its plans and its recipes. The question is not what is going to happen in twenty or thirty years' time – at that date, of course, things will be much better – but of how today to struggle out of our ruins, how immediately to distribute labour-power, how today to raise the productivity of labour, and how, in particular, to act in the case of those 4,000 skilled workers whom we combed out of the army in the Ural. To dismiss them to the four corners of the earth, saying "Seek for better conditions where you can find them, Comrades"? No, we could not act in this way. We put them into military echelons, and distributed them amongst the factories and the works.

'"Wherein, then, does your socialism", Abramovich cries, "differ from Egyptian slavery? It was just by similar methods that the pharaohs built the pyramids, forcing the masses to labour." Truly an inimitable analogy for a "socialist"! Once again the little insignificant fact has been forgotten – the class nature of the government! Abramovich sees no difference between the Egyptian regime and our own. He has forgotten that in Egypt there were pharaohs, there were slave-owners and slaves. It was not the Egyptian peasants who decided through their soviets to build the pyramids; there existed a social order based upon hierarchical caste; and the workers were obliged to toil by a class that was hostile to them. Our compulsion is applied by a workers' and peasants' government, in the name of the interests of the labouring masses. That is what Abramovich has not observed. We learn in the school of socialism that all social evolution is founded on classes and their struggle, and all the course of human life is determined by the fact of what class stands at the head of affairs, and in the name of what caste it is applying its policy. That is what Abramovich has not grasped. Perhaps he is well acquainted with the Old Testament, but socialism is for him a book sealed with seven seals.

'Going along the path of shallow liberal analogies, which do not reckon with the class nature of the state, Abramovich might (and in the past the Mensheviks did more than once) identify the Red and the White Armies. Both here and there went on mobilizations, principally of the peasant masses. Both here and there the element of compulsion has its place. Both here and there were not a few officers who had passed through one and the same school of tsarism. The same rifles, the same cartridges in both camps. Where is the difference? There is a difference, Gentlemen, and it is defined by a fundamental test: who is in power? The working class or the landlord class, pharaohs or peasants, White Guards or the Petrograd proletariat? There is a difference, and evidence on the subject is furnished by the fate of Yudenich, Kolchak and Denikin. Our peasants were mobilized by the workers; in Kolchak's camp, by the White Guard officer class. Our army has pulled itself together, and has grown strong; the White Army has fallen asunder in dust. Yes, there is a difference between the Soviet regime and the regime of the pharaohs. And it is not in vain that the Petrograd proletarians began their revolution by shooting the Pharoes on the steeples of Petrograd.[2]

'One of the Menshevik orators attempted incidentally to represent me as a defender of militarism in general. According to his information, it appears, do you see, that I am defending nothing more or less than German militarism. I proved, you must understand, that the German NCO was a marvel of nature, and all that he does is above criticism. What did I say in reality? Only that militarism, in which all the features of social evolution find their most finished, sharp and clear expression, could be examined from two points of view. First from the political or socialist – and here it depends entirely on the question of what class is in power; and second, from the point of view of organization, as a system of the strict distribution of duties, exact mutual relations, unquestioning responsibility and harsh insistence on execution. The bourgeois army is the apparatus of savage oppression and repression of the workers; the socialist army is a weapon for the liberation and defence of the workers. But the unquestioning subordination of the parts to the whole is a characteristic common to every army. A severe internal regime is inseparable from the military organization. In war every piece of slackness, every lack of thoroughness, and even a simple mistake, not infrequently bring in their train the most heavy sacrifices. Hence the striving of the military organization to bring clearness, definiteness, exactness of relations and responsibilities, to the highest degree of development. "Military" qualities in this connection are valued in every sphere. It was in this sense that I said that every class prefers to have in its service those of its members who, other things being equal, have passed through the military school. The German peasant, for example, who has passed out of the barracks in the capacity of an NCO was for the German monarchy, and remains for the Ebert Republic, much dearer and more valuable than the same peasant who has not passed through military training. The apparatus of the German railways was splendidly organized, thanks to a considerable degree to the employment of NCOs and officers in administrative posts in the transport department. In this sense we also have something to learn from militarism. Comrade Tsyperovich, one of our foremost trade union leaders, admitted here that the trade union worker who has passed through military training – who has, for example, occupied the responsible post of regimental commissary for a year – does not become worse from the point of view of trade union work as a result. He is returned to the union the same proletarian from head to foot, for he was fighting for the proletariat; but he has returned a veteran – hardened, more independent, more decisive – for he has been in very responsible positions. He had occasions to control several thousands of Red soldiers of different degrees of class-consciousness – most of them peasants. Together with them he has lived through victories and reverses, he has advanced and retreated. There were cases of treachery on the part of the command personnel, of peasant risings, of panic – but he remained at his post, he held together the less class-conscious mass, directed it, inspired it with his example, punished traitors and cowards. This experience is a great and valuable experience. And when a former regimental commissary returns to his trade union, he becomes not a bad organizer.

'On the question of the collegiate principle, the arguments of

Abramovich are just as lifeless as on all other questions – the arguments of a detached observer standing on the bank of a river.

'Abramovich explained to us that a good board is better than a bad manager, that into a good board there must enter a good expert. All this is splendid – only why do not the Mensheviks offer us several hundred boards? I think that the Supreme Economic Council will find sufficient use for them. But we – not observers, but workers – must build from the material at our disposal. We have specialists, we have experts, of whom, shall we say, one-third are conscientious and educated, another third only half-conscientious and half-educated, and the last third are no use at all. In the working class there are many talented, devoted and energetic people. Some – unfortunately few – have already the necessary knowledge and experience. Some have character and capacity, but have no knowledge or experience. Others have neither one nor the other. Out of this material we have to create our factory and other administrative bodies; and here we cannot be satisfied with general phrases. First of all, we must select all the workers who have already in experience shown that they can direct enterprises, and give such men the possibility of standing on their own feet. Such men themselves ask for one-man management, because the work of controlling a factory is not a school for the backward. A worker who knows his business thoroughly desires to control. If he has decided and ordered, his decision must be accomplished. He may be replaced – that is another matter; but while he is the master, the Soviet, proletarian master, he controls the undertaking entirely and completely. If he has to be included in a board of weaker men, who interfere in the administration, nothing will come of it. Such a working-class administrator must be given an expert assistant, one or two according to the enterprise. If there is no suitable working-class administrator, but there is a conscientious and trained expert, we shall put him at the head of an enterprise, and attach to him two or three prominent workers in the capacity of assistants, in such a way that every decision of the expert should be known to the assistants, but that they should not have the right to reverse that decision. They will, step by step, follow the specialist in his work, will learn something, and in six months or a year will thus be able to occupy independent posts.

'Abramovich quoted from my own speech the example of the hairdresser who has commanded a division and an army. True! But what, however, Abramovich does not know is that, if our Communist comrades have begun to command regiments, divisions and armies, it is because previously they were commissars attached to expert commanders. The responsibility fell on the expert, who knew that, if he made a mistake, he would bear the full brunt, and would not be able to say that he was only an "adviser" or a "member of the board". Today in our army the majority of the posts of command, particularly in the lower – i.e., politically the most important – grades, are filled by workers and foremost peasants. But with what did we begin? We put officers in the posts of command, and attached to them workers as commissars; and they learned, and learned with success, and learned to beat the enemy.

'Comrades, we stand face to face with a very difficult period, perhaps the most difficult of all. To difficult periods in the life of peoples and classes there correspond harsh measures. The further we go the easier things will become, the freer every citizen will feel, the more imperceptible will become the compelling force of the proletarian state. Perhaps we shall then even allow the Mensheviks to have papers, if only the Mensheviks remain in existence until that time. But today we are living in the period of dictatorship, political and economic. And the Mensheviks continue to undermine that dictatorship. When we are fighting on the civil front, preserving the revolution from its enemies, and the Menshevik paper writes: "Down with the civil war", we cannot permit this. A dictatorship is a dictatorship, and war is war. And now that we have crossed to the path of the greatest concentration of forces on the field of the economic rebirth of the country, the Russian Kautskys, the Mensheviks, remain true to their counter-revolutionary calling. Their voice, as hitherto, sounds as the voice of doubt and decomposition, of disorganization and undermining, of distrust and collapse.

'Is it not monstrous and grotesque that, at this congress, at which 1,500 representatives of the Russian working class are present, where the Mensheviks constitute less than 5 per cent, and the Communists about 90 per cent, Abramovich should say to us: "Do not be attracted by methods which result in a little band taking the place of the people." "All through the people", says the representative of the Mensheviks, "no guardians of the labouring masses! All through the labouring masses, through their independent activity!" And, further, "It is impossible to convince a class by arguments." Yet look at this very hall: here is that class! The working class is here before you, and with us; and it is just you, an insignificant band of Mensheviks, who are attempting to convince it by bourgeois arguments! It is you who wish to be the guardians of that class. And yet it has its own high degree of independence, and that independence, it has displayed, incidentally, in having overthrown you and gone forward along its own path!'

KARL KAUTSKY, HIS SCHOOL
AND HIS BOOK

The Austro-Marxist school (Bauer, Renner, Hilferding, Max Adler, Friedrich Adler) in the past more than once was contrasted with the school of Kautsky, as veiled opportunism might be contrasted with true Marxism. This has proved to be a pure historical misunderstanding, which deceived some for a long time, some for a lesser period, but which in the end was revealed with all possible clarity. Kautsky is the founder and the most perfect representative of the Austrian forgery of Marxism. While the real teaching of Marx is the theoretical formula of action, of attack, of the development of revolutionary energy, and of the carrying of the class blow to its logical conclusion, the Austrian school was transformed into an academy of passivity and evasiveness, because of a vulgar historical and conservative school, and reduced its work to explaining and justifying, not guiding and overthrowing. It lowered itself to the position of a handmaid to the current demands of parliamentarism and opportunism, replaced dialectic by swindling sophistries, and, in the end, in spite of its great play with ritual revolutionary phraseology, became transformed into the most secure buttress of the capitalist state, together with the altar and throne that rose above it. If the latter was engulfed in the abyss, no blame for this can be laid upon the Austro-Marxist school.

What characterizes Austro-Marxism is repulsion and fear in the face of revolutionary action. The Austro-Marxist is capable of displaying a perfect gulf of profundity in the explanation of yesterday, and considerable daring in prophesying concerning tomorrow – but for today he never has a great thought or capacity for great action. Today for him always disappears before the wave of little opportunist worries, which later are explained as the most inevitable link between the past and the future.

The Austro-Marxist is inexhaustible when it is a question of discovering reasons to prevent initiative and render difficult revolutionary action. Austro-Marxism is a learned and boastful theory of passivity and capitulation. Naturally, it is not by accident that it was just in Austria, in that Babylon torn by fruitless national antagonisms, in that state which represented the personified impossibility to exist and develop, that there arose and was consolidated the pseudo-Marxist philosophy of the impossibility of revolutionary action.

The foremost Austrian Marxists represent, each in his own way, a certain 'individuality'. On various questions they more than once did not see eye to eye. They even had political differences. But in general they are fingers of the same hand.

Karl Renner is the most pompous, solid and conceited representative of this type. The gift of literary imitation, or, more simply, of stylistic forgery, is granted to him to an exceptional extent. His May Day article represented a charming combination of the most revolutionary words. And, as both words and their combinations live, within certain limits, with their own independent life, Renner's articles awakened in the hearts of many workers a revolutionary fire which their author apparently never knew. The tinsel of Austro-Viennese culture, the chase of the external, of title, of rank, was more characteristic of Renner than of his other colleagues. In essence he always remained merely an imperial and royal officer, who commanded Marxist phraseology to perfection.

The transformation of the author of the jubilee article on Karl Marx, famous for its revolutionary pathos, into a comic-opera chancellor, who expresses his feelings of respect and thanks to the Scandinavian monarchs, is in reality one of the most instructive paradoxes of history.

Otto Bauer is more learned and prosaic, more serious and more boring than Renner. He cannot be denied the capacity to read books, collect facts and draw conclusions adapted to the tasks imposed upon him by practical politics, which in turn are guided by others. Bauer has no political will. His chief art is to reply to all acute practical questions by commonplaces. His political thought always lives a parallel life to his will – it is deprived of all courage. His words are always merely the scientific compilation of the talented student of a university seminar. The most disgraceful actions of Austrian opportunism, the meanest servility before the power of the possessing classes on the part of the Austro-German Social Democracy, found in Bauer their grave elucidator, who sometimes expressed himself with dignity against the form, but always agreed in the essence. If it ever occurred to Bauer to display anything like temperament and political energy, it was exclusively in the struggle against the revolutionary wing – in the accumulation of arguments, facts, quotations, against revolutionary action. His highest period was that (after 1907) in which, being as yet too young to be a deputy, he played the part of secretary of the Social Democratic group, supplied it with materials, figures, substitutes for ideas, instructed it, drew up memoranda, and appeared almost to be the inspirer of great actions, when in reality he was only supplying substitutes, and adulterated substitutes, for the parliamentary opportunists.

Max Adler represents a fairly ingenuous variety of the Austro-Marxist type. He is a lyric poet, a philosopher, a mystic – a philosophical lyric poet of passivity, as Renner is its publicist and legal expert, as Hilferding is its economist, as Bauer is its sociologist. Max Adler is cramped in a world of three dimensions, although he had found a very comfortable place for himself within the framework of Viennese bourgeois socialism and the Habsburg state. The combination of the petty business activity of an attorney and of political humiliation, together with barren philosophical efforts and the cheap tinsel flowers of idealism, have imbued that variety which Max Adler represented with a sickening and repulsive quality.

Rudolf Hilferding, a Viennese like the rest, entered the German Social Democractic Party almost as a mutineer, but as a mutineer of the Austrian stamp, i.e., always ready to capitulate without a fight. Hilferding took the external mobility and bustle of the Austrian policy which brought him up for revolutionary initiative; and for a round dozen of months he demanded – true, in the most moderate terms – a more intelligent policy on the part of the leaders of the German Social Democracy. But the Austro-Viennese bustle swiftly disappeared from his own nature. He soon became subjected to the mechanical rhythm of Berlin and the automatic spiritual life of German Social Democracy. He devoted his intellectual energy to the purely theoretical sphere, where he did not say a great deal, true – no Austro-Marxist has ever said a great deal in any sphere – but in which he did, at any rate, write a serious book. With this book on his back, like a porter with a heavy load, he entered the revolutionary epoch. But the most scientific book cannot replace the absence of will, of initiative, of revolutionary instinct and political decision, without which action is inconceivable. A doctor by training, Hilferding is inclined to sobriety, and, in spite of his theoretical education, he represents the most primitive type of empiricist in questions of policy. The chief problem of today is for him not to leave the lines laid down for him yesterday, and to find for this conservative and bourgeois apathy a scientific, economic explanation.

Friedrich Adler is the most balanced representative of the Austro-Marxist type. He has inherited from his father the latter's political temperament. In the petty exhausting struggle with the disorder of Austrian conditions, Friedrich Adler allowed his ironical scepticism finally to destroy the revolutionary foundations of his world outlook. The temperament inherited from his father more than once drove him into opposition to the school created by his father. At certain moments Friedrich Adler might seem the very revolutionary negation of the Austrian school. In reality, he was and remains its necessary coping-stone. His explosive revolutionism foreshadowed acute attacks of despair amidst Austrian opportunism, which from time to time became terrified at its own insignificance.

Friedrich Adler is a sceptic from head to foot: he does not believe in the masses, or in their capacity for action. At the time when Karl Liebknecht, in the hour of supreme triumph of German militarism, went out to the Potsdamerplatz to call the oppressed masses to the open struggle, Friedrich Adler went into a bourgeois restaurant to assassinate there the Austrian premier. By his solitary shot, Friedrich Adler vainly attempted to put an end to his own scepticism. After that hysterical strain, he fell into still more complete prostration.

The black-and-yellow crew of social-patriotism (Austerlitz, Leitner, etc.) hurled at Adler the terrorist all the abuse of which their cowardly sentiments were capable.

But when the acute period was passed, and the prodigal son returned from his convict prison into his father's house with the halo of a martyr, he proved to be doubly and trebly valuable in that form for Austrian Social Democracy. The golden halo of the terrorist was transformed by the experienced counterfeiters of the party into the sounding coin of the demagogue. Friedrich Adler became a trusted surety for the Austerlitzes, and Renners in face of the masses. Happily, the Austrian workers are coming less and less to distinguish the sentimental lyrical prostration of Friedrich Adler from the pompous shallowness of Renner, the erudite impotence of Max Adler, or the analytical self-satisfaction of Otto Bauer.

The cowardice in thought of the theoreticians of the Austro-Marxist school has completely and wholly been revealed when faced with the great problems of a revolutionary epoch. In his immortal attempt to include the soviet system in the Ebert–Noske constitution, Hilferding gave voice not only to his own spirit but to the spirit of the whole Austro-Marxist school, which, with the approach of the revolutionary epoch, made an attempt to become exactly as much more left than Kautsky as before the revolution it was more right. From this point of view, Max Adler's view of the Soviet system is extremely instructive.

The Viennese eclectic philosopher admits the significance of the soviets. His courage goes so far that he adopts them. He even proclaims them the apparatus of the social revolution. Max Adler, of course, is for a social revolution. But not for a stormy, barricaded, terrorist, bloody revolution, but for a sane, economically balanced, legally canonized and philosophically approved revolution.

Max Adler is not even terrified by the fact that the soviets infringe the 'principle' of the constitutional separation of powers (in Austrian Social Democracy there are many fools who see in such an infringement a great defect of the Soviet system!). On the contrary, Max Adler, the trade union lawyer and legal adviser of the social revolution, sees in the concentration of powers even an advantage, which allows the direct expression of the proletarian will. Max Adler is in favour of the direct expression of the proletarian will; but only not by means of the direct seizure of power through the soviets. He proposes a more solid method. In each town, borough and ward, the workers' councils must 'control' the police and other officials, imposing upon them the 'proletarian will'. What, however, will be the 'constitutional' position of the soviets in the republic of Zeiz, Renner and company? To this our philosopher replies: 'The workers' councils in the long run will receive as much constitutional power as they acquire by means of their own activity' (*Arbeiterzeitung*, no. 179, 1 July 1919).

The proletarian soviets must gradually grow up into the political power of the proletariat, just as previously, in the theories of reformism, all the proletarian organizations had to grow up into socialism; which consummation, however, was a little hindered by the unforeseen misunderstandings, lasting four years, between the Central Powers and the Entente – and all that followed. It was found necessary to reject the economic programme of a gradual development into socialism without a social revolution. But, as a reward, there opened the perspective of the gradual development of the soviets into the social revolution, without an armed rising and a seizure of power.

In order that the soviets should not sink entirely under the burden of borough and ward problems, our daring legal adviser proposes the propaganda of social-democratic ideas! Political power remains as before in the hands of the bourgeoisie and its assistants. But in the wards and the boroughs the soviets control the policemen and their assistants. And, to console the working class and at the same time to centralize its thought and will, Max Adler on Sunday afternoons will read lectures on the constitutional position of the soviets, as in the past he read lectures on the constitutional position of the trade unions.

'In this way,' Max Adler promises, 'the constitutional regulation of the position of the Workers' Councils, and their power and importance, would be guaranteed along the whole line of public and social life; and – without the dictatorship of the soviets – the soviet system would acquire as large an influence as it could possibly have even in a Soviet Republic. At the same time we should not have to pay for that influence by political storms and economic destruction' (ibid.). As we see, in addition to all his other qualities, Max Adler remains still in agreement with the Austrian tradition: to make a revolution without quarrelling with his Excellency the Public Prosecutor.

The founder of this school, and its highest authority, is Kautsky. Carefully protecting, particularly after the Dresden party congress and the first Russian revolution, his reputation as the keeper of the shrine of Marxist orthodoxy, Kautsky from time to time would shake his head in disapproval of the more compromising outbursts of his Austrian school. And, following the example of the late Victor Adler, Bauer, Renner, Hilferding – altogether and each separately – considered Kautsky too pedantic, too inert, but a very reverend and a very useful father and teacher of the church of quietism.

Kautsky began to cause serious mistrust in his own school during the period of his revolutionary culmination, at the time of the first

Russian revolution, when he recognized as necessary the seizure of power by Russian Social Democracy, and attempted to inoculate the German working class with his theoretical conclusions from the experience of the general strike in Russia. The collapse of the first Russian revolution at once broke off Kautsky's evolution along the path of radicalism. The more plainly was the question of mass action in Germany itself put forward by the course of events, the more evasive became Kautsky's attitude. He marked time, retreated, lost his confidence; and the pedantic and scholastic features of his thought more and more became apparent. The imperialist war, which killed every form of vagueness and brought mankind face to face with the most fundamental questions, exposed all the political bankruptcy of Kautsky.

He immediately became confused beyond all hope of extrication, in the most simple question of voting the war credits. All his writings after that period represent variations of one and the same theme. 'Me and my muddle'. The Russian Revolution finally slew Kautsky. By all his previous development he was placed in a hostile attitude towards the November victory of the proletariat. This unavoidably threw him into the camp of the counter-revolution. He lost the last traces of historical instinct. His further writings have become more and more like the yellow literature of the bourgeois market.

Kautsky's book, examined by us, bears in its external characteristics all the attributes of a so-called objective scientific study. To examine the extent of the Red Terror, Kautsky acts with all the circumstantial method peculiar to him. He begins with the study of the social conditions which prepared the great French Revolution, and also the physiological and social conditions which assisted the development of cruelty and humanity throughout the history of the human race. In a book devoted to Bolshevism, in which the whole question is examined in 234 pages, Kautsky describes in detail on what our most remote human ancestor fed, and hazards the guess that, while living mainly on vegetable products, he devoured also insects and possibly a few birds (see p. 122). In a word, there was nothing to lead us to expect that from such an entirely respectable ancestor – one obviously inclined to vegetarianism – there should spring such descendants as the Bolsheviks. That is the solid scientific basis on which Kautsky builds the question? . . .

But, as is not infrequent with productions of this nature, there is hidden behind the academic and scholastic cloak a malignant political pamphlet. This book is one of the most lying and conscienceless of its kind. Is it not incredible at first glance, that Kautsky should gather up the most contemptible stories about the Bolsheviks from the rich table of Havas, Reuters and Wolff, thereby displaying from under his learned nightcap the ears of the sycophant? Yet these disreputable details are only mosaic decorations on the fundamental background of solid, scientific lying about the Soviet Republic and its guiding party.

Kautsky depicts in the most sinister colours our savagery towards the bourgeoisie, which 'displayed no tendency to resist'.

Kautsky attacks our ruthlessness in connection with the Social Revolutionaries and the Mensheviks, who represent 'shades' of socialism.

KAUTSKY DEPICTS THE SOVIET ECONOMY
AS THE CHAOS OF COLLAPSE

Kautsky represents the Soviet workers, and the Russian working class as a whole, as a conglomeration of egoists, loafers and cowards.

He does not say one word about the conduct of the Russian bourgeoisie, unprecedented in history for the magnitude of its scoundrelism; about its national treachery; about the surrender of Riga to the Germans, with 'educational' aims; about the preparations for a similar surrender of Petrograd; about its appeals to foreign armies – Czechoslovakian, German, Romanian, British, Japanese, French, Arab and Negro – against the Russian workers and peasants; about its conspiracies and assassinations, paid for by Entente money; about its utilization of the blockade, not only to starve our children to death, but systematically, tirelessly, persistently to spread over the whole world an unheard-of web of lies and slander.

He does not say one word about the most disgraceful misrepresentations of and violence to our party on the part of the government of the SRs and Mensheviks before the November revolution; about the criminal persecution of several thousand responsible workers of the party on the charge of espionage in favour of Hohenzollern Germany; about the participation of the Mensheviks and SRs in all the plots of the bourgeoisie; about their collaboration with the imperial generals and admirals, Kolchak, Denikin and Yudenich; about the terrorist acts carried out by the SRs at the order of the Entente; about the risings organized by the SRs with the money of the foreign missions in our army, which was pouring out its blood in the struggle against the monarchical bands of imperialism.

Kautsky does not say one word about the fact that we not only repeated more than once, but proved in reality our readiness to give peace to the country, even at the cost of sacrifices and concessions, and that, in spite of this, we were obliged to carry on an intensive struggle on all fronts to defend the very existence of our country, and to prevent its transformation into a colony of Anglo-French imperialism.

Kautsky does not say one word about the fact that in this heroic struggle, in which we are defending the future of world socialism, the Russian proletariat is obliged to expend its principal energies, its best and most valuable forces, taking them away from economic and cultural reconstruction.

In all his book, Kautsky does not even mention the fact that first of all German militarism, with the help of its Scheidemanns and the apathy of its Kautskys, and then the militarism of the Entente countries with the help of its Renaudels and the apathy of its Longuets, surrounded us with an iron blockade; seized all our ports; cut us off from the whole of the world; occupied, with the help of hired White bands, enormous territories, rich in raw materials; and separated us for a long period from the Baku oil, the Donetz coal, the Don and Siberian corn, the Turkestan cotton.

Kautsky does not say one word about the fact that in these conditions, unprecedented for their difficulty, the Russian working class for nearly three years has been carrying on a heroic struggle against its enemies on a front of 8,000 *versts*; that the Russian working class learned how to exchange its hammer for the sword, and created a mighty army; that for this army it mobilized its exhausted industry and, in spite of the ruin of the country, which the executioners of the whole world had condemned to blockade and civil war, for three years with its own forces and resources it has been clothing, feeding, arming, transporting an army of millions – an army which has learned how to conquer.

About all these conditions Kautsky is silent, in a book devoted to Russian communism. And his silence is the fundamental, capital, principal lie – true, a passive lie, but more criminal and more repulsive than the active lies of all the scoundrels of the international bourgeois press taken together.

Slandering the policy of the Communist Party, Kautsky says nowhere what he himself wants and what he proposes. The Bolsheviks were not alone in the arena of the Russian Revolution. We saw and see in it – now in power, now in opposition – SRs (not less than five groups and tendencies), Mensheviks (not less than three tendencies), Plekhanovists, Maximalists, Anarchists ... Absolutely all the 'shades of socialism' (to speak in Kautsky's language) tried their hand, and showed what they would and what they could. There are so many of these 'shades' that it is difficult now to pass the blade of a knife between them. The very origin of these 'shades' is not accidental: they represent, so to speak, different degrees in the adaptation of the pre-revolutionary socialist parties and groups to the conditions of the greater revolutionary epoch. It would seem that Kautsky had a sufficiently complete political keyboard before him to be able to strike the note which would give a true Marxian key to the Russian Revolution. But Kautsky is silent. He repudiates the Bolshevik melody that is unpleasant to his ear, but does not seek another. The solution is simple: the old musician refuses altogether to play on the instrument of the revolution.

IN PLACE OF AN EPILOGUE

This book appears at the moment of the Second Congress of the Communist International. The revolutionary movement of the proletariat has made, during the months that have passed since the First Congress, a great step forward. The positions of the official, open social-patriots have everywhere been undermined. The ideas of communism acquire an ever wider extension. Official dogmatized Kautskianism has been gradually compromised. Kautsky himself, within that 'Independent' Party which he created, represents today a not very authoritative and a fairly ridiculous figure.

Nonetheless, the intellectual struggle in the ranks of the international working class is only now blazing up as it should. If, as we just said, dogmatized Kautskianism is breathing its last days, and the leaders of the intermediate socialist parties are hastening to renounce it, still Kautskianism as a bourgeois attitude, as a tradition of passivity, as political cowardice, still plays an enormous part in the upper ranks of the working-class organizations of the world, in no way excluding parties tending to the Third International, and even formally adhering to it.

The Independent Party in Germany, which has written on its banner the watchword of the dictatorship of the proletariat, tolerates in its ranks the Kautsky group, all the efforts of which are devoted theoretically to compromise and misrepresent the dictatorship of the proletariat in the shape of its living expression – the Soviet regime. In conditions of civil war, such a form of cohabitation is conceivable only and to such an extent as far and as long as the dictatorship of the proletariat represents for the leaders of 'Independent' Social Democracy a noble aspiration, a vague protest against the open and disgraceful treachery of Noske, Ebert, Scheidemann and others, and – last but not least – a weapon of electoral and parliamentary demagogy.

The vitality of vague Kautskianism is most clearly seen in the example of the French Longuetists. Jean Longuet himself has most sincerely convinced himself, and has for long been attempting to convince others, that he is marching in step with us, and that only Clemenceau's censorship and the calumnies of our French friends Loriot, Monatte, Rosmer and others hinder our comradeship in arms. Yet is it sufficient to make oneself acquainted with any parliamentary speech of Longuet's to realize that the gulf separating him from us at the present moment is possibly still wider than at the first period of the imperialist war? The revolutionary problems now arising before the international proletariat have become more serious, more immediate, more gigantic, more direct, more definite, than five or six years ago; and the politically reactionary character of the Longuetists, the parliamentary representatives of eternal passivity, has become more impressive than ever before, in spite of the fact that formally they have returned to the fold of parliamentary opposition.

The Italian Socialist Party, which is within the Third International, is not at all free from Kautskianism. As far as the leaders are concerned, a very considerable part of them bear their internationalist honours only as a duty and as an imposition from below. In 1914–15, the Italian Socialist Party found it infinitely more easy than did the other European parties to maintain an attitude of opposition to the war, both because Italy entered the war nine months later than other countries, and particularly because the international position of Italy created in it even a powerful bourgeois group (Giolittians in the widest sense of the word) which remained to the very last moment hostile to Italian intervention in the war.

These conditions allowed the Italian Socialist Party, without the fear of a very profound internal crisis to refuse war credits to the government, and generally to remain outside the interventionist bloc. But by this very fact the process of internal cleansing of the party proved to be unquestionably delayed. Although an integral part of the Third International, the Italian Socialist Party to this very day can put up with Turati and his supporters in its ranks. This very powerful group – unfortunately we find it difficult to define to any extent of accuracy its numerical significance in the parliamentary group, in the press, in the party, and in the trade union organizations – represents a less pedantic, not so demagogic, more declamatory and lyrical, but nonetheless malignant opportunism – a form of romantic Kautskianism.

A passive attitude to the Kautskian, Longuetist, Turatist groups is usually cloaked by the argument that the time for revolutionary activity in the respective countries has not yet arrived. But such a formulation of the question is absolutely false. Nobody demands from socialists striving for communism that they should appoint a revolutionary outbreak for a definite week or month in the near future. What the Third International demands of its supporters is a recognition, not in words but in deeds, that civilized humanity has entered a revolutionary epoch; that all the capitalist countries are speeding towards colossal disturbances and an open class war; and that the task of the revolutionary representatives of the proletariat is to prepare for that inevitable and approaching war the necessary spiritual armory and buttress of organization. The internationalists who consider it possible at the present time to collaborate with Kautsky, Longuet and Turati, to appear side by side with them before the working masses, by that very act renounce in practice the work of preparing in ideas and organization for the revolutionary rising of the proletariat, independently of whether it comes a month or a year sooner or later. In order that the open rising of the proletarian masses should not fritter itself away in belated searches for paths and leadership, we must see to it today that wide circles of the proletariat should even now learn to grasp all the immensity of the tasks before them, and of their irreconcilability with all variations of Kautskianism and opportunism.

A truly revolutionary, i.e., a communist wing, must set itself up in opposition, in face of the masses, to all the indecisive, half-hearted groups of doctrinaires, advocates and panegyrists of passivity, strengthening its positions first of all spiritually and then in the sphere of organization – open, half-open and purely conspirative. The moment of formal split with the open and disguised Kautskians, or the moment of their expulsion from the ranks of the working-class party, is, of course, to be determined by considerations of usefulness from the point of view of circumstances; but all the policy of real communists must turn in that direction.

That is why it seems to me that this book is still not out of date – to my great regret, if not as an author, at any rate as a communist.

17 June 1920

NOTES

FOREWORD

[1] Another more specific theoretical limitation is that Trotsky, not unlike Lenin, continues to oppose the 'good' (orthodox Marxist) early Kautsky to the late 'bad' renegade, not seeing how the seeds of his regression are all already there in his earlier 'orthodoxy'.

[2] Leon Trotsky, *Sochineniya* (Moscow: Gosizdat 1925), vol. 17, pp. 480–5. One cannot but admire Trotsky's ruthless honesty in this appraisal, which went up to fully admitting the vital role of the black economy in the survival of the Soviet state: apropos illegal home-brewing (*samogonka*), he wrote that it is 'the protest of local needs against the centralism that does not satisfy them . . . I am speaking about the semi-contraband or completely contraband production that occurs in the localities and plays an enormous economic role, because otherwise the country will be ruined.'

[3] Vladimir N. Brovkin, *Behind the Front Lines of the Civil War: Political Parties and Social Movements in Russia, 1918–1922* (Princeton, NJ: Princeton University Press 1994), p. 270.

[4] Martin Malia, *Soviet Tragedy: A History of Socialism in Russia* (New York: Free Press 1995), p. 130.

[5] Robert Conquest, *Harvest of Sorrow: Soviet Collectivization and the Terror-Famine* (New York: Oxford University Press 1986), p. 48.

[6] Isaac Deutscher, *The Prophet Armed: Trotsky 1879–1921* (London: Verso 2003), p. 489.

[7] Ibid., pp. 515–16.

[8] Orlando Figes, *A People's Tragedy: The Russian Revolution 1891–1924* (London: Jonathan Cape 1996), pp. 722–3.

[9] Deutscher, *The Prophet Armed*, pp. 490–1.

[10] Although, even here, one should not forget a crucial fact: the Soviet state apparatus we all know and love did *not* have its roots in war communism, but is a fully legitimate child of the NEP. The reasoning of the party elite was: since we are withdrawing from direct control over economy, we should make sure that this will not cost us real power – so, to counteract the unleashed market forces, we need a strong state apparatus able to intervene and squash the enemy . . .

[11] See Lars T. Lih, '"Our Position Is in the Highest Degree Tragic": Bolshevik "Euphoria" in 1920', in *History and Revolution: Refuting Revisionism*, eds Mike Haynes and Jim Wolfreys (London and New York: Verso 2007).

[12] Quoted from Massimo Salvadori, *Karl Kautsky and the Socialist Revolution* (London: Verso 1979), p. 290.

[13] Even today – Negri, in a book which has good words even for Stalin, dismisses me in a footnote of his last book as 'Žižek the Slovene, who now became more or less Trotskyist', see Antonio Negri, *Goodbye Mister Socialism* (Paris: Éditions du Seuil 2007), p. 61.

[14] J. Arch Getty and Oleg V. Naumov, *The Road to Terror: Stalin and the Self-Destruction of the Bolsheviks* (New Haven, CT, and London: Yale University Press 1999), p. 249.

[15] Georg Lukács, 'Hölderlin's Hyperion', in *Goethe and His Age* (London: Allen & Unwin 1968), p. 137.

[16] The reference is to George Leggett, *The Cheka: Lenin's Political Police* (Oxford: Oxford University Press 1981).

[17] Lesley Chamberlain, *The Philosophy Steamer* (London: Atlantic Books 2006), pp. 315–16.

[18] V.I. Lenin, *Collected Works*, vol. 33 (Moscow: Progress Publishers 1966), p. 479.

[19] Georgi Dimitroff, *Tagebücher 1933–1943* (Berlin: Aufbau Verlag 2000).

[20] Fredric Jameson, *The Seeds of Time* (New York: Columbia University Press 1994), p. 89.

[21] Ibid., p. 90.

[22] Quoted from Orlando Figes, *Natasha's Dance* (London: Allen Lane 2001), p. 447.

[23] Leon Trotsky, *Diary in Exile 1935* (Cambridge, MA: Harvard University Press 1976), pp. 145–6.

[24] The dream is analysed by Lacan in his seminar VI on *Le désir et son interprétation*, the session of 7 January 1959 (unpublished).

[25] Fredric Jameson, 'Lenin and Revisionism', in *Lenin Reloaded*, SIC series, vol. 7, eds S. Budgen, S. Kouvelakis and S. Žižek (Durham, NC: Duke University Press 2007), p. 59.

[26] G.W.F. Hegel, *Lectures on the Philosophy of World History* (Cambridge: Cambridge University Press 1980), p. 263.

INTRODUCTION

[1] [*Editorial note* from Trotsky's *Military Writings*, Volume 3: By the end of 1919, the Red Army had beaten back the White Guards on all fronts. British and French imperialism, at first so confident of crushing the October Revolution, were now encountering not only the strength of the Soviet state itself, but the opposition to intervention which it inspired in the working class in the imperialist countries. A ceasefire was even signed with the Polish chief Piłsudski, whom the French intended to spearhead the renewal of their attack.

The work of economic reconstruction in Russia was interrupted in March 1920 with the Polish invasion of the Ukraine. The Bolsheviks responded by setting out to teach the Polish gentry and bourgeoisie a lesson once and for all. The whole country was mobilized. It was during this campaign that the strength of the Red Army grew to five million. Trotsky organized the whole front.

This campaign differed from the previous phase of the civil war, in that it was not against White Guard bands or direct imperialist intervention; it was against the lackeys of imperialism in the Polish ruling class. In his orders throughout the campaign Trotsky was firm in resisting all chauvinist pressure to wage the war on a national basis. He suspended publication of the paper *Voyennoye Dyelo* because of its chauvinist attacks on the Polish nation, issued instructions that soldiers taken prisoner were not to be mistreated, and constantly appealed to the Polish workers and peasants to resist Piłsudski and join forces with their Soviet brothers.

By July, the Polish forces were retreating. The Bolshevik leadership decided to pursue Piłsudski's armies to Warsaw. Behind his public upholding of this line, Trotsky held grave reservations. He opposed Lenin within the Politburo, concerned that the Red Army's advance would rouse nationalist sentiments among broad sections of the Polish masses, rather than bring them out to greet the Soviet forces as liberators. In the event, the brave efforts of Tukhachevsky's northern armies were defeated outside Warsaw, while the southern armies under Budyonny, with Stalin as commissar, were too far away to assist. The Red Army withdrew; and Lenin soon supported Trotsky in concluding peace with Poland.]

THE BALANCE OF POWER

[1] [*Editorial note*: Reference to the Hungarian Soviet Republic formed 21 March 1919 and overthrown in August 1919, after which a wave of White Terror was unleashed against the left.]

[2] [*Editorial note*: The Romanian army entered Budapest on 6 August 1919, thus ending the experience of the Soviet Republic.]

THE DICTATORSHIP OF THE PROLETARIAT

[1] [*Translator's note*: For convenience sake, the references throughout have been altered to fall in the English translation of Kautsky's book. Mr. Kerridge's translation, however, has not been adhered to.]

[2] [*Editorial note*: The 'June days of 1848' refers to the French workers' uprising of 21–26 June, 1848 ferociously suppressed by General Cavaignac. 'Commune': in the aftermath of the defeat of French forces in the Franco-Prussian War of 1870–71, the Paris Commune was established in March 1871 and governed with the support of the popular classes until its bloody repression at the end of May by the troops loyal to the government based at Versailles.]

DEMOCRACY

[1] In order to charm us in favour of a Constituent Assembly Kautsky brings forward an argument based on the rate of exchange to the assistance of his argument, based on the categorical imperative. 'Russia requires', he writes, 'the help of foreign capital, but this help will not come to the Soviet Republic if the latter does not summon a Constituent Assembly, and does not give freedom of the press; not because the capitalists are democratic idealists – to tsarism they gave without any hesitation many milliards – but because they have no business faith in a revolutionary government' (p. 218). There are scraps of truth in this rubbish. The Stock Exchange did really support the government of Kolchak when it relied for support on the Constituent Assembly. From its experience of Kolchak the Stock Exchange became confirmed in its conviction that the mechanism of bourgeois democracy can be utilized in capitalist interests, and then thrown aside like a worn-out pair of puttees. It is quite possible that the Stock Exchange would again give a parliamentary loan on the guarantee of a Constituent Assembly, believing, on the basis of its former experience, that such a body would prove only an intermediate step to capitalist dictatorship. We do not propose to buy the 'business faith' of the Stock Exchange at such a price, and decidedly prefer the 'faith' which is aroused in the realist Stock Exchange by the weapon of the Red Army.

THE PARIS COMMUNE AND SOVIET RUSSIA

[1] It is not without interest to observe that in the Communal elections of 1871 in Paris there participated 230,000 electors. At the town elections of November 1917 in Petrograd, in spite of the boycott of the election on the part of all parties except ourselves and the left Social Revolutionaries who had no influence in the capital, there participated 300,000 electors. In Paris, in 1871, the population numbered two million. In Petrograd, in November 1917, there were not more than two million. It must be noticed that our electoral system was infinitely more democratic. The Central Committee of the National Guard carried out the elections on the basis of the electoral law of the empire.

THE WORKING CLASS AND ITS SOVIET POLICY

[1] Available at http://www.marxists.org/archive/trotsky/1918/03/work.htm.
[2] [The Vienna *Arbeiterzeitung* opposes, as is fitting, the wise Russian Communist to the foolish Austrians. 'Did not Trotsky,' the paper writes, 'with a clear view and understanding of possibilities, sign the Treaty of Brest-Litovsk of violence, notwithstanding that it served for the consolidation of German imperialism? The Treaty of Brest-Litovsk was just as harsh and shameful as is the Treaty of Versailles. But does this mean that Trotsky had to be rash enough to continue the war against Germany? Would not the fate of the Russian Revolution long ago have been sealed? Trotsky bowed before the unalterable necessity of signing the shameful treaty in anticipation of the German revolution.' The honour of having foreseen all the consequences of the Treat of Brest-Litovsk belongs to Lenin. But this, of course, alters nothing in the argument of the organ of the Viennese Kautskians.]
[3] *Labour, Discipline, and Order Will Save the Socialist Soviet Republic* (Moscow 1918). Kautsky knows this pamphlet, as he quotes from it several times. This, however, does not prevent him passing over the passage quoted above, which makes clear the attitude of the Soviet government to the intelligentsia.

PROBLEMS OF THE ORGANIZATION OF LABOUR

[1] Since that time – June 1920 – the percentage has been considerably lowered.
[2] This was the name given to the imperial police, whom the Minister for Home Affairs, Protopopoff, distributed at the end of February 1917, over the roofs of houses and in the belfries.